MW01067580

U.S. CENTRAL AMERICANS

EDITED BY
KARINA O. ALVARADO
ALICIA IVONNE ESTRADA
ESTER E. HERNÁNDEZ

U.S. CENTRAL
AMERICANS

Reconstructing Memories, Struggles, and
Communities of Resistance

THE UNIVERSITY OF
ARIZONA PRESS
TUCSON

The University of Arizona Press
www.uapress.arizona.edu

© 2017 by The Arizona Board of Regents
All rights reserved. Published 2017

Printed in the United States of America

22   21   20   19   18   17   7   6   5   4   3   2

ISBN-13: 978-0-8165-3406-7 (paper)

Cover design by Carrie House, HOUSEdesign llc
Cover art: "El Muro" Tlaloc's Journey, 2007, by Alicia Maria Siu

Library of Congress Cataloging-in-Publication Data
Names: Alvarado, Karina Oliva, editor. | Estrada, Alicia I., editor. | Hernández, Ester E., editor.
Title: U.S. Central Americans : reconstructing memories, struggles, and communities of resistance /
    edited by Karina O. Alvarado, Alicia I. Estrada, and Ester E. Hernández.
Description: Tucson : The University of Arizona Press, 2017. | Includes bibliographical references
    and index.
Identifiers: LCCN 2016031031 | ISBN 9780816534067 (pbk. : alk. paper)
Subjects: LCSH: Central American Americans. | Central Americans—United States. | Central
    American Americans—California, Southern. | Central Americans—California, Southern.
Classification: LCC E184.C34 U35 2017 | DDC 305.868/728073—dc23 LC record available at
    https://lccn.loc.gov/2016031031

♾ This paper meets the requirements of ANSI/NISO z39.48-1992 (Permanence of Paper).

We dedicate this volume to Central American diasporic communities in the United States, and to the scholars, activists, and community organizers actively working with (im)migrant communities, and in sustaining Central American cultures, lifeways, and histories. We also dedicate the volume to U.S. Central American youth in their attempts to redefine their identities and familial and communal stories as a generation that uncovers, recovers, and transforms.

CONTENTS

PREFACE

Our Process as Subjects Within Diasporic Communities and Fields

U.S. CENTRAL AMERICANS: Reconstructing Memories, Struggles, and Communities of Resistance began with the three editors, Karina O. Alvarado, Alicia Ivonne Estrada, and Ester E. Hernández, in conversation about our research as Central American–born scholars writing on intersected Central American and U.S. communities. Our *charlas* (talks) included experiences in the classroom, teaching about U.S. Central Americans, and what we saw as a need to shift beyond civil wars and political factions to community emplacement and social justice within the United States. Because scholars who teach on U.S. Central Americans are usually the sole expert on said topic within a department, typically as the only U.S. Central American faculty member, our meetings also solidified the need for a scholarly U.S. Central American community. We recognize that U.S. Central American scholars are made to seek alternate spaces in creating our own support systems in the absence of pathways to institutionalize this interdisciplinary field. As the project for a U.S. Central American studies anthology developed into a plan of action, we decided to purposely seek the work of established U.S. Central Americanists and scholars in the process of completing their doctoral programs. The anthology reflects knowledge production of U.S. Central Americans, our academic and community networks, and an explicit commitment to mentoring emerging scholars.

This volume provides an alternative framework of analysis for Latina/o studies through its inclusion of U.S. Central Americans. For instance, Latina/o theory has often used 1848 and 1898 as the genesis of Latina/o communities. In doing so, this historical point of origin limits discussions on Latinidad to Puerto Rico, Mexico, and Cuba. Yet, as presented in the anthology, Central America is similarly tied to U.S. imperialistic projects—starting with the construction of nation-states, railroads, Pan-American highways, and canal zones to serve the commercial needs of U.S. companies. In expanding the historical references used to discuss Latina/o communities in the United States, U.S. Central Americans engage notions of Latinidad and call attention to the shared historical (neo)colonial conditions, which created U.S. Central American diasporas. Partial inclusion of U.S. Central American communities in ethnic studies and Latin American studies scholarship is evident in the ways U.S. Central Americans and their communities are often viewed as "newcomers," situating U.S. Central American communities, scholarship, culture, and experiences on the sidelines. Latina/o work on citizenship similarly does not include scholarship on Central Americans, though it could be argued that the Temporary Protected Status (TPS) program established in 1989 is an important moment whereby U.S. Central Americans were assigned pseudocitizenship. Not quite refugee, not quite immigrant, but occupying what U.S. Central American scholar Cecilia Menjívar calls a "liminal" status (2008). The same can be said about U.S. Central American studies within academia.

For instance, Central American studies curriculum exists as a full major at only one (California State University at Northridge [CSUN]) of the twenty-three California State University campuses. Only a few institutions offer a U.S. Central American studies minor. Often Central American topics and courses are housed in Latin American Studies, Area Studies, Latina/o Studies, or Chicana/o and Ethnic Studies departments and programs. Some university campuses offer courses that make up a minor or a certificate. This is typically administered jointly, such as at California State University, Los Angeles (CSULA), between Chicana/o Studies, Latin American Studies, or separately by either department or program. This type of institutional organization limits the development of Central American studies as a field on its own since it relies on the primacy of a more established area of study. Piecemeal courses are never enough to cover the heterogeneity of Central American histories and communities. Hence, this anthology emphasizes the heterogeneity of Central American histories as well as the multiple disciplines and locations from which U.S. Central American scholars study and frame Central American communities in the isthmus and the United States.

We actively sought to include scholars that moved away from national identities and that centered their scholarship on Central American topics of research in the United States. We selected articles after soliciting abstracts and receiving completed work. All three editors reviewed each submission in several iterations. Though we sought work from Nicaraguan and Honduran scholars in California, only scholars working with Guatemalan, Maya, and Salvadoran communities committed to this project. We acknowledge these gaps and hope that the anthology contributes to the ongoing theorizing of the place of Central American scholars within the U.S. academy, and we propose a second anthology focused on communities from Nicaragua, Honduras, Belize, Panama, and Costa Rica. While acknowledging said gaps, the anthology's generational, spatial, urban, indigenous, women, migrant, and public and cultural memory foci contribute highly to the development of U.S. Central American thought, theory, and methods. This volume begins a conversation about the need for U.S. Central American academics to be key players in further institutionalizing Central American studies.

ACKNOWLEDGMENTS

W E THANK OUR editor and peer reviewers for their insightful suggestions. We are deeply grateful to our contributors for their commitment to this project and for their work with U.S. Central American and Latina/o communities. We thank our family, partners, and friends for their love and encouragement as they went through this process with us. We would like to express our gratitude to UCLA's Institute for Research on Labor and Employment, Dr. Abel Valenzuela, and the Chicana/o Studies Department at California State University at Northridge, as well as the Chicano/Latino Studies Department at California State University at Los Angeles for their generous support.

As co-editors, we committed to collaborate, often meeting late at night at the end of already long workdays. We had the best time when we met for work lunches at Homegirl Cafe. We navigated this new terrain as editors, an exciting but sometimes challenging process, especially as first-generation scholars from immigrant backgrounds and working-class origins. We strongly believe that we need to support each other to make a pathway for others and that collaborating makes our efforts more meaningful and nourishing. Thank you, co-editors, for your vision, friendship, and dedication.

This project is a labor of love for our communities, for those who came before us, and for all those to come. All errors contained are ours.

U.S. CENTRAL AMERICANS

INTRODUCTION

U.S. Central American (Un)Belongings

KARINA O. ALVARADO, ALICIA IVONNE ESTRADA,
AND ESTER E. HERNÁNDEZ

A T THE CLOSE OF 2015, an image of a drowned Syrian boy shook the international community, inciting outrage while calling attention to the Syrian refugee crisis.[1] The tragedy of the situation mirrored similar struggles for U.S. Central Americans and Latina/o migrants, since undocumented migration from Central America and Mexico causes hundreds of deaths yearly. We are too familiar with the thousands of unidentified bodies buried in mass graves in places like Texas[2] and the mutilated bodies of people who fall off the "beast,"[3] or those who die when it derails. The Syrian refugee crisis triggered memories of our dead and of our migrants who also continue to seek refuge.

In 2011 and by the summer of 2014, a surge of Central American unaccompanied child migrants gained mainstream visibility, becoming sensationalized as a crisis by U.S. politicians and media. Yet, unaccompanied migrations have been happening for decades. Within our own academic and advocacy communities, many Central Americans residing in the United States remember the journey taken as children or young adults. However, though unaccompanied child migration is not a new occurrence, it currently unfolds in a different enforcement context of border militarization and "deportation terror" (Buff 2008). For example, at the close of 2015 President Obama's administration proclaimed Central Americans as targets for persecution and expedited deportations. Whether migrants experience(d) physical, emotional, or sexual abuse on trek to the United States, our migration experiences and enforceable deportations have left an indelible mark on the consciousness of Central Americans that constitutes a personal, familial, and communitarian crisis created not by communities but by nation-states. These types of embodied experiences and witness set the social context for U.S. Central American cultural memories.

The 2014 "child migrant crisis" that captivated North Americans presented immigrant children of color as a social problem. U.S. media outlets reproduced images of Central American migrant mothers and children, representing them as a threat to North American resources, and resurrecting the 1980s term *anchor baby*. Central Americans had fallen off the radar of visibility since the 1990s with the signing of peace accords in war-torn Guatemala and El Salvador. This new crisis focused on children and hid many truths known by U.S. Central Americans: We are a diverse community of peoples who have long histories of migration as a result of U.S. interventions in the isthmus. Our political struggles, which include civil wars, have been as ongoing and extensive as the ones incurred within the internal colonial model experienced by Mexican Americans and Caribbean Americans. Moreover, as long as the isthmus continues to experience economic poverty and vast disparity between the rich and the economic poor at local, binational, and geopolitical levels, the context for civil strife and migrant escape remains present. Our migrant communities come from countries that have been made to occupy the geopolitical margins as some of the most geodisenfranchised and georacialized people within the Americas. This bottom placement within global hierarchies is reproduced at local levels, influencing representations of Central Americans as silent and invisible. Thus, economic underdevelopment is transposed onto the people, shaping stereotypes around the tropes of impoverishment and violence. Central Americans and U.S. Central Americans maintain hope, resistance, creativity, agency, voice, and memory as part of our identities and cultures that are often overlooked.

The anthology enters here to interrupt assumed silences of diverse U.S. Central American communities. As the chapters show through oral histories, interviews, murals, *mercados*, textiles, festivals, and literature, U.S. Central Americans have a lot to say about their own lives. While much literature is available on U.S. and Central American military, economic, and political relations, our communities are more than historical facts and political theories. We are a people with rich cultures, stories, and memories in flux. The anthology insists on U.S. Central Americans' own identities while exploring and presenting the contradictions found within groups. Understanding U.S. Central Americans means doing away with stereotypes of subalternity. It means looking at experiences of violence and traumas without essentializing U.S. Central Americans as traumatized people. It also means hearing us tell our own stories and then listening to our interpretations in order to open a dialogue between us. When a group of people insists that they are marginalized and tokenized, the more dominant groups must choose an ethical response that includes making room within communities and institutions. While this anthology represents some of the groundbreaking work being done by U.S. Central American scholars, we do not propose for it to be an end-all. We hope the anthology marks a turning point in how Central America has been spoken for, mainly through social science and political theory that includes humanities and cultural approaches, to bring to the fore our complexity, richness, beauty, and resiliency. Understanding U.S. Central Americans means getting to know who we are as people with particular stories, cultural memories, and practices as we contribute to the knowledge building of our countries of origin and diasporas, divulging a complex U.S. Latinidad.

U.S. INTERVENTIONIST HISTORIES: CREATING DIASPORAS

To understand the Central American Northern Triangle (Honduras, El Salvador, and Guatemala) as the source of current migration, it is necessary to look back at the history of the isthmus in relationship to the United States' political, economic, and military agendas beginning in the late nineteenth century. The (mis)fortunes of the Central American countries have been tied to the creation of the Canal Zone and the development of the banana plantation economy and other export crops, such as coffee. Imperialist adventurers and capitalist magnates had designs on Central American territory since the nineteenth century. They dreamed of a railroad system, built a canal, took over the land, and turned it into a plantation, which produced the twentieth-century golden crop—bananas and, later, coffee plantations. This land takeover would later produce the internal social upheaval of the 1980s, subdued to U.S. international interests in confrontation with the socialist bloc. Today, the notion of a security zone dominates the policies and investment in the Central American region, which continues to be the scene of the United States flexing its military, economic, and political influence.

Thirty-five years after the initial mass civil war migrations primarily from Guatemala and El Salvador from the '70s to the '90s, out-migration continues because of postwar economic free-trade programs, growing economic dependence, and the proliferation of *maras* (gangs). Central Americans have grown permanent roots in the United States. The U.S. Census bureau brief estimates Central Americans to be the third-largest Latina/o group in the United States at 4.8 million (8%) (Stoney and Batalova 2013; Zong and Batalova 2015). Their numbers near the 4.9 million (9.2%) of the Puerto Rican population. The closing differential between the Central American and Puerto Rican populations is significant in that Central Americans have never been formally colonized by the United States. They do not have protectorate status and are not U.S.-born citizens as are Puerto Ricans on or off the island. While Latinas/os account for 17 percent of the U.S. population, Mexicans represent the largest Latina/o majority at 64.6 percent. Like Puerto Ricans, Mexicans are direct colonial subjects with longstanding histories of circular migration. Yet, while Mexico and the United States have been described as two nations with one economy, Central America's development has been historically disrupted and interrupted to promote U.S. economic interests since the inception of each Central American nation. U.S. economic, military, and corporate interventions in the isthmus have been just as long and extensive as the United States' relationship with Mexico and the Caribbean.

Civil wars initiated the flows and migratory movements during the 1980s and 1990s; the United States was directly involved in the duration and extremity of these wars. For example, Nicaragua's Sandinista government (1979–1990) was not able to establish itself, nor its socialist vision, since it was forced to concentrate its time and economy to fight the U.S.-funded Contra War (1981–1990). Forty percent (158,000) of the estimated U.S. Nicaraguan population today (395,000) entered in 1990 after the defeat of the Sandinista regime. During the Reagan era, Central America became the bull's-eye to the Reagan Doctrine that formally deployed an overt and covert fight against communism. While Reagan epitomized the hegemonic Cold War belief that constructed communism as the antithesis and enemy of North American democracy and values, it can also be theorized that the claim of communism served as an economic and military strategy for intervention. Thus, of all the Central American nations, Nicaraguans' reception by the United States was comparable to that of Cuban exiles, in which both were seen, presented, and promoted as anticommunist "freedom fighters," so that today an estimated 53 percent of the Nicaraguan

U.S. population are U.S. citizens.[4] In comparison, Salvadorans and Guatemalans have a much smaller proportion of citizens, which aligns with the use of the Cold War rhetoric to define refugee status.

Historically, raising the specter or possibility of communism would always provide an immediate justification for forcible U.S. intervention and internal nation-state violence (Zea 1963). Such was the case for the other Central American countries. In 1930s Nicaragua, Augusto C. Sandino stood against U.S. imperialism and occupation and foreshadowed the Contra War that would ensue fifty years later; in El Salvador, the shadow of communism was also deployed to further disenfranchise indigenous peasant communities since the early 1900s. Following the end of an era of labor organizing within El Salvador, the 1930s global depression, compelled by the U.S. economic crash, provided the context to local social repression against the nascent labor movement. Indigenous communities seeking land restitution and working alongside labor unions, some of which were communist, came under direct attack by the Salvadoran state. Between the months of January and March of 1932, 30,000 Salvadorans, mostly indigenous, peasant, and male, were massacred in what is now called *La Matanza* (the Salvadoran Slaughter) (Gould and Lauria-Santiago 2008). The nation-state called war on its own people through an anticommunist mission deployed in the 1930s that extended into the civil war roughly half a century later. Naming itself after one of the leaders of the 1932 uprising, the Salvadoran guerrilla group Farabundo Martí National Liberation Front (FMLN) would postwar (after 1992) become the most viable political party to counter the political group on the right, Alianza Republicana Nacionalista (ARENA). The FMLN indeed espoused socialist goals. Yet, the majority of those killed in the war were not ideologically compelled. Out of the 75,000 lives lost and 10,000 disappeared, most Salvadorans fell completely under the definition of victims of war. While the 1932 Slaughter and the civil war have not been proclaimed or acknowledged as genocide against what is mostly an indigenous rural population, both direct and indirect outcomes reproduced ethnocide as indigenous peasant communities were compelled to drop or hide language, clothing, and cultural markers that the regime tied to communist sympathizers. In other words, simply looking indigenous implied dissent to, and was proscribed by, the nation-state. Both El Salvador and the United States constructed communism as an identity of villainy and insurgency throughout the twentieth century. Being considered a rebel sympathizer or possible communist held transnational ramifications for those seeking refuge in the United States. For example, the

United States granted asylum to 2.6 percent of Salvadoran refugee seekers (García 2006). As has been written about extensively by scholars on Central America, the U.S. government could not implicate itself in the atrocities committed by a military state it was funding, thus the systemic denial of asylum for Salvadorans fleeing the civil war.

The funding and support of a military state followed U.S. hemispheric political, economic, and military interests. Since the 1960s the emphasis of U.S. assistance, such as the Alliance for Progress (1961–1969), shifted to military agendas and the buildup of a security apparatus, which gave rise to the infamous death squads that terrorized the country throughout the civil war period (Chomsky 1987, 319). Initially, this program was meant to support reforms and economic projects but quickly changed to prioritize U.S. economic and security interests. Chomsky argues that the military was charged with policing and ensuring internal security. Consequently, demands for equitable distribution of resources such as land reform met with recalcitrant forces.

Progressive forces representing religious communities, teachers' unions, and peasant organizations would find themselves defined as a threat and face repression due to their demands for land reform and greater investment in social programs such as education, health care, and infrastructure. It is important to remember that the need for the Alliance for Progress was rooted in the unequal distribution of resources that left the majority of the population landless, undereducated, and with few opportunities. One of the goals of the Alliance was to improve the conditions of the recipient nations, such as alleviating hunger. Moreover, it sought to strengthen state bureaucracies to enhance tax collection and revenue as well as produce "integration" of the region. This integration often favored U.S. corporations and interests. As coffee production became the cash crop in the country, land consolidated in the hands of a few elite families. Peasants became primarily wage laborers. Their efforts to form cooperatives and to demand better working conditions in plantations were heavily repressed by the security apparatus of the state. Elites focused on controlling the coffee industry or in diversifying their assets. The system produced gross inequalities, hunger, and malnutrition for the rural sectors.

Democratic elections occurred in the 1970s. However, when the elections threatened established elites, they were quickly squelched with the assistance and collusion of the military. Such was the outcome of the 1972 elections that resulted in the exile of José Napoleón Duarte and his vice president Ernesto Claramount of the Partido Demócrata Cristiano. In 1977, Ernesto Claramount ran for the presidency again. However, he was ousted by General Carlos Humberto Romero's regime after Romero was declared the winner of the fraudulent election. A series of military juntas and the consolidation of opposition forces into the Frente Democrático Revolucionario (FDR) and the Farabundo Martí Frente de Liberación Nacional (FMLN) took place. After death squads tortured and killed leaders of the opposition in 1980, the civil war deepened. U.S. military funding to El Salvador continued despite pleas to stop it from U.S. and Salvadoran sectors of civil society. More than 70,000 would die at the hands of the death squads, in combat, and through military operations in rebel-controlled territories that included air bombings assisted by the United States.

When Salvadorans began to arrive in large numbers in the 1980s, the official U.S. response was thus to deny the need for granting asylum. Two-thirds, or 64 percent, of Salvadoran immigrants arrived in the United States during and after 1990; 29 percent are now U.S. citizens. To date, Salvadorans and Guatemalans continue to be defined as economic migrants. The nonreception of Central Americans as refugees has had enduring consequences for their economic and social adaptation in the United States. The U.S. denial of refugee status relegated large proportions to undocumented status and predetermined their precarious economic and social stability. While some were granted Temporary Protected Status (TPS), which has at minimum allowed for stable employment, it is a far cry from official designation of refugee or legal permanent-resident status as, for example, extended to Cubans fleeing the Castro regime.[5]

Guatemalan migration to the United States needs to be understood as a result of decades of U.S.-sponsored dictatorships and interventions in that country. In 1944, after a series of U.S.-supported regimes, President Juan José Arévalo was elected. During his presidency Arévalo made vast improvements to public education and social services. Once his term ended on March 15, 1951, President Jacobo Arbenz Guzmán was elected by 65 percent of the vote. Arbenz Guzmán continued and expanded the social reforms created by Arévalo's administration. For instance, he legalized the Communist Party (Guatemalan Labor Party, CTG) and encouraged labor organizing. During Guatemala's own golden era of labor organizing, twenty-five peasant unions emerged. Additionally, Arbenz Guzmán immediately attempted to address the nation's economic dependence through its import/export relationship to the United States that was mediated by the United Fruit Company. In 1952 his Agrarian Reform Law challenged the United States' Good Neighbor Policy, which was supposed to respect Latin American nations' self-governance without U.S. intervention.

Moreover, the 2 percent of the population that owned 72 percent of farmland depended on work servitude that Arbenz Guzmán's administration sought to end. The redistribution of land allocated forty-two acres per campesino of the expropriated unused land within large plantations. The oligarchs were paid 3 percent for a 25-year bond for their unused, though now expropriated, lands (LaFeber 1993). According to LaFeber, by 1954, 100,000 families had received land, bank credit, and technical aid. Arbenz Guzmán's administration promoted leadership among the rural communities since the law stipulated that it was to be administered locally and by department. To protect U.S. interests, in particular the profits of the United Fruit Company, the CIA orchestrated a coup d'état. Two days after the coup, a military junta supported by the United States and led by Colonel Carlos Castillo Armas was established. The junta would signal a return to military repression in the country and end what historians have called Guatemala's ten years of spring. The series of imposed dictatorships that followed created the conditions that fueled the thirty-six-year civil war (1960–1996).

In Guatemala, the civil war was also marked by genocide.[6] For Maya-Jakaltek anthropologist Victor Montejo the genocide of the Guatemalan civil war was not unprecedented but was as equally violent and massive as those committed by the Spanish invasion in 1492 (Montejo 1987). The United Nations Truth Commission as well as the Commission for Historical Clarification confirmed that by the end of the civil war, 93 percent of the atrocities occurred through the state's military and paramilitary forces. To put the Guatemalan violence in a hemispheric context, the over 45,000 disappeared and 200,000 killed during the war represent half of the total forcefully disappeared and killed during the entire Cold War in Latin America between 1966 and 1986 (REMHI 1998; CEH 1999; Grandin 2004; Kisler 2010). Of the approximately 200,000 killed and forcefully disappeared, 83 percent were Maya. The "Silent Holocaust" climaxed between 1978 and 1983 with the regimes of General Fernando Romeo Lucas García and General Efraín Ríos Montt. In 1982 alone, there were 18,000 documented murders. The scorched-earth policy implemented by Ríos Montt contributed to the systematic eradication of over four hundred Maya villages.

Historically seen as a threat to the economic and social development of the nation, Maya communities, whether participants in the resistance movements or not, were violently and systematically murdered. As 1992 Nobel Peace Prize winner Rigoberta Menchú Tum has vividly denounced in her testimonial, *Me llamo Rigoberta Menchú y así me nació la conciencia* (1983), men were captured, tortured, and brutally murdered. Some of these captured men were at times buried alive (REMHI 1998; CEH 1999). Boys were forcibly conscripted, kidnapped, or murdered. Women and girls were often publicly raped, tortured, and later, killed. The elderly, children (including newborns), and entire communities were repeatedly executed collectively. In addition, the Human Rights Commission report notes that the heads of Maya infants were frequently smashed against walls and the wombs of pregnant women were cut open in an effort to completely eradicate the "bad seeds" they carried. While the majority of those murdered and forcefully disappeared by the state were Mayas in the highlands, ladino and Mayas in urban areas were also tortured and murdered. Though the civil war officially ended on December 29, 1996, with the signing of the peace accords, a continuum of centuries of violence continues to afflict indigenous and rural communities enforced in the postwar and neoliberal periods.

Following the signing of the 1996 Guatemalan Peace Accords on March 12, 1999, President Bill Clinton publicly apologized to the Guatemalan people for the role the United States played in supporting the military repression. His apology came a month after the publication of the Historical Clarification Commission report, which explained that the United States was also responsible for the human rights abuses that took place during the civil war. Though Bill Clinton's public apology promised that the United States would "not repeat the mistake [of violating human rights]," U.S. interventions continued through the implantation of neoliberal policies that included the creation of megadevelopment projects and the criminalization of Maya and ladino activists. Clinton's apology[7] did not provide much-needed support to the thousands of Guatemalans who were forced to migrate to the United States escaping the civil war, postwar, and neoliberal periods.

As Guatemalans migrated to the United States for refuge, the United States took a similar stance toward the Salvadoran refugee seekers, systematically denying any form of legal entry and residency. The over one million displaced during the civil war and the thousands that followed in the postwar period were mostly displaced to the United States and Mexico. During the civil war, through the United Nations High Commissioner for Refugees and Mexico's Comisión Mexicana de Ayuda a Refugiados, refugee camps were established in the Yucatán region. According to historian Cristina García, Guatemalans who refused refuge in camps, such as those in Quintana Roo, were thus positioned as economic migrants by the United States so that only 1.8 percent of Guatemalans received U.S. asylum. Initially, most Guatemalans migrated during the peak of the Guatemalan civil war. The Pew Research Center reports that 74 percent entered after 1990. Since migration has continued and increased according to the Migration Policy Institute (MPI), the majority of Guatemalan immigrants actually arrived after 2000.[8] Though the census and Pew statistics do not distinguish between Maya and ladino Guatemalan immigrants, grass-roots Maya organizations estimate that half of the Guatemalan migrants in the United States are Maya. Today, an estimated 23 percent of the total U.S. Guatemalan population are U.S. citizens.

Unlike its three adjoining neighbors, Honduras did not experience a civil war during the last half of the twentieth century. However, the United States relied on Honduras throughout the 1800s and 1900s as an ally against the specter of communism in Guatemala, El Salvador, and Nicaragua. Honduras has often been placed in the middle by the United States and also by its adjoining nations. For example, U.S. filibuster William Walker's story is linked to Nicaragua through his occupation and self-appointed presidency of Nicaragua from 1856 to 1857 (Lancaster 1994). Yet, Honduras played a vital role in stopping his repeated attempts at occupying its neighbor. In 1860, after yet another attempt to take Nicaragua, the British Royal Navy captured Walker near Trujillo, Honduras. To ensure that Walker would not stir rebellions in British Honduras (Belize) and the Mosquito Coast (on the Atlantic Coast of Honduras and Nicaragua), the British Royal Navy turned him over to the Honduran government, which executed him by firing squad. Anti-imperialists champion Honduras's actions in putting a final stop to the occupation attempts of a man set on conquering Central America. Regardless, Honduras acted on the behalf of the British. After Britain lost its Central American colonies, Honduras would be made a facilitator of U.S., rather than British, strategy.

Honduran international trade and investment was increasingly tied to the United States from the 1870s. Foreign interests dominated in shipping, most notably bananas from the north coast, and railway expansion. The Tropical Trading and Transport Company established itself in 1877 and merged with the Boston Fruit Company in 1899 to become the infamous United Fruit Company (now Chiquita Banana). Known as *el pulpo* (the octopus), the company's tentacles penetrated the rest of the isthmus. Along with the Standard Fruit Company (Dole) and Cuyamel Fruit Company, Honduras came to epitomize the "banana republic," as coined by writer O. Henry in 1904. The corporations that came to own much of Honduras's only farmable lands built the nation's transportation infrastructure. However, this was accomplished to promote U.S. companies' profits, which were disinvested from the Honduran economy. The United States began its military presence in 1903 with the goal of protecting these monopoly companies. As Honduran activist Elvia Alvarado denounced in her testimony *Don't Be Afraid, Gringo: A Honduran Woman Speaks from the Heart* (1987), U.S. imperialism made Honduras one of the poorest nations in the Americas.

Honduras's contiguous borders to Nicaragua, Guatemala, and El Salvador made it a strategic military site, especially for the United States' war against communism. In 1954, the Honduran military provided support to the United Fruit Company's coup d'état in Guatemala. In 1965, as part of the Organization of American States, Honduras, El Salvador, Costa Rica, Nicaragua, and Brazil joined the United States' occupation of the Dominican Republic to restore order as the "Constitutionalists" sought the return of Juan Bosch to the presidency. Bosch had been democratically elected but in 1963 was ousted, and civil strife ensued in the Dominican Republic, providing a reason for U.S. occupation. An election was held in 1966, which Bosch ran for but lost to U.S.-backed Joaquín Balaguer, who became a dictator, ruling the Dominican Republic for the next twenty-two years. In this case, we see the United States using its interventionist methods in the Caribbean.

Honduras's position(ing) was made most prominent during the Contra War (1981–1990). The Reagan administration based its covert military operations and attacks on Nicaragua from Honduras. LaFeber notes that the U.S. covert military posts contributed to Honduran deforestation. Most notable is that the CIA trained the death squad Battalion 3–16, which enacted tortures and disappearances of Hondurans suspected of being communist Sandinista sympathizers. During this timeline, U.S. military aid increased tenfold to Honduras. By 1986, Sandinistas fought the Contras within Honduras, thus crossing the Nicaraguan border. This included the United States deploying its own special forces through Operation Golden Pheasant (1988). U.S. troops landed at a Honduran Air Force base that was, in fact, the headquarters for the U.S. military. Though the Contras would eventually assist in the defeat of the Sandinista government, Battalion 3–16 remained in Honduras and continued to practice its torture tactics. It is closely linked to both the proliferation of *maras* in twenty-first-century Honduras and in influencing the national police, who rule corruptly and with total impunity, contributing to Honduras being named today as one of the most dangerous and deadliest nations in the Western Hemisphere.

Honduras's placement as middleman at times seemed contradictory. While in 1988 Honduras headquartered the U.S. military in its war against the

Nicaraguan Sandinistas, it established refugee camps for Salvadorans fleeing the atrocities of civil war. The irony is that El Salvador's civil war was also funded, and its military similarly trained, by the U.S. government. According to John Brown, the U.S. military commands and staff that worked together in Honduras were then deployed by the CIA in Operation Just Cause, the incursion and attack into Panama in 1989.[9]

From October 29 to November 1998, Hurricane Mitch struck Honduras, Guatemala, and Nicaragua. Referred to as one of the most powerful and destructive hurricanes in the history of the Americas, it is estimated that it left nearly 18,000 dead and thousands missing. Of the three Central American countries, Honduras was the most devastated with over 7,000 people killed, 1.5 million displaced (approximately 20 percent of the total population), 35,000 houses destroyed, and another 50,000 homes damaged. Additionally, approximately 70 percent of the crops were lost, which left thousands unemployed and homeless. The vast economic disparity, unemployment, and inequalities further reinforced a political crisis in the nation. By 2009, this crisis escalated with the ouster of President Manuel Zelaya.

Though Zelaya had been elected as a centrist and a member of the Liberal Party of Honduras (PLH) in 2005, his growing leftist changes alienated the Honduran military and conservative businesses and institutions. Zelaya began to address some of the deep historical and social inequalities by raising the minimum wage, lowering energy prices, and attempting to prioritize the poor. These moves placed him under suspicion by conservatives and elites who aligned Zelaya with Venezuela's Hugo Chávez and Bolivia's Evo Morales, especially after he joined the Alianza Bolivariana para los Pueblos de Nuestra América as a direct response to the United States' Central American Free Trade Agreement. As Nikolas Kozloff reported in *Democracy Now*, Zelaya critiqued the United States' war on drugs and called for legalization of certain drugs in order to nullify drug violence (2009). While a "mythology" exists that Zelaya was attempting to enact a constitutional referendum that would extend his presidency,[10] in fact, Zelaya attempted to run a constitutional survey "of public opinion on convoking a national constitutive assembly" to review whether to amend the constitution (Joseph 2009). Thus, "Zelaya never did anything illegal or extralegal" but was executing his rights as president while maintaining the Honduran constitution (Joseph 2009). Regardless of whether changes would have come about through the national constitutive assembly, Zelaya could not have run for reelection. According to Shaun Joseph, the Honduran oligarchy was threatened by Zelaya's preparing a lawsuit against several elite families who had stopped paying their electricity bill for their mansions and businesses for at least two decades, costing the nation a minimum of $20 million. His lawsuit was preempted by congress, which passed an amnesty for "anyone" who had not paid their electricity bill. Though Zelaya has been accused of attempting to violate the Honduran constitution, governments installed by armed force are in fact rendered unconstitutional under Article 3, which states,

> No one owes allegiance to a usurping government nor to those who assume office or public service by force of arms or by using means or procedures which violate or ignore the provisions established by this Constitution and other laws. The acts adopted by such authorities are null. The people have the right to resort to insurrection in defense of the constitutional order.[11]

Zelaya was forcibly removed from office in June 28, 2009, and exiled to Costa Rica. He was replaced by Roberto Micheletti, his one-time opponent in the PLH's primary elections. Though the constitution's Article 3 grants the people the right to insurrection, the state responded with force against Zelaya's supporters and Micheletti's anticoup protesters. While free speech and press are supposed to be protected under the Honduran constitution, to date, Honduras has been declared one of the most dangerous nations for journalists and activists.

It is under this context of an unofficial war on the people that Hondurans, especially Honduran youth, who constitute the largest and most recent Central American group out-migrating, seek refuge. Like most Central American migrants, an estimated 79 percent of Hondurans living in the United States entered after 1990. The Temporary Protected Status (TPS) program granted in 1998 because of Hurricane Mitch registered 64,000 Hondurans in 2014 and has been renewed through 2016. As the more recent migrants, Hondurans constitute the most impoverished (22%) and least formally educated, with 75 percent of their U.S. population being undocumented. The economic displacement and political and social instability of the region can be traced directly to U.S. economic development agendas and foreign policy.

While Honduras epitomizes U.S. financial expansionism as protected by the U.S. military in the banana republic, Panama is exemplary of foreign interventionist manipulation of land, water, and people through the creation of a nation-state in order to construct a canal that would facilitate U.S. commerce and military security by sea. Though this anthology does not include an article on U.S. Panamanians, it is important to understand the significance of Panama in the construction of Central America as a region dependent on U.S. commerce and militancy. In 1890, military strategist Alfred T. Mahan published *The Influence of Sea Power*, which established a blueprint for U.S. expansionism as a global superpower. By 1898, the United States had reached the limits of consolidating its continental borders. As it looked out toward the Pacific, the Atlantic, the Gulf of Mexico, and the Caribbean, it sought to complete a manifest destiny beyond its borders. It also strived to protect itself as a nation, especially since, according to world-systems theorist Ramón Grosfoguel, the United States was aware of a German military attack via the seizure of Puerto Rico (2003, 51). In order to achieve both goals, the United States needed to establish its naval power, especially since it was suspicious that newly freed Cuba would develop a nationalist, anticolonial movement that might spread throughout Latin America. Thus, the United States strategized to occupy and attain Puerto Rico and Cuba, especially since they stood as the only islands within the four maritime routes. Access to these maritime routes—and to the U.S. island possessions that in 1898 included Puerto Rico, Cuba, Hawaii, Guam, and the Philippines—was absolutely necessary for the United States to establish itself as a superior economic and military power. Mahan's naval strategy included a plan for building and controlling a canal in Central America. Grosfoguel explains, "A United States-controlled canal in Central America would enable fleet unity. The fleet would move with greater speed and security from one ocean to the other by way of the canal" (50). It is significant that a strategic plan for a canal predated Panama as a sovereign nation-state. This plan would eventually shape the map and politics of the isthmus for centuries to come since it also established Central America as a military satellite and economic farm for the United States. Central America came to produce primarily food and manufactured products for the United States. Consequently, the United States has historically extracted Central America's natural resources, which includes the labor of its people.

As the United States settled on the region of what is now Panama, the nation of Panama needed to be constructed as a separate nation-state from Colombia. Explaining Mahan's strategy that highly influenced the interventionist events that took shape in the decade of 1890 to 1900, Grosfoguel states, "The relation of forces, alliances, and struggles in the world interstate system provides a context to better understand the constant imperialist interventions suffered by the Caribbean. It can also explain why the Caribbean has been a battlefield for different core states of the world-system throughout the past five centuries" (49). Therefore, in the historical conceptualization of the Caribbean by core nations, Central America was shaped as an east–west passageway and north–south route for semiperipheral and core nations that erased it as an axis point. We shift the axis from the Caribbean to Central America to underscore how the region turned into a bull's-eye for violent U.S. interventionist policies that ensured its access to the rest of the Americas throughout the twentieth century. Situated in the position of both target and bystander, Central America occupied a contradictory position of both fringe and center to U.S. economic and military interests to the Caribbean. Moreover, the United States has maintained its own economic and political stability (relative to Central America and much of the rest of the world) through its ability to regulate the rest of the Americas. Thus, while Latin America continues to be conceived as an outcome of Spanish imperial colonialism, U.S. imperial intervention continues to shape the land, political, and economic boundaries of each nation within Central America. For example, Spanish colonial powers had, prior to the building of the canal, established Panama as a passageway from the Atlantic basin for the importation of African slaves and to access the riches of South America. The Panama that emerged as a nation in 1903 had already existed as a region for almost four centuries. However, it took geopolitical maneuvers to get from the place of region to the site of a nation in the project of "dividing the isthmus" (Rodríguez 2009). Like the rest of Central America, Panama obtained independence in 1821, soon to join the Great Republic of Colombia. By 1823, the nations within the isthmus included the Federal Republic of Central America (the union included Guatemala, El Salvador, Honduras, Nicaragua, and Costa Rica), the British settlement of Belize, and the Colombian Republic (which included Panama, Colombia, Northern Peru, Ecuador, Venezuela, and North-western Guyana). In 1889, the War of a Thousand Days provided the entryway for U.S. intervention that encouraged Panamanian sedition from Colombia and emboldened it by establishing its military presence to deter a Colombian attack.

With the signing of the Hay-Bunau-Varilla Treaty in 1903 and the purchased shares of the Compagnie Nouvelle de Canal (1904), the United States established its right to land five miles on either side of the canal and its occupation of said lands "in perpetuity." The concept of "in perpetuity" should not be glossed over since it highlights the U.S. intention to forever attempt to control the rights to land, air, and water within Central America. The treaty included "a sixteen-kilometer-wide strip of territory and extensions of three nautical miles into the sea from each terminal."[12] It also gave the United States rights to all bodies of water for transportation purposes surrounding lands and islands within the zone and to the "the construction, maintenance, and operation of any system of communication dealing with the canal."[13] The canal, moreover, created a stratified and racialized society shaped by U.S. racial Jim Crow practices and policies within what was supposed to be a sovereign nation. The reracialization of Panama, which occurred because of North American beliefs of biological-environmental determinism, is still present today through Panama's racially stratified society. The treaty established the canal as more than a passageway but as an actual moment of social, economic, topographical, and political transformation. The treaty remained a site of contestation as a symbol of limited sovereignty for Panamanians that would erupt in conflict in 1964 and in U.S. occupation in 1989. In relation to the rest of Central America, 1903 represents the consolidation of the isthmus divided, mapping the topographical borders we know today.

Similar to the rest of the Central American nations, Panama felt the repercussions of the United States' early involvement. In 1977, the first treaty, the Permanent Neutrality Treaty, was signed by President Jimmy Carter and Brigadier General Omar Torrijos, declaring the canal neutral and open to vessels of all nations. The Panama Canal Treaty followed, which provided for joint control of the canal until December 31, 1999, when control of the Canal Zone would be transferred over completely from the United States to Panama. However, ten days before the transfer of control was to begin in January 1, 1990, the United States bombed and occupied Panama under the directive Operation Just Cause. The reason given was at least twofold: that the Panamanian Defense Forces (PDF) had killed a U.S. soldier and that the operation was an attempt to rescue Panama from the dictatorial rule of President Manuel Noriega. However, the justification of occupation for salvation contradicts Panamanian organizations' charge that it resulted in the death of 6,000 Panamanians. Moreover, the U.S. School of the Americas trained Noriega, and he rose to presidency (1983–1989) with U.S. aid. On the CIA payroll, Noriega collaborated in the anti-Sandinista or "Contra" war on Nicaragua; he provided the planes used for the traffic of drugs that funded weapons for the Contras. Operation Just Cause occurred between the fall of the Berlin Wall and Operation Desert Shield/Desert Storm, thus providing a training and testing ground for weapons and maneuvers that would be used in Iraq eight months later (Trent 2002).

U.S. Panamanian demographics have been shaped by the Panama Canal history. This relationship shaped Panama's language, racial, and out-migration populations. According to Pew Research,[14] Panamanians are a significant part of the 4 percent of foreign-born black Latina/o immigrants in the United States, with their numbers being at 32,000 of total U.S. Panamanians (165,456 according to the U.S. 2010 census). The Pew Research Center explains, "Black immigrants are somewhat more likely to hold U.S. citizenship than all immigrants—54 percent versus 47 percent. Given that many black Panamanian immigrants are from English-speaking Caribbean nations, they're also more likely to be proficient in English compared with all immigrants (74% versus 50%). Black immigrants are also less likely to be in the U.S. illegally than all immigrants (16% versus 26%)." It is also significant that along with Nicaragua, Belize, and Costa Rica, immigrants from Panama tend to be women (64%).[15] As reported by MPI, Panamanians in the U.S. have the second-highest rate of English proficiency (English-only or speaking English "very well") at 73 percent. Belizean immigrants struggle the least with English-language proficiency (95 percent), followed by Costa Ricans (61%).[16] Panamanian adult immigrants represent the most formally educated Central American immigrants with 27 percent holding a bachelor's degree or higher. According to MPI, 23 percent of adult immigrant Costa Ricans report holding a BA or higher. While Hondurans and Guatemalans constitute the most recent Central American migrants (who are also the most impoverished and least formally educated), Panamanians, Costa Ricans, and Belizeans represent some of the oldest settlements in the United States. According to statistics from the MPI reports, "In 2011, immigrants from Panama (59 percent), Nicaragua (59 percent), and Belize (58 percent) were most likely to have arrived before 1990." U.S. Panamanians are the least impoverished at 15 percent, especially when compared to Hondurans and Guatemalans. U.S. Panamanians are considered part of a Central American diaspora and also part of a black international diaspora.

We provide this historical context to highlight that the U.S.-Central America relation is not a new phenomenon, nor is Central American immigration to the United States. Moreover, the influx of migration that occurred post-1980s as well as current diasporas and recent migration trends are intrinsically connected to the economic, political, and military strategies the United States planned and then deployed onto Central America as a region and to each Central American nation. At times this placed Central American nations in contradictory positions to their neighbors in order to meet the demands of the United States as a core, global economic and military power. As explained, U.S. policies toward Central America were often promoted for the safety and prosperity of Central

Americans, though wealth is disinvested and profits return to companies of the Global North. Moreover, postcommunist justifications have now transmuted to anti-gang and drug trafficking regulations that continue to permit U.S. military presence in Central America. This, in turn, ensures Central American migration to the U.S. rather than mitigate it. While U.S. involvement in Central America helped to establish U.S. affluence at global and local levels, it also shaped Central American poverty and the disenfranchisement of marginalized peoples. The United States, however, cannot be held solely accountable for the dependency and distortions that continue to take place in Central America. Each national state apparatus perpetuated the legacies of colonialism that promote patriarchal ideologies of whiteness and male heterosexual superiority and that have, through global consumerism, idealized economic materialism as a purpose in life. It is at this summit, at the crux of neocolonial and global outcomes, that we situate the chapters within the anthology. Having this historical understanding should also help us grasp just how complex the negotiations of space, nations, ethnicities, narratives, locations, identities, and visual and linguistic codes are for each segment of diasporic Central Americans explored in each chapter.

Central American countries also sought to create a regional economy and institutional collaboration among all five nations in the '50s, '60s, and '70s that were derailed by the U.S. role in the rise of military dictatorships at the end of the 1970s and through the 1980s. The 1980s are known as the "lost decade" in terms of the political and economic losses incurred during the height of the civil wars that drew the region into the Cold War conflict. Through the Central American Common Market, the Central American peso was created, which was worth one U.S. dollar and pursued import-substitution industrialization to overcome economic dependency on exports. Regional integration succumbed to conflict over land and the uneven benefits the common market brought to each nation, meaning agricultural and industrial policies did not benefit all countries equally. The 1969 war between Honduras and El Salvador (known as the Soccer War) threw into relief the conflicts over industrial and agricultural agendas of integration and the unresolved factors that pitted regional interest against national ones. Currently, new versions of the common market seek to revive regional economic and institutional collaboration that includes Panama, Belize, and the Dominican Republic through the Central American Integration System known as SICA (Sistema de la Integración Centroamericana). The peace process also led to the Diálogo de San José,[17] which established cooperation between the European Union and Central America with the aim of promoting democratic institutions, political infrastructure, and the economic integration of the region. From 1984, these meetings with various trade agreements took place, but the urgency that led to the meetings and European assistance with favorable trade conditions shifted to other regions.

In sum, Central America has been integrally connected to U.S. politics and economy since the nineteenth century. It is in this context that we frame the migrations of Central American populations to the United States. Central American populations in the United States have grown as a result of economic processes that displaced them from their land and drove them to migrate and to organize in response to the massive political and economic changes they confronted. The mobilized populations met military repression, particularly in Nicaragua, Guatemala, El Salvador, and Honduras. During the civil wars and military repression that ensued, thousands were killed, forcefully disappeared, and displaced locally and regionally. Today, the postwar processes of democratization and the economic vitality in the region remain uncertain as violence continues to affect the populations of Honduras, Guatemala, and El Salvador and drives its youngest citizens toward the United States in flight without any guarantee of refuge. This anthology aims to generate conversations about the hemispheric significance of the region as we embrace continuities but also shifts that emphasize processes of political and cultural transformation.

CONTEXTUALIZING CENTRAL AMERICAN MIGRATIONS

There are various reasons why Central American countries have established their largest diasporas in the United States. The causes have never been purely economic. For example, economic restructuring in California and the shift from Fordist to post-Fordist production have been referenced as a reason why Central Americans chose to migrate to the United States in the 1990s (Baker-Cristales 2004; Hamilton and Stoltz Chinchilla 2001). But these economic developments could not have occurred without the simultaneous implementation of the Sistema de la Integración Centroamericana (SICA) in 1991 and the North American Free Trade Agreement (NAFTA) in 1994 that further destabilized the national economies south of the U.S.-Mexico border. U.S.-sponsored civil wars and internal governmental corruption had already devastated Central American economies, a problem compounded further by natural disasters like Hurricanes Mitch and Stan as well as the rapid exploitation of natural resources.

The exploitation of natural resources intensified with the 2006 Central American Free Trade Agreement, which has not reduced economic problems but in fact intensified them. At local levels, illicit economies and gang culture emerged tied to the militarization of civilians, traces of the U.S.-Contra cocaine trade for weaponry, and the expedited deportation of U.S.-made gang members into Central America in keeping with 1996's Illegal Immigration Reform and Immigrant Responsibility Act. However, unless probed, migrants often claim the desire for a better life as the reason why they migrated to the United States. A better life can mean a life free of violence (from the military, police, gangs, and patriarchal restrictions), an opportunity for education, access to medical care, and a stable and well-paying job. What might seem the most personal of decisions, upon examination, are tied to politics and national and internal trade and laws. The compelling factor of a restructured economy, therefore, intersects the personal and political, such as with gender, since domestic and state gendered forms of violence buttress one another (Zentgraf 2005) and influence gender migration flows (Hondagneu-Sotelo 2003). As stated, once in the United States, Central Americans became caught in a legislative and criminal profiling cycle that expedited the expulsion of Central American immigrants, including those who held legal permanent residency, back to Guatemala, El Salvador, and Honduras (Zilberg 2011; Bibler Coutin 2007; Golash-Boza 2015). The dream of creating an economically viable life with the priority on attaining a higher education continues to motivate parent migration to the United States (Abrego 2014). This, in turn, influences some unaccompanied children to migrate and seek to reunite with their parents. In view of transregional conditions of struggle, Central Americans have made a significant mark in labor and immigrant organizing, especially in Los Angeles but also throughout the United States. Though Central American immigrants and their U.S.- born or raised children are a visible presence, especially in California, U.S. scholarship continues to neglect the significance of these populations in relation to their own growing communities and to other U.S. Latinidades, ethnicities, and neighborhoods.

Latina/o and immigrant visibility in Los Angeles rose to the forefront in 2002 with the May Day marches in which 12,000 people mobilized to proclaim their presence, citizenship, and social equity demands (Ochoa and Ochoa 2005). In 2006, according to social activist and journalist Sharat G. Lin, "The May Day demonstrations for immigrants' rights in cities across the United States were the largest collective outpouring of street protest since the Vietnam War and the Civil Rights movement of the 1960s and 1970s. Over 650,000 people participated in two marches in Los Angeles, 400,000 in Chicago, 250,000 in San Jose, 75,000 in Denver, and 30,000 each in San Francisco, Sacramento, Fresno, Houston, and New York City" (251).[18] It is significant that all cities mentioned are the primary areas of destination and settlement for Central Americans, particularly Guatemalans and Salvadorans, with both Los Angeles and San Francisco as the top two cities. However, Central Americans as a whole continue to be undercounted. In California,[19] the 2010 U.S. Census listed the total Guatemalan and Salvadoran population at the exclusion of other Central Americans, estimating Guatemalans and Salvadorans at 907,000. According to the Migration Policy Institute, "In 2011, the greater Los Angeles metropolitan area hosted the largest number of Central American immigrants, with about 575,200 (19 percent of the Central American born in the United States)."[20] The Pew Research Center estimates that "Los Angeles County has by far the largest Hispanic population at 4.8 million."[21] Central Americans, both immigrant and native born, continue to be the second-largest Latina/o group in California. To the detriment of our ethnic diversity, state statistics erase regional, racial, and cultural differences, as noted by our contributors in the anthology.

While sociologists have proposed Florida and specifically Miami to be part of Latin America, Los Angeles has historically been a gateway, and first point of entry, for immigrants from throughout Latin America. From the 1970s into the late 1990s, Angeleno churches and Central American–led organizations offered sanctuary to Salvadorans, Guatemalans, Nicaraguans, and Hondurans fleeing military-state civil wars, and more recently state police and *mara* civil violence. Moreover, since 1989, San Francisco has been known officially as a city of refuge. The city's official website explains, "In recent years, the Sanctuary Movement has experienced a rebirth, as grassroots organizations, faith communities, and local government have stood firmly against repressive immigration proposals in Congress and immigration raids that separate families. In February 2007, Mayor Gavin Newsom reaffirmed San Francisco's commitment to immigrant communities by issuing an Executive Order that called on City departments to develop protocol and training on the Sanctuary Ordinance."[22] Though Los Angeles can be considered the Ellis Island of the Pacific, Central Americans often choose to relocate and to settle in suburban areas with significant Central American populations such as Long Beach and Pacoima. Guatemalans and Salvadorans share the top three rankings of cities populated by them with (1) Los Angeles–Long Beach, (2) San Francisco–Oakland–Vallejo, and (3) San Bernardino–Riverside.[23] Moreover, Central American immigrants settle within the Great Central Valley as undocumented migrant fieldworkers. For many Central Americans, Los Angeles is but a stop on their northern route to cities like San Francisco, where prior Central American immigrants established themselves as early as the late 1800s (Menjívar 2008). However, Los Angeles and especially the neighborhoods of Pico-Union and Westlake/MacArthur Park region (known as Little Central America) remain the oldest settlements in the most populated city by Central American and Maya immigrants. These dynamic neighborhoods are the focus of various articles in the anthology.

U.S. Central Americans fills the void on U.S.-based scholarship that has historically neglected the fastest growing Latina/o group in the United States. The set of original articles is groundbreaking in that it represents the first collection of cutting-edge work being done by U.S. Central American scholars in U.S. Central American studies. Most of the articles deal with transforming space, place, cultural practices, performativities, and identities by complicating nation and engaging lenses of intersectionality, subjectivity, performativity, experience, and cultural memory. This interdisciplinary collection, thus, begins to anthologize scholarly work researched and written by Central Americans born or raised in the United States on U.S. Central American populations.

We employ U.S. Central American and not hyphenated national identities such as Guatemalan-American, Salvadoran-American, or Honduran-American because we emphasize the shared histories, cultures, and struggles of Central American diasporic communities in the United States. While a U.S. Central American positionality highlights shared experiences, asserting a regional (and not a national) identity also foregrounds the diverse ethnic identities (Maya, Garifuna, Xinca, Lenca, Pipil, ladino/mestizo) within the Central American diasporas. This interdisciplinary analytical frame allows us to expand studies on Central Americans in the United States since earlier scholarship has often been based on specific nation-states, which tends to blur the shared experiences, contributions, and struggles of U.S. Central American communities. However, the communities discussed within the anthology are primarily Salvadoran, Guatemalan, and Maya. In conceptualizing this anthology, we approached U.S. Central American scholars writing on Nicaraguan, Garifuna, and Honduran diasporas. As is often the case in academia, timing makes a world of difference. Though these scholars were unavailable, we hope that this anthology marks a turning point for ongoing publication and dialogue on U.S. Central Americans.

The anthology situates one of its most important clusters: California, which is home to one in three Central Americans. As the most prominent location of migrant entry, as a political site of mobilization in the 1990s, and as the state that holds a significant number of universities with U.S. Central American scholars, California remains vital in the relationship between the United States, Central America, and its diasporas. The volume dialogues with a select body of sociological, social science, ethnological, and cultural studies scholarship pertinent to anyone interested in the study of Latina/o diversity, U.S. Central American people and communities, ethnic studies, and intergenerational differences among Central Americans living in the United States. The co-editors and the contributors share a commitment to interdisciplinary scholarship and to promoting dialogue and understanding across ethnic and generational groups. The editors and contributors have published widely on issues related to U.S. Central Americans, Latinas/os, Chicanas/os, feminisms, comparative ethnicities, cultural studies, sociology, and the Maya diaspora.

Research on U.S. Central Americans has grown within the last decade as a response to the growing visibility of Central American populations, the sensationalizing of youth as unaccompanied migrants and *maras*, and the coming of age of 1.5- and second-generation Central Americans. As the third-largest national Latina/o group and second-largest California Latina/o population, Central Americans have crossed a threshold that requires institutions and other American cultures to learn about U.S.- born and raised Central Americans. U.S. Central Americans embody both an establishing and emergent status that make them and their communities, cultures, histories, and narratives dynamic. A focus on U.S. Central Americans has become fundamental for understanding diversity within U.S. immigrant experiences.

Social science scholarship on Central American migration has burgeoned in the past few decades. This important body of work covers events and topics of the '80s and '90s that explore the reasons for migration, such as poverty and civil war, the journey, and the context of reception and its impact on family separation and immigrant political activism. Work on Central American migratory movements by Menjívar (2000), Coutin (2000), Hamilton and Stoltz Chinchilla (2001), Baker-Cristales (2004), Cordova (2005), and Abrego (2014) primarily focus on California, while Hagan (1994) and Mahler (1996) focus on Texas and New York, respectively. These studies give us the poignant stories of new immigrants navigating an increasingly restrictive immigration climate and the burden of "illegality," because they were continuously denied official refugee status. Concerned with the immigrant generation and its activism and struggles, some of these books begin to analyze Central American experiences in the United States in particular, solely in the last chapter. The anthology centers this last chapter as a much-needed collection of work that tells how Central Americans are creating new yet historically and culturally tied communities, identities, subjectivities, narratives, discourses, memories, and cultural products through studies, literature, and art that reimagine and reshape Central America within the United States.

Central American Maya scholarship has employed a similar historical approach on immigration, transnational links such as hometown associations, and remittances while minimally exploring emergent practices situated in the United States. Scholarship on Maya diasporic communities has mainly focused on the reason for immigration to the United States (see Burns [1993]; Foxen [2008]; Hamilton and Stoltz Chinchilla [2001]; LeBaron [2012]; Loucky and Moors [2000]; and Popkin [2005]). The cited studies examine the reception of Mayas in cities like Los Angeles; Houston; and Indiantown, Florida, primarily between the decades of the 1980s and 1990s and as illustrated also by Hagan (1994) and Rodríguez (1987). Fewer studies focus on the struggles for survival in the United States. Burns (1993), Foxen (2008), Hagan (1994), and Popkin (2005) highlight the importance of social and church organizations that maintain transnational links to specific hometowns in Guatemala. Additionally, Patricia Foxen (2008) has expanded these studies through her ethnography on Guatemalan Maya communities in Providence, Rhode Island. While historian Leon Fink's *The Maya of Morganton: Work and Community in the Nuevo New South* stands as an exception since the book focuses on Maya labor struggles in Morganton, North Carolina's poultry industry (2003), *U.S. Central Americans: Reconstructing Memories, Struggles, and Communities of Resistance* builds on and complements work on the Maya diaspora by focusing on other forms of community formation like memory, language, textiles, and public space. This anthology addresses various characteristics of the burgeoning Maya diaspora by including the experiences of first- and second- generation Mayas and placing them in dialogue with other indigenous and nonindigenous U.S. Central Americans.

Most research texts on Central Americans in the United States focus on Central American history, politics, and economies. There are only two formative texts that include and analyze literature written by Central Americans in the United States. These are Ana Patricia Rodríguez's *Dividing the Isthmus: Central American Transnational Histories, Cultures, and Literatures* (2009) and Arturo Arias's *Taking Their Word: Literature and Signs of Central America* (2007). Though historically rich and comprehensive, as the titles suggest, Central American literature and cultural production by authors born or raised in the United States does not remain the primary focus. In fact, literature and cultural production by U.S. Central American writers is limited in each text; after all, the methods are transnationalist in that U.S. literature written by Central Americans is framed and analyzed in relation also to Central America, adding to U.S.-based scholarship on the writers and literatures from the isthmus. Yajaira Padilla's *Changing Women, Changing Nation* (2012) examines U.S. Central American works in the last two chapters. The literature and cultural-text articles in this anthology dialogue with Rodríguez, Arias, and Padilla's influential work. Moreover, scholars such as Alicia Ivonne Estrada, Karina O. Alvarado, Maritza E. Cárdenas, and Oriel Siu are significantly impacting the study of U.S. Central American literature. The anthology's multi-interdisciplinary lens turns its complete focus on the literature and cultural texts produced by U.S. Central Americans as part of cultural-memory practices in the United States.

As a landmark anthology, *U.S. Central Americans: Reconstructing Memories, Struggles, and Communities of Resistance* brings together innovative and needed research by eminent and emerging U.S. Central American scholars from within various fields and disciplines. As these works demonstrate, migrant imaginaries, subjectivities, communities, and experiences are transnational, and to date, the focus of much research has remained on the practices by Central Americans as they relate to their countries of origin. The co-editors and contributors rely on the importance of that work as they aim to build and expand on it by including the 1.5 and second generation of U.S.- born or raised Central Americans. The 1.5 generation and beyond brings to the fore how these transnational dynamics manifest in California, which holds one of the largest U.S. Central American populations. The anthology situates Central Americans firmly within Latina/o, Chicana/o, ethnic, American, and Latin American studies, not as a chapter introducing an Othered ethnic experience but as central to the greater conversations on diaspora, U.S. intercommunity relations, and Latinidad. Equally important is U.S. Central Americans centralizing our presence and cultural practices of memory and voice. The collection offers nine chapters that explore a range of multidisciplinary topics promoting inclusivity and understanding across ethnic, gender, class, and generational divides.

FRAMING U.S. CENTRAL AMERICANS: OUR LATINIDAD

Central American regional economic and political integration and unity efforts are not recent. In the period after Spanish independence (1821) the Central

American region created a federal republic that initially united the present-day nation-states of Guatemala, El Salvador, Honduras, Nicaragua, and Costa Rica. During the period of the Federal Republic of Central America (1821–1841), liberal political leaders viewed the isthmian union as an imagined *patria grande*. Though the Federal Republic of Central America ended in 1841 with the succession led by Guatemala, the imagined notion of a patria grande continued to manifest itself through symbolic articulations of a shared regional culture evident in independence parades, a regional newspaper (*Diario de Centro América* [1880 to present]), economic trade, and immigration laws that create links between and within the Central American nations.[24] Moreover, history texts like *Historia de la América Central* by José Milla and *Reseña histórica de Centro América* by Lorenzo Montúfar discursively unify the region, affirming the notion of a patria grande. Central American diasporas in the United States bring and maintain this imagined greater Central America community and its symbolic discourse. The notion of patria grande continues in the yearly independence parades recreated by the U.S. Central American diasporas in Los Angeles. As with the Republic of Central America, which historians have noted maintained a "complex combination of conflicts between and within the five states" (Palmer 1993, 517), U.S. Central American diasporic identities are constructed between and within complex spaces of collaboration and conflict.

In the U.S. academy, Arturo Arias was one of the first to theorize on a broader U.S. Central American community by deploying the term coined by Maya Chinchilla "Central American-American" and Arias's American Central American (1991, 2003). However, scholars have continued to work with the imagined community, highlighting and situating diaspora, diasporic, and transnational in their titles and studies (Craft 2005; Hernández 2006; Rodríguez 2005, 2009; Padilla 2013; Estrada 2013). Country-specific terms include the Salvadoran Departamento 15 / *hermanos lejanos* (Rodríguez 2005; Baker-Cristales 2004), Rodríguez's *Salvadoreñidades* (2005), and reworkings of prior frames to offer new concepts such as U.S. Salvadoran and Padilla's trans-Salvadoran (2012). Rodríguez's "transisthmus" encapsulates the diasporas and transnationalist movements within Central America and between it and the United States (2009). Most scholars writing on Central Americans from the U.S. diasporas are working with or through terms like U.S. Central American. In 2007, Alvarado raised the question of a "U.S. Central American" identity in "discussing our name or lack of one, in order to highlight a U.S. Central American social political position" (2007, 12–13).

U.S. Central American is not only an alternative term to *American Central American* but also a "reclamation [that] includes differentiating [our]selves from a purely Central American [and North American] banner" (Alvarado 2013, 372). However, U.S. Central American, Central American–American, and *centralamericanos*, a term employed by Maritza E. Cárdenas in this anthology, share an effort to affirm a historical isthmian union in the diaspora. These terms illustrate the multiple articulations of U.S.-based regional Central American identities that aim at challenging static national and U.S.-recognized hyphenated national identities. They show a process in which Central Americans in the United States actively engage the construction of their own identities and communities, even if in contestation.

The placement of "U.S." before Central American recognizes the social and national location from which we as members of the Central American diaspora construct our identities, histories, communities, and cultures. It brings attention to the presence, often via violent interventions, of the United States in the isthmus, which resulted in the migration of thousands of Central Americans to the United States. The removal of the hyphen contests its historical use to mark ethnic identities (Mexican-American, Asian-American, African-American). Refusing the hyphenation and assumed Americanization that comes with "-American," we choose U.S. Central American. In so doing, our claims to a hemispheric identity confront the act of appropriation and erasure in using "American" to refer only to North Americans. Moreover, "U.S. Central American" stresses a shared isthmian identity—Central American, instead of articulating traditional national identities like Guatemalan-American, Salvadoran-American, or Honduran-American. This cognizant identification emphasizes a continued sense of historical and cultural unity while recognizing the varied differences that make up the isthmus. By situating the U.S. and Central America next to each other, we emphasize the multiple ways in which Central American diasporas experience belonging and nonbelonging in both the United States and Central America. As Alvarado explains, "U.S. Central American identity is beyond the binational and bicultural since Central American and American creates a third space" that is purely distinctive from North American, South American, and Central American as an embodied location and identity (2007, 36). As illustrated in this collection of critical essays, U.S. Central American-ness emphasizes fluidity, multiplicity, and solidarities like those historically created in Los Angeles to the isthmus against the repressive regimes in both regions. U.S. Central American makes visible the ways in which diasporas reconstruct spaces to assert their agency and unity as a group. All the essays in this anthology emphasize the ways in which U.S. Central American diasporas construct community and historical memory and assert their subjectivity in a country that often criminalizes their ethnicities or attempts to erase them.

NOTES

1. Hannah Bloch, "That Little Syrian Boy: Here's Who He Was," NPR September 3, 2015. http://www.npr.org/sections/parallels/2015/09/03/437132793/photo-of-dead-3-year-old-syrian-refugee-breaks-hearts-around-the-world.

2. "Mass Graves of Immigrants Found in Texas, But State Says No Laws Were Broken." July 16, 2015. http://www.democracynow.org/2015/7/16/mass_graves_of_immigrants_found_in.

3. Refers to the network of freight trains that migrants use to travel through Mexico to reach the Mexico-U.S. border. It is called the beast to personify the train(s) as a living creature that mangles bodies and disappears people. See Villegas (2014).

4. Anna Brown and Eileen Patton. "Hispanics of Nicaraguan Origin in the United States, 2011," June 19, 2013. http://www.pewhispanic.org/2013/06/19/hispanics-of-nicaraguan-origin-in-the-united-states-2011/.

5. In 2016, the United States continues to receive Cubans arriving at ports of entry as political refugees but places Central Americans arriving at a port of entry in detention and/or in expedited deportation proceedings.

6. The United Nation's 1948 *Convention on the Prevention and Punishment of the Crime of Genocide* (CPPCG) stipulates that genocide occurs when there is an attempt to destroy in whole or in part an ethnic/racial group through the systematic eradication of the elderly, children, women, and men.

7. In 2011, in a ceremony at the National Palace, Guatemalan President Álvaro Colom apologized to Jacobo Arbenz Guzmán's son Juan Jacobo and to the nation of Guatemala for the "great crime" of forcibly removing, humiliating, and exiling Arbenz Guzmán. While maligned in the past, Arbenz Guzmán's biography will be rewritten and included in Guatemala's historical memory. While the Colom government apologized for the Arbenz Guzmán ouster, it continued a close military aid and economic alliance with the United States. See Elizabeth Malkin, "An Apology for a Guatemalan Coup, 57 Years Later," *New York Times*, October 20, 2011, http://www.nytimes.com/2011/10/21/world/americas/an-apology-for-a-guatemalan-coup-57-years-later.html?_r=1.

8. See Zong and Batalova (2015).

9. John S. Brown, "Operation Just Cause, The Incursion into Panama," 14, http://www.history.army.mil/html/books/070/70-85-1/cmhPub_70-85-1.pdf.

10. After the ouster, and once Zelaya was removed, a referendum was passed that now allows Honduran presidents to serve more than one term.

11. "Honduras's Constitution of 1982 with Amendments Through 2012," trans. by Maria del Carmen Gress and Jefri J. Ruchti. William S. Hein and Co., Inc., https://www.constituteproject.org/constitution/Honduras_2012.pdf.

12. Convention for the Construction of a Ship Canal (Hay-Bunau-Varilla Treaty), November 18, 1903. http://avalon.law.yale.edu/20th_century/pan001.asp.

13. See the 1903 Treaty and Qualified Independence at http://countrystudies.us/panama/8.htm.

14. Monica Anderson, "A Rising Share of the U.S. Black Population Is Foreign Born," Pew Research Center, April 9, 2015, http://www.pewsocialtrends.org/2015/04/09/a-rising-share-of-the-u-s-black-population-is-foreign-born/.

15. See note 12. Convention for the Construction of a Ship Canal (Hay-Bunau-Varilla Treaty).

16. See Zong and Batalova (2015).

17. *Las conferencias ministeriales del diálogo de San Jose 1984-2002.* Oficina de la Delegación de Comisión Europea en Costa Rica. Report can be located online at http://www.sciencespo.fr/opalc/sites/sciencespo.fr.opalc/files/Las_Conferencias_Ministeriales_del_Dialogo_de_San Jose1984-20021_0.pdf; see also Background Negotiations of the Central America-European Union Trade Policy Developments, Organization of American States, which can be found at www.sice.oas.org/TPD/CACM_EU/CACM_EU_s.ASP.

18. See Lin (n.d.).

19. U.S. Census data for 2014 estimates that California's total population is 38,802,500. In 2010 the total California population is said to have been 37,253,956, of which 14,013,719 were Latina/os representing 37.6 percent of the population. PEW tallies Latinos at 38 percent and non-Latina/o whites at 40 percent of California's population. While other states such as Texas and New Mexico have higher percentages of Latina/os, California has the highest total number of Latina/os.

20. See note 12.

21. See the United States Census Bureau QuickFacts website at http://quickfacts.census.gov/qfd/states/06/06037.html.

22. See the City and County of San Francisco Sanctuary Ordinance found in General Services Agency at http://sfgov.org/ccsfgsa/sanctuary-ordinance.

23. "Hispanic Population in Select U.S. Metropolitan Areas, 2011," Pew Research Center, http://www.pewhispanic.org/2013/08/29/hispanic-population-in-select -u-s-metropolitan-areas-2011/.

24. In *Culling the Masses: The Democratic Origins of Racist Immigration Policy in the Americas* (2014), David Scott FitzGerald and David Cook-Martín note that the Central American nations' membership to the Federal Republic of Central America facilitated citizenship and migration among the nations (362–65).

REFERENCES

Abrego, Leisy. 2014. *Sacrificing Families: Navigating, Laws, Labor, and Love Across Borders*. Stanford: Stanford University Press.

Alvarado, Elvia, and Medea Benjamin. 1987. *Don't Be Afraid, Gringo: A Honduran Woman Speaks from the Heart*. San Francisco: Institute for Food and Development Policy.

Alvarado, Karina O. 2013. "An Interdisciplinary Reading of Chicana/o and (US) Central American Cross-Cultural Narrations." *Latino Studies* 11 (3): 366–87.

———. 2007. *Transnational Lives and Texts: Writing and Theorizing US/Central American Subjectivities*. PhD diss. University of California, Berkeley.

Arias, Arturo. 1999. "Central American-Americans? Re-mapping Latino/Latin American Subjectivities on Both Sides of the Great Divide." Explicación de Textos Literarios. Farmington Hills, MI: Gale Group.

———. 2003. "Central American-Americans: Invisibility, Power and Representation in the U.S. Latino World." *Latino Studies* 1 (1): 168–87.

———. 2007. *Taking Their Word: Literature and the Signs of Central America*. Minneapolis: University of Minnesota Press.

Baker-Cristales, Beth. 2004. *Salvadoran Migration to Southern California: Redefining El Hermano Lejano*. Gainesville: University Press of Florida.

Buff, Ida. 2008. *Immigrant Rights in the Shadow of Citizenship*. New York: New York University Press.

Burns, Allan. 1993. *Maya in Exile: Guatemalans in Florida*. Philadelphia: Temple University Press.

Chomsky, Noam. 1987. "Central America." In *The Chomsky Reader*, 313–68. New York: Pantheon Books.

Comisión para el Esclarecimiento Histórico (CEH). 1999. *Guatemala: Memoria del silencio*. Guatemala City: United Nations Operating Projects Services.

Cordova, Carlos B. 2005. *The Salvadoran Americans.* Westport, CT: Greenwood.

Coutin, Susan B. 2000. *Legalizing Moves: Salvadoran Immigrants' Struggles for U.S. Residency.* Ann Arbor: University of Michigan Press.

———. 2007. *Nations of Emigrants: Shifting Boundaries of Citizenship in El Salvador and the United States.* Ithaca, NY: Cornell University Press.

Craft, Linda J. 2005. "Mario Bencastro's Diaspora: Salvadorans and Transnational Identity." *MELUS* 30 (1): 149–67.

Ennis, Sharon R., Merarys Ríos-Vargas, and Nora G. Albert. May 2010. "The Hispanic Population: 2010, Census Briefs." U.S. Census Bureau: Department of Commerce Economics and Statistics Administration. http://www.census.gov/prod/cen2010/briefs/c2010br-04.pdf.

Estrada, Alicia I. 2013. "Ka Tzij: The Maya Diasporic Voices from *Contacto Ancestral.*" *Latino Studies* 11 (2): 208–27.

Fink, Leon. 2003. *The Maya of Morganton: Work and Community in the Nuevo New South.* Chapel Hill: University of North Carolina Press.

FitzGerald, David, and David Cook-Martín. 2014. *Culling the Masses: The Democratic Origins of Racist Immigration Policy in the Americas.* Cambridge, MA: Harvard University Press.

Foxen, Patricia. 2008. *In Search of Providence: Transnational Mayan Identities.* Nashville: Vanderbilt University Press.

García, Cristina. 2006. *Seeking Refuge: Central American Migration to Mexico, the United States, and Canada.* Berkeley: University of California Press.

Golash-Boza, Tanya. 2015. *Deported: Immigrant Policing, Disposable Labor, and Global Capitalism.* New York: New York University Press.

Gould, Jeffrey L., and Aldo Lauria-Santiago. 2008. *To Rise in Darkness: Revolution, Repression, and Memory in El Salvador, 1920–1932.* Durham, NC: Duke University Press.

Grosfoguel, Ramón. 2003. *Colonial Subjects: Puerto Ricans in a Global Perspective.* Berkeley: University of California Press.

Hagan, Jacqueline Maria. 1994. *Deciding to Be Legal: A Maya Community in Houston.* Philadelphia: Temple University Press.

Hamilton, Nora, and Norma Stoltz Chinchilla. 2001. *Seeking Community in a Global City: Guatemalans and Salvadorans in Los Angeles.* Philadelphia: Temple University Press.

Hernández, Ester E. 2006. "Confronting Exclusion in the Latino Metropolis: Central American Transnational Communities in the Los Angeles Area, 1980s–2006." *Journal of the West* 45 (4): 48–56.

Hondagneu-Sotelo, Pierrette, ed. 2003. *Gender and U.S. Migration: Contemporary Trends.* Berkeley: University of California Press.

Informe del Proyecto Interdiocesano de Recuperación de la Memoria Histórica (REMHI). 1998. *Guatemala: Nunca Más.* Guatemala City: Oficina de Derechos Humanos del Arzobispado de Guatemala.

Joseph, Shaun. Eyewitness HONDURAS—Resistance to the Coup D'état. Accessed September 2, 2009. https://youtu.be/GRLAxKoaaMc?t=10m23s.

Kisler, Amanda. 2010. "Disappeared but Not Forgotten: A Guatemalan Community Achieves a Landmark Verdict." *NACLA* 43 (1): 9–13.

Kozloff, N. 2009. "What's Behind the Honduran Coup? Tracing Zelaya's Trajectory." *Democracy Now,* July 1. https://youtu.be/7DFEbyhpjgk.

LeBaron, Alan. 2012. "When Latinos Are Not Latinos: The Case of Guatemalan Maya in the United States, the Southeast and Georgia." *Latino Studies* 10 (1-2): 179.

LaFeber, Walter. 1993. *Inevitable Revolutions.* 2nd ed. New York: Norton and Company.

Lin, Sharat G. n.d. "Undocumented Immigrants in the United States: From Impoverishment to May Day Resurgence." Accessed June 30, 2015. San Jose Peace and Justice Center. http://www.sanjosepeace.org/article.php/20090422101506446.

Loucky, James, and Marilyn M. Moors. 2000. *The Maya Diaspora: Guatemalan Roots, New American Lives.* Philadelphia: Temple University Press.

Mahler, Sarah J. 1996. *Salvadorans in Suburbia: Symbiosis and Conflict.* New Immigrants Series. 1st ed. New York: Pearson.

Menchú, Rigoberta, and Elisabeth Burgos-Debray. 2000. *Me llamo Rigoberta Menchú y así me nació la conciencia.* México, D.F.: Siglo Veintiuno Editores.

Menjívar, Cecilia. 2000. *Fragmented Ties: Salvadoran Immigrant Networks in America.* Berkeley: University of California Press.

———. 2008. "Educational Hopes, Documented Dreams: Guatemalan and Salvadoran Immigrants' Legality and Educational Prospects." *The Annals of the American Academy of Political and Social Science.* Vol. 620, "Exceptional Outcomes: Achievement in Education and Employment among Children of Immigrants," 177–93.

Montejo, Victor. 1987. *Testimony: Death of a Guatemalan Village.* Translated by Victor Perera. Willimantic, CT: Curbstone Press.

Ochoa, Enrique, and Gilda L. Ochoa. 2005. *Latino Los Angeles: Transformation, Communities, and Activism.* Tucson: University of Arizona Press.

Padilla, Yajaira M. 2013. "The Central American Transnational Imaginary: Defining the Transnational and Gendered Contours of Central American Immigrant Experience." *Latino Studies* 11 (2): 150–66.

Palmer, Steven. 1993. "Central American Union or Guatemalan Republic? The National Question in Liberal Guatemala, 1871–1885." *The Americas* 49 (4): 513–530.

Popkin, Eric. 2005. "The Emergence of Pan-Mayan Ethnicity in the Guatemalan Transnational Community Linking Santa Eulalia and Los Angeles." *Current Sociology* 53 (4): 675–706.

Rodríguez, Ana Patricia. 2005. "'Departamento 15': Cultural Narratives of Salvadoran Transnational Migration." *Latino Studies* (3): 19–41.

———. 2009. *Dividing the Isthmus: Central American Transnational Histories, Literatures, and Cultures.* Austin: University of Texas Press.

Rodriguez, Nestor P. 1987. "Undocumented Central Americans in Houston: Diverse Populations." *The International Migration Review* 21 (1) (Spring): 4–26. Center for Migration Studies of New York, Inc.

Stoney, Sierra, and Jeanne Batalova. 2013. "Central American Immigrants in the United States." http://www.migrationpolicy.org/article/central-american-immigrants-united-states-1.

Trent, Barbara. 1992. *The Panama Deception: Exposing the Cover Up!* Chapel Hill, NC: Empowerment Project, 2002, DVD.

Villegas, Rodrigo Dominguez. 2014. "Central American Migrants and 'La Bestia': The Route, Dangers, and Government Responses." September 10, Migration Policy Institute. http://www.migrationpolicy.org/article/central-american-migrants-and-la-bestia-route-dangers-and-government-responses.

Zea, Leopoldo. 1963. *Latin America and the World.* Norman: University of Oklahoma Press.

Zentgraf, Kristine M. 2005. "Why Women Migrate, Guatemalan and Salvadoran Women in Los Angeles." In *Latino Los Angeles: Transformation, Communities, and Activism,* edited by Enrique Ochoa and Gilda L. Ochoa, 63–82. Tucson: University of Arizona Press.

Zilberg, Elana. 2011. *Space of Detention: The Making of Transnational Gang Crisis Between Los Angeles and San Salvador.* Durham, NC: Duke University Press.

Zong, Jie, and Jeanne Batalova. 2015. "Central American Immigrants in the United States." http://www.migrationpolicy.org/article/central-american-immigrants-united-states.

PART I

GENERATIONAL ORAL HISTORIES OF
EDUCATION, AND GENDERED LABOR
AND RESISTANCE LITERATURE

T HE ANTHOLOGY ENGAGES with multiple generations, starting with
Ana Patricia Rodríguez's chapter, which examines the pioneers who
arrived in San Francisco soon after the 1965 Immigration Act. Chapters in part 1 also tackle questions of solidarity as immigrant generations made
spaces for support that the second generations expanded. Oral history methods
play a large role in this section as the contributors use them to explore various
issues and topics. The anthology begins with Ana Patricia Rodríguez's chapter
since it creates a longer history to the 1.5 generation while employing the 1.5 as
an analytical tool. "Salvadoran Immigrant Acts and Migration to San Francisco
(circa 1960s and '70s)" calls for a layered analysis of overlapping 1.5 generations
within their historical context and cultural milieu, specifically in San Francisco.
Rodríguez asks that we consider prior 1.5 generations and their significance in
understanding the multiple waves of Central American migration. Who were
these "pioneers," and how is it that each new migrant and settled generation are
pioneers in their own right? Moreover, while clandestinity has been considered
as a fundamental part of the Central American experience (both in Central
America and the United States), Rodríguez's chapter reminds us that Central
Americans, both documented and not, have deployed visibility to access U.S.
law in order to promote immigrant rights. Her chapter ends by drawing these
multiple connections (1.5, pioneer actions, activism, and law) to the rise of unaccompanied child migration, which leaves us with the question of the legal and

cultural changes this new migrant and 1.5 generation will bring. Rodríguez and Abrego call to examine how multiple forms of oppression shape immigrants' socioeconomic conditions; they suggest that we need to pay attention to gender and gendered economies as well as how particular cohorts are impacted by state policies.

Leisy Abrego's "Hard Work Alone Is Not Enough: Blocked Mobility for Salvadoran Women in the United States" reminds us of the inequity and inequality present in Salvadoran communities in Los Angeles and not just in El Salvador. This is an especially poignant and contradictory situation since Salvadoran migrants are often generalized as economic migrants. Yet, as her study of a Salvadoran migrant woman shows, the move from El Salvador to Pico-Union can be a lateral one within the global economy for the most disenfranchised in Central America. In this instance, the American dream of social mobility falters into an economic cycle of precarity. While North Americans often define Central America with narratives of extreme poverty, it is at the erasure of U.S. populations who also contend with great economic poverty such as having to face the weekly possibility of homelessness and the daily worry of hunger. Abrego's study of a Salvadoran woman street vendor highlights the discrepancy between the desire for betterment and the gendered social, historical, political, and economic intersections that block achievement regardless of a person's effort. Her chapter seeks to challenge any Central American complacency both in regards to community building and specifically in support of women.

Turning to the experiences of children of mixed parentage, Steven Osuna in "'Obstinate Transnational Memories': How Oral Histories Shape Salvadoran-Mexican Subjectivities" explains and analyzes the hybrid identities of children of Mexican and Salvadoran immigrants and how they work to piece together their parents' life stories. His study explores cultural erasure to North American and Mexican assimilation. The youth of his study are shown to discover, digest, and hold on to their parents' stories of their home countries, which include competing narratives that privilege Mexicanidad. These "obstinate" memories or parent-to-child transmission of cultural meanings help the youth come to terms with all sides of their cultural narratives. Osuna examines the oral histories of Salvadoran-Mexican children whose parents migrated due to the Salvadoran civil war and to whom they attribute their political consciousness about immigration and civic engagement. This chapter is vital in considering the growing U.S. population of bicultural, pan-Latina/o youth perspectives. In this way, the first chapter closes with the hybrid identities and experiences of bicultural youth and their desire to bridge Mexican American and U.S. Central American fragmentations of community and self.

The section closes with Karina O. Alvarado's long view. "A Gynealogy of Cigua Resistance: La Ciguanaba, Prudencia Ayala, and Leticia Hernández-Linares in Conversation" situates women's struggles for sovereignty and social justice within a longer time span and explores temporal and spatial flows shaping how the second generation engages with these histories. She does this through three feminine narratives to illustrate crossings and transboundaries that women have tackled and that span multiple borders and eras. Reading the legend of the *Ciguanaba* linked to the Spanish colonial period and its postcolonial context, Alvarado then moves to address El Salvador's first woman presidential candidate at the turn of the twentieth century. Lastly, she brings us to the present in how young intellectuals in the twenty-first century are making these stories their own to assert their identities and memories as U.S. Central Americans. Her chapter creates historical linkages and transnational connections among women from El Salvador, Los Angeles, and San Francisco through a hemispheric consciousness of gendered resistance. She proposes the Pipil-Nahuat term *Cigua* to showcase and analyze the intersection of a gendered, indigenous, mestiza, and migrant movement. Her chapter encourages dialogues of solidarity to highlight stories of female hemispheric resilience as imagined by poet Hernández-Linares. As Alvarado shows, female hemispheric resilience emerges not simply from a poetic imaginary but through the life and work of community leaders, such as Prudencia Ayala, and contemporary U.S. Salvadorans as part of the postmemory of U.S. Central Americans.

This section considers the different ways generations dialogue and fill in the silences, demonstrating that oral histories, law, and oral literature constitute different forms of subject and personhood within familial and (trans)national frameworks. The authors use generations in drawing chronological and political meanings. These oral histories and storytelling capture and rearticulate a sociohistorical moment and transitional/transnational space shared by collectivities beyond the immediate family to a greater U.S. Central American experience and communities. Their ethnographies, biographies, and stories, therefore, utilize intimacy to consider larger cultural and gendered experiences.

1

SALVADORAN IMMIGRANT ACTS AND MIGRATION TO SAN FRANCISCO (CIRCA 1960S AND '70S)

ANA PATRICIA RODRÍGUEZ

O N THE FOURTH OF JULY of 1968, my father landed at the San Francisco International Airport aboard a Pan American 747, on the same airline carrier that transported thousands of immigrants from Latin America and the Caribbean to the United States in the late 1960s and early 1970s. It was flower power season in San Francisco, and my father was part of a cohort of Salvadoran immigrants arriving in the United States after the passing of the watershed amendment to U.S. immigration law known as the 1965 Immigration and Nationality Act, or the Hart-Celler Act.[1] At thirty-three years of age, my father entered the United States with "green card" in hand, an auto repair job waiting for him, and plans to reunite shortly with my mother, my sister, and myself. We would arrive at the same airport one year later on May 5, 1969. My family and others like us were direct beneficiaries of the 1965 Immigration and Nationality Act, which eliminated national-origin quotas and exclusions and opened new flows of immigration, especially from Asia and Latin America, to the United States for years to come. In their respective works, Córdova (2005), Hamilton and Stoltz Chinchilla (2001), Menjívar (2000), Mahler (1995a, 1995b), and Repak (1995) write about early Central American immigrants like my parents, the so-called *pioneras/os* (pioneers) who settled in and helped build Central American immigrant enclaves in cities like San Francisco, New York, and Washington, DC, before the war-induced exoduses of the 1980s and thereafter.[2]

Studies of Central American immigration, however, largely overlook the 1960s and '70s immigration narratives of Salvadoran families like my own, who made their way through unchartered ground before the larger waves of Central American migration would arrive in the 1980s. According to Carlos B. Córdova, the 1965 Immigrant and Nationality Act "allowed numerous young working-class and middle-class Central American families to resettle in the United States" (2005, 64). In this chapter, I chart the story of my father and his immigrant cohort, who arrived in the San Francisco Bay Area in the late 1960s.[3] Their migration was a consequence of the gendered recruitment of skilled blue-collar labor as determined and specified by the Hart-Celler Act. Through their stories, I seek to understand the precedents of the larger story of Salvadoran migration to the United States, particularly in sites like the San Francisco Bay Area. Through my father's story, filtered through oral history, historical documents, and my own memories as a 1.5-generation child of migration, I propose to examine the Salvadoran immigrant acts (following the work of Lisa Lowe in *Immigrant Acts: On Asian American Cultural Politics*), which brought a budding number of Salvadoran migrants to the United States. In this context, I discuss the prewar sociohistorical conditions of El Salvador that pushed people like my parents to emigrate, the U.S. immigration policies and labor demands sanctioned by the Hart-Celler Act that pulled them to the United States, and finally the daily acts, actions, and agency that early Salvadoran migrants exercised in their migration. My family's immigrant story, I hope to show here, represents some of the issues faced by pre-1980s Salvadoran immigrants. Theirs are Salvadoran immigrant acts that need to be known.[4]

Providing an overview of the conditions that brought Salvadoran male heads of household like my father to San Francisco in the late 1960s, I attempt to piece together my own story as a 1.5-generation immigrant,[5] who as a child was subject to her parents' decisions, plans, and actions, all situated within the larger field of systemic immigrant (legal) acts and cultural politics of the 1960s and '70s (Lowe 1996). For Salvadoran immigrants, Córdova explains, "the decision to migrate is always made by the heads of the family, and children do not always participate in the decision-making process" (2005, 58), although this may have dramatically changed with more recent child migrations (UNHRC 2014). In *Keeping the Immigrant Bargain: The Costs and Rewards of Success in America*, Vivian S. Louie insists that in order to understand the 1.5-generation immigration story, "we first need to consider the journeys their parents have made to and in America [*sic*]" (2012, 1). So in that vein, I draw from my childhood memories of coming to and growing up in the San Francisco Bay Area as well as my father's immigrant sto-ries,[6] which shape my sense of diasporic belongings as a "child of immigration" (Suárez-Orozco and Suárez-Orozco 2001) and as an intercultural adult today. I acknowledge that to immigrate to a politically and culturally liberal city like San Francisco in the late 1960s at age five with legal resident status alongside one's parents (as I did) is not the same as to flee war forcibly as a child refugee (with or without one's parents and papers) in the 1980s or to cross multiple territorial borders as an unaccompanied minor displaced by violent neoliberal and global-izing forces in 2014 (UNHRC 2014). Indeed, specificities and factors of gender, class, race, sexuality, age of arrival, migration origins, routes and destinations, geopolitics, and historical contexts shape all migration experiences, as I show in the next section.

SALVADORAN IMMIGRANT ACTS

As noted by immigration scholars, it is important to examine "the greater con-ceptual and historical specificity" lived and shared by migrants upon leaving their homelands and arriving in United States (Levitt and Waters 2006, 21; Eckstein 2006, 212). Moreover, we must understand the historical geopolitical contexts generating and governing international migration to and from specific sites (Rumbaut 2006, 45). In *Immigrant Acts: On Asian American Cultural Pol-itics*, Lowe examines the contradictions of Asian American racialization as an ethnic minority in the United States in the context of U.S. political and military interventions in Asia and the legal exclusionary acts and practices that have constructed Asian Americans as a perennial immigrant and foreign group in the United States. While Lowe makes visible the all-important contributions of Asian immigrants and Asian Americans to the production of U.S. capital and nation building in the nineteenth and twentieth centuries, herein I wish to draw parallels to the centrality of Central America and Central Americans to U.S. global power and empire building in the neoliberal era. Like Asians, Central Americans have immigrated to the United States since at least the nineteenth century (Córdova 2005, 60), in great part as a result of conditions produced by U.S. foreign policies and interventions in the isthmus. Upon arrival in the United States, Central American immigrants, refugees, and political asylum seekers have experienced legal exclusion, political and social marginalization, economic exploitation, and racialization as criminal aliens, although they make great material and cultural contributions to the United States and Central American nation-states.

More recently, Central American migrants, particularly youth from the so-called Northern Triangle region (El Salvador, Honduras, and Guatemala), have been demonized as undesirable people, criminalized as violent gang members, and pathologized as "disease-ridden children" even before they make entry into the United States (Kleiner 2014). Focusing for the most part on border protection, the mainstream media reinforces the image of Central Americans as "illegal" border crossers while popular culture represents Central Americans in film and television as unauthorized border crossers, gang members, and law breakers (Rodríguez 2001). Once in U.S. territory, Central American migrants are subject to violent exclusion, persecution, and deportation measures, supported by an extensive anti-immigrant apparatus and imaginary that Leo Chavez has identified as the "Latino threat narrative" (Chavez 2008). As the poet Roque Dalton wrote in "Poema de Amor" (Love poem) ([1974] 2000), Salvadorans continue to be cast as *los eternos indocumentados* (the eternally undocumented), *los siempre sospechos de todo* (under suspicion of everything), and in constant migration in search of work and refuge.

Successively throughout the late nineteenth, twentieth, and now twenty-first centuries, Salvadoran migration waves have been closely tied to U.S. military, political, economic, and even humanitarian interventions, such as those associated with the Alliance for Progress in the isthmus (e.g., the Peace Corps). Enabled early on by U.S. foreign policies such as the Monroe Doctrine (1823) and the Roosevelt Corollary (1904) and more recently by trade agreements and hemispheric security treaties such as the Dominican Republic-Central American Free Trade Agreement (CAFTA-DR 2007) and the Plan of the Alliance for Prosperity in the Northern Triangle (2014), among others, the U.S. government has justified numerous economic, political, and de facto military interventions in El Salvador as well as Nicaragua, Guatemala, Honduras, Costa Rica, and Panama (Rodríguez 2009; Dunkerley 1994). U.S. economic, political, and military interventions in Central America have supported the extraction of natural resources (e.g., mining in Honduras) and cash crops (e.g., production of bananas in Guatemala, Nicaragua, and Costa Rica, and coffee throughout the region), control of infrastructure (e.g., the Panama Canal and the modern system of highway dry canals and roads), and the expansion of transnational networks, putting Central American economies at the service of U.S. exports and finance and displacing local producers and laborers (Rodríguez 2009).

With the Alliance for Prosperity, the U.S. government has enforced greater control over the Northern Triangle countries of El Salvador, Honduras, and Guatemala. In this neoliberal and high-security age, Central Americans, particularly from these countries, are undergoing never before seen levels of out-migration as social, economic, and political conditions worsen for the general population.

In her *Immigrant Acts*, Lowe argues that Asians arrived originally in the United States as exploited labor migrants, displaced just as Central Americans were by U.S. interventions and imperialism in their countries. Once in the United States, Asian immigrants and Asian Americans were racialized as the "foreigner-within" (1996, 5) through a series of immigration laws and acts.[7] I would like to suggest here that, like Asian immigrants and Asian Americans, Central Americans, too, have been denied access to full citizenship in the United States through specific exclusionary immigration acts and naturalization laws. Like Asian immigrants and Asian Americans in the United States, Central Americans have provided important labor, yet many have been denied, in great measure, the right to permanent residency and citizenship in the United States. At best, Salvadorans, Hondurans, and Nicaraguans may presently attain Temporary Protected Status (TPS) under certain immigrant acts (Baker-Cristales 2004; Coutin 2003; Hamilton and Stoltz Chinchilla 2001). Lowe writes, "Immigration exclusion acts and naturalization laws have thus been not only means of regulating the terms of the citizen and the nation-state but also an intersection of the legal and political terms with an orientalist discourse that defined Asian as culturally and racially 'other' in times when the United States was militarily and economically at war with Asia" (1996, 5). Much as Asian Americans have been configured as the excludable Other, "perpetual immigrant," and "foreigner-within" (Lowe 1996; Takaki 1993), Central American immigrants today are "tropicalized" (Benz 1997), for the most part rendered as "illegal," violent, and criminal figures, turned out of their homelands and largely denied entry, belonging, and citizenship in the United States. As an invisible, unauthorized labor force, many Salvadorans remain a flexible, expendable, and exploitable people in the global economy, or what Dalton called poetically "los hacelotodo, los vendelotodo, los comelotodo" (the do, sell, eat everything) ([1974] 2000). I would like to suggest here, following Arturo Arias's work on Central American invisibility (2007), that what makes some Central American migrants, among them Salvadoran, "invisible" in the global economy is precisely the obfuscation and reification of their exploitable surplus labor. In particular, the labor of undocumented Central Americans is made cheap and invisible by the same immigrant acts that produce their undocumented status.

Starting with the 1965 Immigration Act, a number of specific immigrant acts and laws have served to regulate and control Central American immigration to date. They include the Immigration Reform and Control Act of 1986, the Illegal Immigration Reform and Immigrant Responsibility Act of 1996, the Nicaraguan Adjustment and Central American Relief Act of 1997, the USA Patriot Act (2001), and the Development, Relief, and Education for Alien Minors Act (DREAM Act), said to be spurring the migration of children in 2014–2015. Indeed, "the present wave of immigration was triggered by the 1965 Immigration Act as well as by subsequent changes in American asylum and refugee policies" (Portes and Schauffler 1996, 9), which excluded Central Americans from legal entry into the United States due to larger geopolitical forces, including Cold War deployments and U.S. military interventions in the isthmus throughout the twentieth century.

In what follows, I examine how Salvadoran immigrant acts, namely the 1965 Immigration Act, shaped the departure of emigrants from El Salvador and their entry and incorporation in locations like San Francisco in 1968 and 1969. Like other immigrants of their generation, my parents decided to leave El Salvador because they sought better opportunities for themselves and their children. In part, they were motivated to emigrate by increasingly difficult economic and political conditions in El Salvador. In the late 1960s, the oligarchic elite supported by military dictators held power in El Salvador. Violent political repression increased steadily in the countryside and cities, the country's economic situation deteriorated, and leftist organizations gained momentum and popular support. Migration to the United States became an important valve for Salvadorans, especially after Honduras expelled long-term Salvadoran residents from its national territory in 1969 (Córdova 2005; Hamilton and Stoltz Chinchilla 1997).

SALVADORAN MIGRATION TO SAN FRANCISCO (CIRCA 1960S AND '70S)

In the late 1960s my father, growing weary of deteriorating economic and political conditions in El Salvador and seeking alternatives for his family's well-being, decided to immigrate to San Francisco, where friends and acquaintances in the auto mechanic industry had already settled. Córdova claims that, according to Salvadoran consular records, by the early 1970s there were 40,000 Salvadorans living in the San Francisco Bay Area (2005, 60). In San Francisco, Salvadoran immigrants like my parents and their peers encountered a dramatically volatile situation as mobilizations against the Vietnam War surged across the country, civil discontent erupted in frequent protests across the city, and, in the Mission District, the Mexican American and Latina/o community faced greater discrimination and violence due to development and revitalization projects encroaching on what was then considered the city's "Latino ghetto" (Brook, Carlsson, and Peters 1998; Heins 1972). On May 1, 1969, a few days before my mother, sister, and I arrived at our apartment at 872 Shotwell Street between 23rd and 24th Streets in the Mission District, seven young Latino men, mostly Salvadoran, were accused of and prosecuted for armed robbery and killing a police officer. The trial against "Los siete" would galvanize different sectors in the Mission District against urban development, racial and economic inequality, police brutality, and discrimination against Latina/o residents (Summers Sandoval 2013). At the same time, families in the neighborhood faced reforms in bilingual education after the passing of the 1968 Bilingual Education Act (BEA) and the implementation of desegregation measures in the public school system designed to bus children to cross-city neighborhoods.

Settling in the epicenter of the largely Chicano/Mexican American neighborhood, my family was among the many Salvadorans and Nicaraguans who resided in the Mission District (Summers Sandoval 2013). The 1965 Immigration and Nationality Act, the 1968 Civil Rights Act and antiwar movements, and the flower power and hippie social scene in San Francisco shaped my early childhood. My friends and I were among the first generation of immigrant children to enroll in bilingual education programs made possible by the Bilingual Education Act, or Title VII of the Elementary and Secondary Education Act of 1968, and *Lau v. Nichols* in 1974. I would learn English under the tutelage of my kindergarten and first grade teachers, Ms. Lee and Ms. Mann, who would start class every morning to the beat of Simon and Garfunkel's "The 59th Street Bridge Song (Feelin' Groovy)." My family's weekend outings regularly included excursions to Golden Gate Park or Aquatic Park to see hippies drumming, singing, and dancing; to Playland at the Beach on the Great Highway; and to the now long-defunct White Front store in Potrero Hill, where they would purchase the ubiquitous striped jeans and flowered shirt-short sets for their children. I remember the night that our family friend Charles was shot while driving his taxi in San Francisco, instilling fear in everyone because his killing was thought to be the work of the Zodiac Killer who terrorized the city between December 1968 and October 1969.

Unknowingly, my parents, like other immigrant parents at the time, engaged in what scholars have called the immigrant bargain, "whereby the parents' sacrifice in leaving home is redeemed by the success of their children in the United States" (Suárez-Orozco and Suárez-Orozco 2001, cited in Smith 2006, 151; see also Louie 2012). Beholden to their parents, children of immigration are brought to new locations, where they are expected to gain an education and to maintain connections to their parents' homelands through language, culture, traditions, and values despite acculturating to facets of life in the United States—in other words, to make good on the promise of building a better future in the United States, if not in the first generation, then in successive generations. In particular, the migration and settlement experiences of immigrant children, in this case members of the 1.5 generation like myself and my peers who arrived in early childhood through adolescence, are acutely tied to the immigrant bargain made by our parents (Louie 2012; Portes 1996). The migration stories of members of the 1.5 generations thus can hardly be told without telling the story of our immigrant parents, their hopes, and their dreams for their children.

SALVADORAN PIONERAS/OS IN SAN FRANCISCO

My father was, thus, part of a large wave of Salvadoran labor migrants, the fourth wave identified as such by Córdova (2005, 63–64).[8] Along with other Salvadorans, my father arrived in San Francisco as a young man with specialized labor skills in auto repair. He also brought with him a deep desire to work as well as a strong work ethic. His story and that of others of his generation is the collective story of immigrants allowed entry into the United States under the provisions of the 1965 Immigration Act, which according to many scholars changed the face and pace of immigration in the United States for years to come (Portes 1996). Indeed, the 1965 Immigration Act opened a new era in U.S. immigration norms and patterns, easing entry into the United States, especially for immigrants from countries like the Philippines, El Salvador, and the rest of Latin America. Whereas the bulk of immigration in the past had been from Western Europe, now immigrants would come in great numbers from the Western Hemisphere—that is, the Caribbean, Mexico, Central and South America, and Asia. U.S. ethnic diversity as we know it today can be linked directly to the post-1965 entry of the so-called new immigrants, their ensuing chain migrations, and their family reunifications, as well as to various immigration acts and reforms that followed.

Like other "new immigrants" after 1965, Salvadorans came to the United States to fill the void of a skilled male labor force drafted into the Korean and Vietnam Wars, consumed by growing civil unrest in major U.S. cities, and redeployed to industries across the country. Little research, however, has focused on these Salvadoran immigrants of the 1960s and '70s, who not only worked where they were needed but moreover added to the ethnic diversity of urban centers like San Francisco and laid the cornerstones for present-day Latina/o ethnic enclaves in the city and elsewhere. In her book *Fragmented Ties: Salvadoran Immigrant Networks in America*, Cecilia Menjívar recognizes that Salvadoran immigrants such as my father were pioneras/os who broke ground for later Salvadoran immigrants seeking refuge and asylum in the United States from the wars in region in the 1980s. Later immigrants would resettle in the San Francisco Mission District and across the San Francisco Bay Area with the help of informal and familial social networks established by those early pioneers, who are called on to assist newcomers even to this day (see Menjívar 2000).

In listening to my father's stories and anecdotes throughout the years, it became clear to me that here was a history of great personal, local, national, and transnational significance, especially in times that grow increasingly hostile and violent toward immigrants from Latin America. One need only take note of the Minute Men vigilantes standing guard at the U.S.-Mexico border, Ku Klux Klan activity targeting Latina/o immigrants in the New South, politicians singling out immigrants as potential terrorists, and the public turning its back on Central American child migrants detained at the border and detention centers across the country after the so-called child-migrant surge in 2014 (UNHRC 2014). How did it come to be, I ask, that Central American immigrants became the latest national immigration problem and unquestionable "Latino threat" to national security (Chavez 2008) and the scapegoats of failed immigration policies and reforms in the United States, when the 1965 Immigration Act made possible the migration of skilled laborers from Central America only a few decades ago? Perhaps revisiting the stories of the not-so-new immigrants of 1965, such as my father and his migrant cohort, holds the key to understanding the significant role that Salvadoran immigrants in the United States have played in building U.S. society, economy, and body politic and to challenging the image of "criminal alien" Central American immigrants that circulates so widely today.

RECOLLECTIONS OF PIONERA/O MIGRANTS

In *The Voice of the Past: Oral History*, Paul Thompson reminds us that oral history evidence and records, such as those of Salvadoran immigrant pioneras/os, may serve "first, as a corrective and supplement to existing sources, and secondly in opening up new problems for consideration" (2000, 83). By recording and examining the oral histories of my father and others of his cohort, I interrogate the greater immigrant myths of the United States and deconstruct, in particular, the current hostile narrative that makes Central American, particularly Salvadoran, immigration a problem in the United States rather than a contributing force to this nation. I also seek to look before and beyond the 1980s Salvadoran war-induced migration narrative to find other narratives of earlier overlooked Salvadoran migrations. In this section, I thus delve into the story of Salvadoran immigration in San Francisco, using the oral histories of post-1965 Salvadoran immigrant pioneras/os.

Because Salvadoran immigration is historically situated and produced, it is important to consider its actors and their motivations, actions, and agency. Through a series of interviews with pioneras/os of the 1960s and '70s migration wave, I ask why they immigrated, how they came, where they arrived, what they experienced upon arrival, how they acculturated, and finally, how, in hindsight, they reflect on their migration experience in the United States. More or less, these were the questions that I posed to the narrators in interviews conducted for the most part in Spanish. Spanish remains these narrators' principal language, although they acquired proficiency in English through their thirty to fifty years of residing in the United States. As we know, experiences are encoded and imagined in and through language. Thus, conducting interviews in one language and translating to another language presents significant challenges. At the crux of their narratives, the narrators poignantly relayed what it was like to leave El Salvador and resettle in San Francisco in the late 1960s and to learn to live in both Spanish and English—in between these languages: outside English at times, inside only Spanish at other times—all within their hybrid diasporic experiences (Rodríguez 2004).

In this study, the narrators immigrated, for the most part, to the United States in the 1960s as young male adults in their early to mid-thirties. In the interviews conducted one on one, they tell of the opportunity presented to them to come to the United States as they learned that their labor skills might qualify them for entry and jobs in the United States. To apply to come to the

United States, they prepared a packet of materials: an application in English, a medical exam, a police record, and a letter verifying labor skills, all submitted for review to the U.S. embassy in San Salvador. Upon approval of their applications, they were given a permanent residency immigrant visa for travel to the United States. All narrators referred to a yellow manila envelope they carried on their person on their flights to San Francisco, containing the materials ensuring them entry into the United States.

The narrators also describe their first experiences upon arrival in the country, passing through U.S. customs, exiting San Francisco International Airport, arriving at their rooming houses, finding their first jobs, looking for apartments in anticipation of their family's arrival, and learning to navigate their new home and city. They describe their first contact with and effort to learn English while seeking community in English as a Second Language (ESL) classes, eateries, and dancehalls like the Centro Obrero in the Mission District. In situ, the men learned to speak, read, and interact in English proficiently—all the result of the hard work, effort, perseverance, resourcefulness, ingenuity, and the flexibility some of them claimed as the qualities that helped them adjust to life in the United States. Although I had hoped to interview Salvadoran female immigrants granted entry by the 1965 Immigration Act, for this project and for aforementioned personal reasons, I interviewed only male heads of household of my father's cohort who had been recruited for skilled manual labor in fields such as welding, automobile repair, shoemaking, and other types of industrial labor. The workers in these skilled areas tended to be male, at least those from El Salvador in the 1960s.

In regards to learning English, one narrator who worked in auto repair explained, "I went to English night classes as much as I could, but I learned my English on the job by reading car repair manuals. I learned all my work vocabulary from those manuals." Similarly, a second narrator explained that he worked in the "foundry" of the old *San Francisco Chronicle-Examiner* newspaper plant, transporting and melting metal letter blocks for reuse. He learned English by reading the paper on the job. And a third narrator explained that he also learned English on the job, joined the labor union, and adapted to San Francisco as time went by, for it was a city that he liked. "Me encantó," he said. He commented that he learned important vocabulary by driving throughout the streets of San Francisco—reading the words *dead end* and seeing the corresponding configuration of such a street, for example. Arriving in the United States for the most part as young adult males with wives and children or long-term girlfriends in El Salvador, they planned to bring their families to San Francisco within one year of their arrival. The narrators explained that finding jobs was their main priority upon arriving. Most found jobs within weeks and, at the most, a few months after arriving through social networks of family, friends, and other contacts. One narrator talked about how his soccer league provided him with not only a social network and recreation outlet but also information about employment and even a $20 stipend per game, as he had been a semiprofessional player in El Salvador. Their skilled jobs in car dealerships and auto-body repair shops paid an average of $4 per hour, excluding union membership fees. The narrators repeatedly and consistently expressed that the labor union (International Association of Machinists) played a significant role in their employment history and acculturation process.

The narrators alluded to the significant role of social networks in finding jobs, housing, ESL classes, and other resources in San Francisco and in learning to navigate the city streets. Almost always, they initially stayed in rooms rented to them by friends, relatives, or acquaintances until they were able to rent apartments in preparation for their families' arrival. For the most part, the narrators describe living first in the Mission District of San Francisco, which by the 1960s had become a Latino and Spanish-speaking enclave with a commercial street, accessible transportation, bilingual education programs (as of the 1968 Bilingual Education Act) for children and ESL classes for adults, free or reduced-payment clinics, and other social services in addition to what were then Mexican restaurants, banks, and other businesses catering to Latina/o neighbors. They described moving away from the Mission District, through a process that cultural geographers and urban studies scholars have called step-migration, to the other working-class neighborhoods or even suburbs, primarily in Daly City, located immediately south of San Francisco.

Notably, the narrators interviewed seemed not to dwell on the difficulties faced in their early years in San Francisco. They talked about feeling *soledad* (lonely), *nostalgia* (nostalgic), and isolated due to lack of English-language skills at the time, but they said that they rarely felt discriminated because they had the company, assistance, and support of their friends. Discrimination and racism were alluded to when, for example, a narrator was fired for being hurt on the job, passed up for promotion or a raise, or assigned irregular work hours, and most experienced miscommunications on account of not understanding English completely. One narrator commented, "Nos sentíamos como mudos" (We felt like mutes). All that was offset, according to one narrator, by his faith in God, his relationships with *buenas personas* (good people), and the satisfaction of having lived with *honradez* (honor). He felt honor in never intentionally doing ill to others, in maintaining friendships, and in looking for *oportunidad* (opportunity) when it presented itself. In particular, this narrator reflected on the qualities that permitted him to live in the United States without *remordimientos* (regrets). He commented on his flexibility, conformity, motivation, courage, dreams, and labor skills as assets and resources that enabled him to forge ahead. He explained that "la vida es como la ola del mar, va para arriba y para abajo" (life is like the ocean wave, it goes up and down), and pondered how he rode the tide of the vicissitudes of life in order to support his family.

The last question that I posed to narrators at the end of each interview was "¿Valió la pena haber venido a los Estados Unidos?" Technically, the English translation of the question would be, Was it worth coming to the United States? Was it of some value or worth? This translation, apt as it may seem, does not capture the larger significance of the word *pena*, which in Spanish also signifies pain, worry, and even shame. Combining the meaning of the word *pena*—worth and pain—all the narrators of my oral histories explained that for them the measurable benefits and outcomes of their migration and labor were seen in the gains made by their children in their educational attainment, professional aspirations, and socioeconomic mobility. Upon his retirement after an extremely active life, one narrator said he felt like "una naranja exprimida" (a squeezed orange). On a personal level, he had worked very hard so that his children could have the educational and employment opportunities that he had envisioned for them when he first left El Salvador. In like fashion, another narrator said that he had gained much *compensación* (compensation or reward) for his sacrifice, for "el pago que da la vida es lo que viene después" (life had paid him with what came after . . . the accomplishments of his children). And still another narrator explained that, while the parents had made "el sacrificio," the children gained "el provecho," the fruits of the sacrifices and labor of their parents. Their children had graduated from high school, some from college, and some owned homes and had families and children of their own. It would seem that, upon reminiscing on their life experiences and migrations, these narrators, who immigrated to the United States in the 1960s and '70s, felt that their immigrant bargain had been fulfilled, if not for them, then for their children.

CONCLUSIONS

Fifty years after the 1965 Immigration and Nationality Act was passed, all of the Salvadoran immigrant pioneras/os that I interviewed had become U.S. citizens in the 1980s and '90s, most in order to petition visas for other members of their families as crisis after crisis hit El Salvador. They were cognizant of being members of a Salvadoran immigrant group that paved the way for successive immigration waves but who are rarely recognized for their central role in opening ground in the United States for subsequent flows of migrations from Central America. Arriving in the late 1960s, my father's immigrant cohort provided essential blue-collar labor to the U.S. economy as wage earners, taxpayers, and immigrant pioneras/os. They opened new routes of migration, settlement, and incorporation for other Central American and Latina/o migrants. Although they experienced discrimination due to language, education, and cultural barriers, they remain positive about their migration experience in the United States and their children's achievements.

Apparently for them, coming to San Francisco, California, was worth the hardships and obstacles faced through the years because they were able to build a new home that "fuse[d] aspects of both cultures—the parental tradition and the new culture" (Suárez-Orozco and Suárez-Orozco 2001, 113) and to raise their children in the Salvadoran tradition and heritage, albeit in the United States. As they age, retire, and live under the threat of diminishing Medicaid and Social Security benefits in the United States, many of the Salvadoran migrant pioneras/os now face extreme challenges affecting not only the Salvadoran immigrant community but also U.S. society as a whole. Their oral histories speak to current issues such as social service cutbacks to poor, aging, and disenfranchised populations in the United States. In the age of diminished Social Security returns, the immigrant bargain made by immigrant parents and pioneras/os obliges the children of immigration, whether of my generation or successive ones, to fulfill our end of the bargain and to ensure that the immigrant pioneras/os have access to universal healthcare and elder care coverage, retirement funds, and affordable housing, among other things.

NOTES

1. Rumbaut (2006) notes that the 1965 Immigration Act was not fully implemented until 1968, the year of my father's arrival in San Francisco.
2. In *Latinos at the Golden Gate: Creating Community and Identity in San Francisco* (2013), Summers Sandoval tells the story of even earlier Central American immigrants who settled in San Francisco at the turn of the twentieth

century, while in "A Gold Rush Salvadoran in California's Latino World, 1857," Hayes-Bautista, Chamberlin, and Zuniga (2009) push the date of arrival of Salvadoran migrants to California to the mid-nineteenth century. The concept of pioneer thus should be understood as relative and situational in the immigration continuum and must be deconstructed for its gendered neocolonialist and expansionist underpinnings. In this chapter, pioneras/os is used to refer to pre-1980 Central American/Salvadoran immigrants, whose movement is tied to the 1965 Immigration and Nationality Act (Córdova 2005).

3. In this chapter, "age cohort" is used to refer to "people of approximately the same age who experienced the same historical events as roughly the same points in their individual development" (Foner and Kasinitz 2007, 270).

4. This paper draws from a set of six oral histories and interviews that I conducted in 2004 with my father and his peers (all male heads of families). Rather than providing long citations of the narratives, I identify and discuss themes and patterns in their narratives in the last part of this chapter (Rodríguez 2004).

5. There are many definitions of the 1.5 immigrant generation drawing from the initial work on the subject (Rumbaut [1976] 2004, 2006; Portes and Rumbaut 2001; Portes 1996). In general, the 1.5 generation is identified as "people born abroad who emigrate as children and are largely raised in the U.S." (Foner and Kasinitz 2007, 270). More precisely at the early end of the spectrum, Rumbaut (2006) distinguishes the 1.75 generation as those who arrive (like myself) before starting school (age five and younger) and "who retain virtually no memory of their birthplace, who are largely socialized here, and whose experiences and adaptive outcomes are most similar to the U.S.-born second generation"; at the mid-range, the 1.5 generation as "preadolescent, school-age children (age six to twelve)"; and at the other end, the 1.25 as "adolescents (ages thirteen to seventeen) . . . whose experiences and adaptive outcomes are closer to those of the first generation of immigrant adults" (Rumbaut 2006, 91–92). Some scholars collapse the 1.5- and second- generation immigrants into the second generation, explaining that "they were born to immigrant parents in the United States, or they came to this country when they were still very young" (Levitt and Waters 2006, 1). The category of immigrant generation, hence, has to be theoretically unpacked and historically situated in time and place if it is to be of critical value in immigration studies. More recently, with Levitt and Waters (2006) and Suárez-Orozco and Suárez-Orozco (2001), the transnationality and transculturation of "children of immigration" are increasingly being studied, although scholars like Rumbaut argue that longitudinal

studies show that transnational connections, "both subjective and objective," in the second generation tend to remain limited (Rumbaut 2006, 89–90) or sporadic over a person's life cycle (Jones-Correa 2006, 227). Inconclusive data suggest that more research on the transnational practices of the 1.5 and successive generations is necessary.

6. Because my mother died when I was twelve years old, I have little access to her stories and memories; consequently, I decided to focus on my father and his cohort's stories of migration in this chapter. This study, hence, is shaped by my own personal search for my family's migration story. I do not purport to tell the "whole" story of my parents' migration, and even less to speak for the whole of post-1965 Salvadoran migration.

7. Lowe notes a number of Asian exclusion acts, in particular the Chinese Exclusion Act of 1882 barring entry of Chinese immigrants into the United States; the Immigration Act of 1917 denying further entry of people from the "barred zone" of South Asia and Southeast Asia; the Immigration Act of 1924 targeting Japanese and Koreans; and the Tydings-McDuffie Act of 1934 limiting the migration quota of Filipinos. She also discusses the laws passed to repeal these acts from 1943 to 1952 (Lowe 1996, 1–36).

8. See Córdova (2005, 55–68) for an overview of Salvadoran migration to the San Francisco Bay Area in the nineteenth, twentieth, and twenty-first centuries. He identifies at least six waves of migration, starting with elite émigrés associated with the international coffee industry headquartered in San Francisco (1870–1930); political exiles in the 1930s and '40s, who often turned to work in the shipping and textile industries; contract laborers brought in to fill the labor gap left by servicemen away fighting during and after World War II in the 1940s and '50s; skilled blue-collar workers in the late 1960s and '70s; displaced migrants fleeing the civil war in the 1970s through the '90s; and transnational migrants forced out of the isthmus by economic conditions made worse by the effects of natural disasters, trade policies, and increasing social violence at the turn of the twenty-first century. See also Hamilton and Stoltz Chinchilla (1997) and Menjívar (2000, 10–12).

REFERENCES

Arias, Arturo. 2007. *Taking Their Word: Literature and the Signs of Central America.* Minneapolis and London: University of Minnesota Press.

Baker-Cristales, Beth. 2004. *Salvadoran Migration to Southern California: Redefining El Hermano Lejano*. Gainesville: University Press of Florida.

Benz, Stephen. 1997. "Through the Tropical Looking Glass: The Motif of Resistance in U.S. Literature on Central America." In *Tropicalizations: Transcultural Representations of Latinidad*, edited by F.R. Aparicio and S. Chávez-Silverman, 51–66. Hanover, NH: University Press of New England.

Brook, James, Chris Carlsson, and Nancy J. Peters, eds. 1998. *Reclaiming San Francisco: History, Politics, Culture*. San Francisco: City Lights Books.

Chavez, Leo R. 2008. *The Latino Threat: Constructing Immigrants, Citizens, and the Nation*. Stanford: Stanford University Press.

Córdova, Carlos B. 2005. *The Salvadoran Americans*. Westport, CT: Greenwood Press.

Coutin, Susan Bibler. 2003. *Legalizing Moves: Salvadoran Immigrants' Struggle for U.S. Residency*. Ann Arbor: University of Michigan Press.

Dalton, Roque. (1974) 2000. "Poema de Amor." In *Las historias prohibidas del pulgarcito*, 199–200. San Salvador: Universidad Centroamericana José Simeón Cañas Editores.

Dunkerley, James. 1994. *The Pacification of Central America: Political Change in the Isthmus, 1987–1993*. London: Verso.

Eckstein, Susan. 2006. "On Deconstructing and Reconstructing the Meaning of Immigrant Generations." In *The Changing Face of Home: The Transnational Lives of the Second Generation*, edited by P. Levitt and M. C. Waters, 211–15. New York: Russell Sage Foundation.

Foner, Nancy, and Philip Kasinitz. 2007. "The Second Generation." In *The New Americans: A Guide to Immigration Since 1965*, edited by M. C. Waters and R. Ueda with H. B. Marrow, 270–82. Cambridge, MA, and London: Harvard University Press.

Hamilton, Nora, and Norma Stoltz Chinchilla. 1997. "Central American Migration: A Framework for Analysis." In *Challenging Fronteras: Structuring Latina and Latino Lives in the U.S.*, edited by M. Romero, P. Hondagneu-Sotelo, and V. Ortiz, 81–100. London and New York: Routledge.

———. 2001. *Seeking Community in a Global City: Guatemalans and Salvadorans in Los Angeles*. Philadelphia: Temple University Press.

Hayes-Bautista, David E., Cynthia L. Chamberlin, and Nancy Zuniga. 2009. "A Gold Rush Salvadoran in California's Latino World, 1857." *Southern California Quarterly* 91 (3): 257–94.

Heins, Marjorie. 1972. *Strictly Ghetto Property: The Story of Los Siete de la Raza*. Berkeley, CA: Ramparts Press.

Jones-Correa, Michael. 2006. "The Study of Transnationalism Among the Children of Immigrants: Where We Area and Where We Should Be Headed." In *The Changing Face of Home: The Transnational Lives of the Second Generation*, edited by P. Levitt and M. C. Waters, 221–41. New York: Russell Sage Foundation.

Kleiner, Sam. 2014. "Right-Wing Xenophobes Area Spreading Lies About Migrant Diseases." *New Republic*, July 15. Accessed March 6, 2016. https://newrepublic .com/article/118700/border-crisis-leads-conservatives-claim-child-migrants -are-diseased.

Levitt, Peggy, and Mary C. Waters. 2006. Introduction to *The Changing Face of Home: The Transnational Lives of the Second Generation*, 1–30. New York: Russell Sage Foundation.

Louie, Vivian S. 2012. *Keeping the Immigrant Bargain: The Costs and Rewards of Success in America*. New York: Russell Sage Foundation.

Lowe, Lisa. 1996. *Immigrant Acts: On Asian American Cultural Politics*. Durham, NC: Duke University Press.

Mahler, Sarah J. 1995a. *American Dreaming: Immigrant Life on the Margins*. Princeton: University of Princeton Press.

———. 1995b. *Salvadorans in Suburbia: Symbiosis and Conflict*. Boston: Allyn and Bacon.

Menjívar, Cecilia. 2000. *Fragmented Ties: Salvadoran Immigrant Networks in America*. Berkeley: University of California Press.

Plan of the Alliance for Prosperity in the Northern Triangle: A Road Map. 2014. Accessed March 6, 2016. http://idbdocs.iadb.org/wsdocs/getdocument.aspx?doc num=39224238.

Portes, Alejandro, ed. 1996. *The New Second Generation*. New York: Russell Sage Foundation.

Portes, Alejandro, and Richard Schauffler. 1996. "Language and the Second Generation: Bilingualism Yesterday and Today." In *The New Second Generation*, edited by A. Portes, 8–29. New York: Russell Sage Foundation.

Portes, Alejandro, and Rubén G. Rumbaut, eds. 2001. *Legacies: The Story of the Immigrant Second Generation*. Berkeley and Los Angeles: University of California Press.

Repak, Terry. 1995. *Waiting on Washington: Central American Workers in the Nation's Capital*. Philadelphia: Temple University Press.

Rodríguez, Ana Patricia. 2001. "Refugees of the South: Central Americans in the U.S. Latino Imaginary." *American Literature* 73 (2): 387–412.

———. 2004. Interviews with Salvadoran Pioneras/os. Daly City, California. February 15–23, 2004.

————. 2009. *Dividing the Isthmus: Central American Transnational Histories, Literatures, and Cultures*. Austin: University of Texas Press.

Rumbaut, Ruben D., and Rubén G. Rumbaut. (1976) 2004. "Self and Circumstance: Journey and Visions of Exile." In *The Dispossessed: An Anatomy of Exile*, edited by P. I. Rose, 331–56. Amherst: University of Massachusetts Press.

Rumbaut, Rubén G. 2004. "Ages, Life Stages, and Generational Cohorts: Decomposing the Immigrant First and Second Generations in the United States." *International Migration Review* 38 (3): 1160–1205.

————. 2006. "Severed or Sustained Attachments? Language, Identity, and Imagined Communities in the Post-Immigrant Generation." In *The Changing Face of Home: The Transnational Lives of the Second Generation*, edited by P. Levitt and M. C. Waters, 43–95. New York: Russell Sage Foundation.

Smith, Robert C. 2006. "Life Course, Generation, and Social Location as Factors Shaping Second-Generation Transnational Life." In *The Changing Face of Home: The Transnational Lives of the Second Generation*, edited by P. Levitt and M. C. Waters, 145–67. New York: Russell Sage Foundation.

Suárez-Orozco, Carola, and Marcelo M. Suárez-Orozco. 2001. *Children of Immigration*. Cambridge, MA, and London: Harvard University Press.

Summers Sandoval, Tomás F., Jr. 2013. *Latinos at the Golden Gate: Creating Community and Identity in San Francisco*. Chapel Hill: University of North Carolina Press.

Takaki, Ronald. 1993. *A Different Mirror: A History of Multicultural America*. Boston: Little, Brown and Company.

Thompson, Paul. 2000. *The Voice of the Past: Oral History*. Oxford: Oxford University Press.

United Nations High Commissioner for Refugees (UNHRC). 2014. *Children on the Run: Unaccompanied Children Leaving Central America and Mexico and the Need for International Protection*. Retrieved March 6, 2016. http://www.refworld.org/docid/532180c24.html.

2

HARD WORK ALONE
IS NOT ENOUGH

Blocked Mobility for Salvadoran Women
in the United States

LEISY ABREGO

N JULY 2013, I conducted interviews in El Salvador. Not focused on any group
in particular, at the core of the conversations was the question, What does it
mean to be Salvadoran? Interestingly, the most common response, from men
and women alike, was something to the effect of "somos gente emprendedora"
(we are enterprising, hardworking people). Indeed, as Salvadorans, we pride
ourselves in being hard workers, telling our children and ourselves stories of a
work ethic of mythic proportions. This is certainly a positive attribute, and we
can find many examples in our history, both in Central America and the United
States, to prove that we have worked together to build communities, centers,
and organizations and changed wherever we have gone (Zimmerman 2010).
There are, however, potential pitfalls to this nationalistic narrative when, without assessing the structural context, we use it to blame individuals who have not
prospered. Blaming individuals is especially likely in the U.S. context, where the
meritocratic worldview so forcefully endorses the belief that anyone, regardless of their social location, is free to be successful through their own merits
(Hochschild 1995). Across nations, moreover, patriarchy and violence play out
in ways that can further block women from thriving. In this piece, I examine
the structural constraints and gendered ideals that make migrant Salvadoran
women particularly vulnerable. Based on the life experiences of a woman I call

Marta, I highlight how these powerful forces contextualize and often delimit our aspirations, actions, and decisions—regardless of how hard we are willing to work. I end by calling for those of us who have benefited from structural advantages—through high school–educated parents, legal permanent residency or U.S. citizenship, and extensive social networks—to work for structural change that will benefit more of the most vulnerable among us.

MARTA'S LIFE AND HER REASONS FOR MIGRATING

Marta is short—probably just under five feet tall—with a beautiful brown complexion and small brown eyes. Often avoiding eye contact, she speaks in a low voice, revealing front teeth lined with silver.[1] I interviewed her in 2004 for a research project about Salvadoran transnational families (see Abrego 2014). With no customers in sight, she agreed to do the interview while she worked. For seventy minutes, we talked next to her vending cart on the sidewalk of a busy street. Under oppressive heat from the summer sun, few people walked by, and not a single person made a purchase. We discussed her reasons for migrating, her journey to the United States, her work history in Los Angeles, and challenges with personal and family relationships.

A long history of what amounts to looting by wealthy transnational corporations and local elites has left much of northern Central America to deal with perpetual inequality and harsh living conditions for the poorest (Barry 1987). In rural El Salvador, labor can begin very early in life for those growing up in poverty. Indeed, this situation made for a difficult life for Marta. Because her family was very poor, she and her siblings could not prioritize or even afford much education. Instead, starting from an early age, they had to go out and work to help provide for the family. For Marta, working since the age of seven meant that she was able to complete schooling only up until the second grade. From a young age, she did domestic work, including laundry for various families, and she sold vegetables at the local market. She learned useful skills and developed tenacity through it all.

However, poverty and its gendered consequences bring new challenges at different life stages. By her teenage years, Marta was a mother of two children, relying on her meager earnings and those of her partner. Like her, the father of her children had little formal schooling, and together they faced a dearth of jobs. The stress of having to provide for themselves, their children, and Marta's aging parents was often overbearing, and with few other outlets, her partner turned to alcohol and became abusive. Indeed, these aggressive forms of masculinity are not uncommon when men face structural barriers that prevent them from living up to society's gendered expectations (Rios 2011). Unable to be the economic providers that society upholds as ideal men, it becomes more feasible to achieve masculinity through expressions of freedom and domination of women (Hume 2004). In this case, Marta, unhappy with the situation, transgressed her own gendered expectations by leaving him. She moved into her parents' home with her two children and tried to work even harder to provide for all of them. Quickly, however, structural realities set in. Domestic or informal work simply did not pay enough money to cover her family's most basic expenses.

Set in a rigidly patriarchal context, jobs available to women in El Salvador with little formal schooling pay unlivable wages that make it impossible for a single mother to provide for her family. Even in the twenty-first century, when *maquiladoras* (factories) with poor working conditions are considered the best option for women with little formal schooling, the pay is set at minimum wage—about $200 per month.[2] This is clearly inadequate to cover a family's basic food necessities, currently estimated to be about $175.[3] There is little left for rent, health care, educational supplies, or other important family expenses. It is understandable, therefore, that most Salvadoran immigrants will state that they migrated to get away from the violence of the civil war or in search of better economic opportunities; but Marta's story also highlights a few key experiences that are prevalent mostly among women. Like many women who come from poor families in El Salvador, Marta had few opportunities for schooling or occupational training that would prepare her for stable employment. Meanwhile, women suffer domestic and other kinds of violence at high rates. Women's migration, therefore, often involves the kind of violence and gendered lack of opportunities that Marta experienced.

Within that context, Marta considered herself quite fortunate. She had a sister, Sonia, who had migrated to Los Angeles a few years earlier. Sonia heard about Marta's troubles and offered her a deal. Sonia would pull together and send the money for a smuggler's fees, and Marta would pay off her debt by coming to Los Angeles, living with Sonia, and caring for Sonia's baby. Seeing no other plausible solution, Marta took on the risky journey by land to join her sister, where she hoped she could soon earn enough money to provide for her children and her parents.

THE MIGRATION JOURNEY: "THERE'S NO OTHER WAY"

It took Marta an entire month to get to the United States by land, as she was undocumented. On that hot summer day, she recounted some of the dangers she faced, including attempted rape, scarce food, and attacks from thieves. As the only woman in her group of travelers, she felt especially vulnerable. Ultimately, she says, she feels lucky to have survived the trip. While she expected the danger, in her desperation she was overcome by the uncertainty:

> Well yes, they tell you, you hear how hard it is to cross and that the trip is danger-ous. But desperation enters you because there is nothing to do and you don't know where the next meal is coming from so you get the strength to hit the road. You know what awaits, but there's no other way.

As the dangers of the journey by land through Central America and Mexico continue to escalate, as human rights abuses rise to plague the various routes north, and as impunity reigns over the horrific crimes committed against Central American migrants en route, many wonder why anyone would pur-sue the risky journey (UNHCR 2015). Migrants' experiences reveal that while they would prefer to travel by plane directly to the United States, this option is unlikely in most cases. Air travel to the United States requires a U.S. visa, and obtaining a visa is close to impossible for the vast majority of Salvador-ans. The nonrefundable visa application fee of $160 is prohibitive for people who earn little more than this per month. In their situation, the likelihood of being denied is high, leading people to rightly view the visa application process as a waste of time and money. Indeed, only those with a large sum in a bank account, stable employment, home ownership, and proof of strong ties keeping them in El Salvador have a chance of being granted a visa. In a highly stratified society marked by class, race, ethnicity, and gender, poor migrants like Marta are pushed to the path of unauthorized migration. When they cannot find the means to feed their children on a daily basis, they become desperate enough to take a risk and sacrifice themselves and their bodies for the opportunity to work and provide for their children. These are the people who in Central America are left unprotected by the state as workers and as women (Sanford 2008). These are the people who then are forced to walk for days, ride the trains, and risk their lives on that treacherous journey north. As Marta succinctly describes, for those in poverty with no feasible options for survival, "there's no other way."

It is important to note that even on this journey, women can expect to be treated differently than men. Targeted for rape on top of all the other kinds of violence and crime that migrants go through while en route (Falcón 2001), women like Marta must often continue to deal with their psychological scars for many years after migrating (Martínez 2010). The healing process is difficult when immigrants find little to no social service resources to help them overcome their trauma (Abrego 2014). In these cases, immigrants are further disadvantaged and pained as they attempt to get settled in the United States.

AFTER MIGRATION

In her desperate attempt to flee the situation and feed her children, Marta had not fully realized what the agreement with her sister would entail. After a month of being on the road, she finally arrived at her sister's home in Los Angeles in 1993 at the age of twenty-one. She was thirty-two years old in 2004 at the time of the interview. Her sister, Sonia, who was rather poor by U.S. standards, left Marta in charge of childcare but did not earn enough to pay her a separate wage. It had been their agreement that Marta would live for free in the home while caring for Sonia's child. Because she was not paying rent, she could not ask Sonia for wages, so she earned nothing. During her stay, after her sister got home from work and on the weekends, Marta relied on her survival skills and tenacity to earn money.

Based on her entrepreneurial experience during her childhood in El Salvador, Marta approached street vendors to offer help in exchange for learning their practices. Through her informal apprenticeship, she learned to make tamales and *atol de elote*—food and warm drinks to sell on the street. From that money, she recalls being able to wire $20 every other week to her children in El Salvador. Clearly, it was not a lack of perseverance that blocked her and her children's well-being. Despite being a self-starter who willingly worked hard, such informal labor did not provide enough to improve her children's lives.

Marta's case also reveals the family-related tensions that can lead to exploitative working conditions when (especially) women receive help from their families in the form of money or free room and board. Many women care for kids, clean the family home, cook, and generally take care of all household chores, thereby using up their time and not being able to earn money to send to their children back in El Salvador. Because of society's assumptions about the kinds of useful skills supposedly innate to women, many migrant women find themselves doing domestic work for relatives or employers and are not paid fair wages. Such patriarchal notions exist across borders but play out in ways specific to each society. In the contemporary United States, sexist and anti-immigrant sentiments reinforce the notions that someone like Marta, because of her racial and gendered social location, can only fulfill domestic responsibilities. Furthermore, because domestic work is devalued, immigrant women are not paid or are paid minimally for their labor.

To make matters worse, out of necessity (and often after being directly threatened by smugglers), paying the smuggler's debt is the first priority for migrants who travel without a visa. This is important because it prevents migrants from sending money to their families as they had initially hoped. Today, as smuggling costs have gone up to anywhere between $8,000 and $10,000 for a single person leaving Central America en route to the United States, women are especially financially burdened. Besides the initial cost of smuggling, migrants take high-interest loans that hike up the price of the journey further (Abrego 2014; UNHCR 2015). For women like Marta who traveled without authorization and stayed with relatives, it is difficult to quickly earn the money to pay back their debt. In Marta's case, after two years, she and her sister agreed—not without great tension—that she had done enough to repay the debt for the smuggler, and Marta moved out as soon as she could. In similar cases, whether they work for family, friends, or unrelated employers, women will go several years making far below minimum wage because their work is devalued and they are expected to be caring individuals who provide this type of work out of the goodness of their heart. Unable to demand higher wages, these women work for a number of hours that exceed a regular full-time job, yet they are paid woefully below minimum wage.

CONTROLLING WOMEN'S BEHAVIOR

While immigrant women may have diverse experiences, many find that upon arriving in the United States to reside with their families, it is also common that they be expected to behave in ways deemed socially appropriate for women (see, for example, Hagan 1994; Menjívar 2000). This means that people like Marta may not be allowed to go out on their own or to make new friends outside of family circles. Unlike men, who are not judged negatively for exploring their new surroundings and speaking with strangers about life in their new country, women like Marta are limited. Unable to go out except for very specific reasons out of necessity, many women immigrants do not have opportunities to expand their social networks. Without access to information from a wider variety of people, many immigrant women cannot find out about jobs, social services, or activities that may help them better integrate into this society. All this further exacerbates the consequences of lack of education, undocumented status, and language disadvantages that keep women in jobs that make it impossible to escape poverty.

In Marta's case, she felt so suffocated by the economic and social limitations that she decided to leave her sister's home only to move in with a new partner she barely knew. Although moving out and sharing expenses with this man were initially freeing, life soon became more difficult for Marta. She explained:

> So I was having problems living with my sister. That's why I got together with the father of my other son. I have a son here too. He's eight now. I met his father two years after getting here, and I got pregnant right away. Things were fine for a while. We rented a single and lived there, helped pay for things together. But almost as soon as my son was born, the man practically disappeared. I think he was doing drugs. Who knows how strong [the drugs] were, but he got really violent. I mean, I wouldn't say that things were good before then, but he wasn't as violent as he got later. At that point, he would leave, and we didn't know anything about him for days, and he would come back at four in the morning one night and threaten to kill me. At that time he was working in construction, and he ended up being like the security guard for the place at night, so he had access to a gun. I was really scared of him because he carried that gun and showed it to me at home.

Feeling economically vulnerable and with no one else to turn to in the city, Marta looked to move in with someone who was practically a stranger. Unfortunately for her, he turned out to be violent. During the time that she lived with him, she worked and they paid rent and bills together, but no matter how hard she worked, her life was not improving. Being a woman with few resources who did not have many people to turn to for help, Marta once again became a target for domestic violence. Her partner had the kind of job (traditionally open only to men) where he could access weapons, thereby increasing Marta's physical vulnerability.

At the end of that relationship, still with very limited resources and still unable to rely on more people in her social network, Marta strategized to protect herself and her son in the only way she knew how. As she explained, the situation was also problematic:

> So what I did was that I invited this one woman, a Mexican woman that I met on the street, to come and live with me. I didn't know her, she was an older woman, but I figured that at least I wouldn't be by myself when my son's father showed up. He kept coming for a while, but when he realized that she was always there, he just stopped coming. It was weird how he just disappeared. And that lady ended up living with me for a whole year. And don't think that things worked out well with her either. I never asked her to pay for anything because I just wanted the company. And she didn't have a job or anything. But eventually she started stealing my things, my money. I think she even stole my underwear at some point! Really, it's true. One time she even took $500!

In her moment of desperation to find a roommate who could, with her very presence, perhaps keep away her violent former partner, Marta invited another complete stranger to live with her. Without the reassurance of a background check, Marta once again fell victim to a roommate who stole from her, making her life difficult yet again.

It was not until a year later that Marta met another man, and at the time of the interview, they had been living together for two years. While far from perfect, the relationship and situation seemed more egalitarian:

> I'm not going to tell you that everything is great with him, because you know that there are always problems, and couples always fight. But at least he's not violent. We pay half and half for everything. So we split the rent and all that. And he has three kids in El Salvador too, so he has to send them money and he understands that I have to send my kids money too.

Despite being able to gain some independence from her sister, Marta continues to struggle due to personal decisions made within the limited options that constrain her. With no social networks, no economic resources, and no options for true upward mobility, Marta strategizes about who to live with and how best to avoid further problems and threats to her life. In the process, she is forced to spend more money on expenses in the United States for her own protection while she sees her limited economic resources wither away. Neither she nor her children in El Salvador or in the United States are experiencing an improvement in their lives, despite the many sacrifices she makes to try to secure a better living for herself and her family.

WORK, LEGAL STATUS, AND REMITTANCES TO FAMILY IN EL SALVADOR

Besides having to provide for her eight-year-old son who lives with her, Marta is still responsible for her two children and her parents in El Salvador. Like hundreds of thousands of Salvadorans abroad, Marta sends remittances to support her loved ones. These monies add up to a significant annual sum—$3.9 billion in 2012—that helps keep afloat the overall economy of the country. But what does it take for individual immigrants to earn the money and send it to their friends and relatives? During our conversation, when I asked Marta to tell me about remittances to her family, she provided extensive details about how she understands this responsibility and the structural reality in which she must make ends meet. Her entire labor history includes examples of labor abuse from a number of employers:

> Sending the money is easy. The hard part is earning the money to actually send it to them. I can say right now that I'm at a pretty stable job, but it hasn't always been that way. When I first got here, I had to take care of my sister's children, but she rarely paid me anything, and since I was living with her, it was very uncomfortable. You know, I couldn't really charge her since I wasn't even paying to live there. Later I got a job. . . . There was this one couple [of employers]—well he was American, but black, and she was Mexican. He was really nice, always made sure to pay me on time and things like that. They owned all these businesses and apartment buildings, so I would clean for them about three times per week. I would clean their hair salon, and then I would go clean one of their apartment buildings. And the deal was that he would write out the check, leave it with her if I wasn't around when he was around, and then she would keep the check. It happened many times and days later, I would tell him that I never got paid and he would try to find out about it, but she would deny that she had kept the money, so they just wouldn't pay me. I worked for them for about two years also until I got tired of her little games. He was a nice man, but she always tried to screw me over.

Like Marta, several women in the larger study recounted similar stories of employers' abuse. Many were paid less than minimum wage and on an irregular basis. They could not demand their rights either because they were uninformed about them, lacked social networks to access help, or were undocumented and felt pressured to stay quiet about any abuse to avoid deportation. For women like Marta in this situation, no matter how hard they work, no matter how many hours they put in, they will not be able to earn enough to provide for their families.

Even when they do not involve domestic work, many of the jobs traditionally available to immigrant women in the Los Angeles economy pay poverty wages. This was certainly true in Marta's case now that she was working as a vendor. Despite having two jobs and working all seven days of the week, she was barely making enough to survive in an expensive city like Los Angeles:

> Well, I usually got paid about $180 per week. Now I work in a restaurant three days a week and I get $120 for those three days every week. Then I can use the vending cart the rest of the week and I usually make another $100 the remaining four days. I have to buy my own merchandise and try to sell it, and that's usually what I make.

Marta makes roughly $220 per week, or about $880 per month, even though she works seven days a week. Such low earnings are not entirely uncommon among Salvadoran female immigrants. In fact, in all of the most common sectors that employ women—whether they work in the garment industry, hotel housekeeping, or as domestic workers—employees often earn less than $300 per week (Abrego 2014). Even when they work full time (or more) like Marta, their hard work does not pay well enough to guarantee them a safe living situation.

In Marta's case, given this context of poverty wages, it is not surprising that she would feel obligated to share expenses with someone, even though she lives in a small single apartment with her son. This context also explains why she does not have enough money to send to her children in El Salvador to make a notable improvement in their daily lives or to facilitate their upward mobility. With those low wages, Marta has several monthly expenses that she cannot avoid:

> Well the first thing is the rent. I live in a single, and the good thing is that we're splitting the costs of everything with my partner right now, so I pay the rent one month and he pays it the other month. I pay $450 per month because I've been

living there for a long time—over on X and Y street. Then the next thing is the money that I send to my kids. I send them every single month $150. And then of course there are those extra expenses, that they need a new backpack or they need new shoes, so I'll try to send them $25 more that month. And what I do is I try to alternate, so that one month I send the extra money for the boy and the next month to the girl. But it's hard. Everything starts adding up because I have to pay for groceries, I have to make sure my kid has some money for school stuff sometimes, because of course I have my son here, and then I have to pay for transportation. Right now I only have to pay for one bus each way, so that's good at least. But everything adds up and it's barely enough to cover all the expenses of every month.

Even the daily expense of public transportation to get to and from work is important in calculating her budget. In another part of the interview, Marta notes that she is sending the money not just for her two children, but for the entire household where they reside. This includes her two elderly parents, who can no longer make a living on their own. Her meager wages, then, must provide for two households, and in the end, neither is thriving.

The country of El Salvador, meanwhile, relies heavily on remittances from people like Marta to maintain the national economy. Over 15 percent of the country's gross domestic product comes from the earnings of Salvadoran migrants abroad who send remittances to their loved ones. Without the sacrifices of migrants like Marta, El Salvador's economy would suffer further (Hernández 2006). To avoid such a disaster, politicians on both the left and the right have expressed their great appreciation for the *hermano lejano*—as they refer to migrants abroad—by building monuments in their honor and aggrandizing their economic efforts in public speeches (Baker-Cristales 2004). Given the particular gendered challenges facing Marta and other women migrants, however, it is difficult to support the reality that El Salvador's national development is taking place largely on the backs of vulnerable women whose labor is heavily exploited.

Along with her level of education, limited social networks, access to poorly paid jobs, and multiple economic responsibilities, legal status is another factor that shapes Marta's life. As an undocumented immigrant woman, not only is she fearful of denouncing corrupt employers who cheat her out of wages but she also has little access to resources that might otherwise help her meet her needs. Therefore, although migration scholars have found that, in general, migrants' job options, earnings, and economic stability improve after ten years of residing in the United States (Myers 2007), Marta has not benefited. Presumably, with time, people learn language and life skills that allow them to better cope and progress in this country, even if they started out with limited resources. Ten years should be enough time to pick up some English, meet more people, and learn to navigate the city in ways that will make it easier to get better jobs. In Marta's case, however, with over a decade in Los Angeles, the passage of time had done little to better position her in the job market. She could not apply for more stable jobs, nor could she explore other possibilities, out of fear of detention and deportation.

Though she has tried to find employment in various sectors, her legal status as an undocumented immigrant gives her access only to jobs in the informal sector, where her poverty wages make it difficult to meet all her children's needs.[4] Her children in El Salvador complain angrily:

> I wish I could say that I did the right thing in coming. Sometimes I think it was the right decision. But when you have your kids yelling at you, being so angry that you left them, it just makes you sad. (Crying.) But there's nothing I can do. I barely make enough for rent and bills here. I don't always have enough left over to send to them, but I do try. And they tell me, "Mami, but things are more expensive now," but they don't understand that it's also expensive here.

Marta's earnings are barely enough to support her son who lives with her and pay rent in Los Angeles. It is not surprising, then, that she does not have enough money to send to her children in El Salvador to markedly improve their daily lives or set them on an upwardly mobile path. Because she is undocumented, moreover, she has no possibility of visiting her children to affirm her commitment to them in person. She cannot leave for El Salvador and then return to the United States.

Feeling abandoned and having little to show for their mother's sacrifices, Marta's children had begun to rebel and get into trouble with drinking and drugs. She was horrified at working so hard and only being able to provide for their basic needs.

> I have to send money for that entire household, which right now is just my two kids and my two parents. My parents are old, and it's hard for my dad to continue to work the land. You know that over there, with the dollar being the main

currency used, everything is really expensive, even if they still pay you in *colones*. So he would have to work really hard just to cover the expenses of the household. So I have to send the money for their food, for all of them. And every so often, you know, more things come up, like you have to go to the doctor for something, or there's some kind of emergency, or the kids need new clothes, and then I have to send extra money.

Like Marta, immigrant parents in similar situations feel they are doing their best, under difficult circumstances, to send money. The children, however, often reproach the parents for what they experience as a form of abandonment. Therefore, while migrants may be doing everything in their power to fulfill their financial obligations to their loved ones, they face notable obstacles that block their ability to thrive both in the United States and in El Salvador.

CONCLUSION

Salvadoran immigrants in the United States are contributing in a number of fields and collectively building their future in this country. With enough students in California colleges and universities to make up an impressive statewide student organization such as the Unión Salvadoreña de Estudiantes Universitarios, it is clear that increasing numbers of children of immigrants are becoming upwardly mobile. In celebrating these students, each of whom is a victory for our community, we can follow our traditional approach and attribute their success to individual efforts. After all, when things go well and we achieve progress, we like to attribute it to our own efforts of mythic proportions. However, in this piece, through the experiences of Marta, it has been my goal to convince readers that more is involved in determining our paths to mobility.

With no shortage of personal drive, entrepreneurial spirit, and tenacity, after eleven years in the United States, Marta continues to be undocumented, poorly educated, exploited for her labor, and generally unable to provide for the needs of all the members in her household in the United States or in El Salvador. Despite expectations that length of residency in the United States will greatly improve life chances and living conditions for immigrants (Myers 2007), Marta has experienced only minimal improvements, even though she matches the expectation of the hardworking Salvadoran. There are many people like Marta in our communities. There is a range of levels of education among Salvadoran immigrants in the United States, but over half of immigrants from El Salvador have less than a high school education (Brick, Challinor, and Rosenblum 2011). This puts the community in a vulnerable position, and indeed this is reflected in the low-wage jobs that predominate among Salvadoran immigrants. In fact, 23 percent of Salvadorans (almost a full quarter of immigrants) live in poverty. This is a rather high rate when compared to 14.3 percent of the overall U.S. population that lives in poverty (Brick, Challinor, and Rosenblum 2011).

Among us, women are especially vulnerable because they cannot access better-paid jobs, they may be targets of domestic violence, their work is devalued, and their social networks are limited. Indeed, women earn much less than men and are more likely to live in poverty (Gammage et al. 2005). In Marta's case, despite all of her best intentions and all of her steady work, her life experiences since migrating have collectively blocked her ability to thrive. Based on poverty wages of her own, Marta's sister, Sonia, was only able to assist Marta in ways that blocked both of their mobility. In response, Marta's decision to start a new relationship with someone as a means to move out did not pay off. Instead, Marta continues to struggle within the limited options that constrain her. With no social networks, no economic resources, no legal protections, and no options for true upward mobility, Marta navigates the system admirably. She strategizes about housing options, who to live with, and how best to avoid further problems and threats to her life. However, in the process she is forced to spend more money on expenses in the United States for her own protection while she sees her few economic resources wither away. Neither she nor her children in El Salvador or in the United States are experiencing an improvement in their lives, despite the many sacrifices she makes to try to secure a better living for all of them.

Based on the many structural challenges evident in Marta's experiences, I make a call for those of us who had the structural advantages—of high school–educated parents, legal permanent residency or U.S. citizenship, extensive social networks, or the sheer good luck of finding or being found by mentors who opened doors for us—to not forget about people like Marta. As we move to advocate for migrants' participation in the national development of El Salvador, as we try to organize people to vote in El Salvador's elections from abroad, and as we continue to develop our community's history in the United States, let us be intentional in including even (and especially) the most vulnerable members of our group in our plans. Too often, immigrant women are bearing the burden for entire families and communities. We can join in the organizing work of labor centers and community organizations, including the Central American Resource Center and other entities established since Salvadorans started migrating to the United States (Zimmerman 2010; Gonzales 2009), to improve working conditions, demand more inclusive immigration policies, and provide opportunities for education and training to make us all stronger and more likely to thrive.

NOTES

1. As is true in much of my work (2013; Forthcoming), I describe research participants' physical traits to humanize them in the analytical process and to remind readers that these voices and experiences are lived in bodies that are also marked by race and gender.

2. All monetary figures included in this chapter refer to U.S. dollars—the currency used in El Salvador.

3. See the website for the Dirección General de Estadística y Censos, accessed on September 1, 2012, at http://www.digestyc.gob.sv/index.php/servicios/en-linea/canasta-basica-alimentaria.html.

4. In fact, stories of undocumented workers who suffer but remain quiet about labor abuses are widespread in many industries and throughout the United States (Holmes 2013; Walter, Bourgois, and Loinaz 2004; Gleeson 2012).

REFERENCES

Abrego, Leisy J. 2013. "Latino Immigrants' Diverse Experiences of Illegality." In *Constructing Immigrant "Illegality": Critiques, Experiences, and Responses*, edited by Cecilia Menjívar and Daniel Kanstroom, 139–60. Cambridge: Cambridge University Press.

———. 2014. *Sacrificing Families: Navigating Laws, Labor, and Love Across Borders.* Stanford: Stanford University Press.

———. Forthcoming. "Illegality as a Source of Solidarity and Tension in Latino Families." *Journal of Latino and Latin American Studies.*

Baker-Cristales, Beth. 2004. *Salvadoran Migration to Southern California: Redefining El Hermano Lejano.* Gainesville: University Press of Florida.

Barry, Tom. 1987. *Roots of Rebellion: Land and Hunger in Central America.* Boston: South End Press.

Brick, Kate, A. E. Challinor, and Marc R. Rosenblum. 2011. *Mexican and Central American Immigrants in the United States.* Washington, DC: Migration Policy Institute.

Falcón, Sylvanna. 2001. "Rape as a Weapon of War: Advancing Human Rights for Women at the U.S.-Mexico Border." *Social Justice* 28 (2): 31–50.

Gammage, Sarah, Alison Paul, Melany Machado, and Manuel Benítez. 2005. *Gender, Migration and Transnational Communities.* Washington, DC: Inter-American Foundation.

Gleeson, Shannon. 2012. *Conflicting Commitments: The Politics of Enforcing Immigrant Worker Rights in San Jose and Houston.* Ithaca and London: Cornell University Press.

Gonzales, Alfonso. 2009. "The FMLN Victory and Transnational Salvadoran Activism: Lessons for the Future." *NACLA Report on the Americas* (July/August): 4–5.

Hagan, Jacqueline Maria. 1994. *Deciding to Be Legal: A Maya Community in Houston.* Philadelphia: Temple University Press.

Hernández, Ester. 2006. "Relief Dollars: U.S. Policies Toward Central Americans, 1980s to Present." *Journal of American Ethnic History* 25 (2–3): 225–42.

Hochschild, Jennifer. 1995. *Facing up to the American Dream: Race, Class, and the Soul of the Nation.* Princeton: Princeton University Press.

Holmes, Seth M. 2013. *Fresh Fruit, Broken Bodies: Migrant Farmworkers in the United States.* Berkeley: University of California Press.

Hume, Mo. 2004. "'It's as if You Don't Know, Because You Don't Do Anything About It': Gender and Violence in El Salvador." *Environment and Urbanization* 16 (2): 63–72.

Martínez, Óscar. 2010. *Los migrantes que no importan: En el camino con los Centroamericanos indocumentados en México.* Barcelona: Icaria.

Menjívar, Cecilia. 2000. *Fragmented Ties: Salvadoran Immigrant Networks in America.* Berkeley: University of California Press.

Myers, Dowell. 2007. *Immigrants and Boomers: Forging a New Social Contract for the Future of America.* New York: Russell Sage Foundation.

Rios, Victor M. 2011. *Punished: Policing the Lives of Black and Latino Boys.* New Perspectives in Crime, Deviance, and Law, edited by John Hagan. New York and London: New York University Press.

Sanford, Victoria. 2008. "From Genocide to Feminicide: Impunity and Human Rights in Twenty-First Century Guatemala." *Journal of Human Rights* 7 (2): 104–22. doi: 10.1080/14754830802070192.

UNHCR. 2015. *Women on the Run: First-Hand Accounts of Refugees Fleeing El Salvador, Guatemala, Honduras, and Mexico.* Washington, DC: United Nations High Commissioner for Refugees.

Walter, Nicholas, Philippe Bourgois, and H. Margarita Loinaz. 2004. "Masculinity and Undocumented Labor Migration: Injured Latino Day Laborers in San Francisco." *Social Science & Medicine* 59: 1159–68.

Zimmerman, Arely M. 2010. Contesting Citizenship Across Borders: Identity, Rights, and Participation Amongst Central Americans in Los Angeles. PhD diss., University of California, Los Angeles.

3

"OBSTINATE TRANSNATIONAL MEMORIES"

How Oral Histories Shape
Salvadoran-Mexican Subjectivities

STEVEN OSUNA

I N THE LAST THIRTY YEARS, Los Angeles has become the epicenter of both
Mexican and Salvadoran transnational migration. Outside of San Salvador, El Salvador, and Mexico City, Mexico, respectively, Los Angeles has
the largest population of Salvadorans, Mexicans, and U.S.-born Mexicans and
Salvadorans (Lipsitz 1999). Due to the political, economic, and various forms
of social struggle in their homelands, Salvadorans and Mexicans have migrated
and created transnational social fields between their countries and Los Angeles (Basch, Schiller, and Blanc 1994; Smith and Guarnizo 1998; Schiller 2005).
Beyond the emergence and transmission of remittances, cultural expressions,
commodities, and material necessities, transnational social fields are also spaces
for the circulation of memories of migration and social struggle. Memories of
migration and nation-state border crossing are not left behind but rather are
permanent traces of the past that are operative in the present. Through oral
histories, transnational migrants' experiences are a critical source of historical
memory that provide testimonies to the struggles and lived experiences of displacement, migration, and diasporic belongings.

There have been numerous waves of Mexican migration, beginning in the
late nineteenth century (Barrera 1979; Valadez Torres 2005). Salvadorans have
been migrating to the United States for the same amount of time, yet not

in large numbers (Menjívar 2000; García 2006). The increase of Salvadoran migration began during the late 1970s and has been continuous since the 1980s (Hernández 2006; Garni and Weyher 2013; Abrego 2014). Both communities have distinct reasons for migration, but in the first instance, many of these migrants serve as the global reserve army of labor for capital in Los Angeles (Valle and Torres 2012; Hall 1986, 43).

Moreover, the unique social positioning of U.S.-born second-generation children of Mexican and Salvadoran migrants, who face numerous forms of oppressions and exploitation, generates unique experiential spaces within these transnational social fields (Ek 2009; Levitt and Waters 2002; Smith and Guarnizo 1998). Although their terrain embodies a transnational social field across nation-state boundaries, it is also locally articulated to a long history of a racialized class struggle in the city. How does the second generation maneuver through this terrain? Do they find strength and empowerment from their parents' histories and memories of migration and struggle? Are the historical memories of migration passed down to the children of Salvadoran and Mexican migrants? If so, how are these histories and memories of migration interpreted from the point of view of the second generation?

Through in-depth, semistructured, qualitative interviews with twenty young adults of mixed Salvadoran-Mexican descent who were raised in Los Angeles, this chapter examines the transmission of historical memories of migration and social struggle, or what I refer to as transnational obstinate memories. These memories connect and signify different spaces, places, and people who have traveled and created transnational social fields throughout Central America, Mexico, and Los Angeles (Basch, Schiller, and Blanc 1994; Smith and Guarnizo 1998; Schiller 2005). They are persistent, enduring, and part of the participants' subjectivities. Through a snowball sampling method and participant observations in student and community organizations, I recruited and reached out to the participants of this research. The participants were between the ages of eighteen and thirty. Half of the participants were women, the other half men; some attended community colleges or universities in Southern California or were either employed full time as custodians and teachers, in a nonprofit organization, or currently unemployed. This population was vital in uncovering the transnational obstinate memories—of economic strife, social movements, and class struggle.

In this chapter I argue that the transnational obstinate memories of the second generation passed down from their immigrant parents provide them with an ideological connection to both Mexico and El Salvador, a social and political consciousness that guides and nurtures them toward social justice organizing, and a foundation to navigate their local terrain in Los Angeles. These transnational obstinate memories are not only persistently operative—they are formative. They produce illuminating critiques of structural processes of inequality while facilitating transnational identities and solidarities between communities. Despite the distinct distances and national borders that must be crossed between the United States, El Salvador, and Mexico, the participants form transnational identities that link them to both their parents' homelands as well as their own. These obstinate transnational memories provide the second generation, and others, with the ability to deploy and use the past as a tool to organize for a more just future and build solidarities between divergent communities.

This chapter emerges from a research study conducted between 2009 and 2011 that interrogated the "dialectical interplay of tension and solidarity" between Salvadoran and Mexican migrants and second-generation communities in Los Angeles (Osuna 2015). It examined the lives of young adults who are children of mixed Salvadoran-Mexican migrant families in Los Angeles, in conjunction with participant observations in community and student organizations. The research contextualized their families' experiences within a larger theoretical, analytical, and historical framework of the global capitalist system; recent transnational processes, including migration and transnational family formation; and the racialization of Latina/os in the United States. Attention to structural and cultural factors that materially and ideologically situate both communities, such as labor market competition and national belonging, assisted in explaining the dialectical interplay of tension and solidarity between the two social groups. What emerged from this research were the dynamic and multiple ways that oral history transmits migratory experiences, which inform the experience of the second generation of Mexicans and Salvadorans in Los Angeles. Privy to both groups' experiences, U.S.-born Salvadoran-Mexicans in this study are uniquely positioned to observe and bridge the infinite Latina/o migrant experiences in Los Angeles. Their lives, and the memories that have been passed down from their parents, complicate the dominant view of a homogenous Latina/o subject in the United States. Moreover, the subjectivity and experiences of these U.S.-born Salvadoran-Mexicans, or Mexican-Salvadorans, is a point of entry in the ongoing conversations around national belonging, identity, ethnic tensions and solidarities, and the struggles of Latina/o communities in the United States.

In his study of decolonization, Frantz Fanon (2004, 167) illustrates the importance of activating historical memory to advance political action. He argues that colonized intellectuals who fight for liberation use the past in order to open the future, foster hope, and spur people into action. Like Fanon's colonized intellectual, some of the participants have taken the memories and experiences of migration of their parents and made political linkages to U.S. foreign policy, critiques of capital, and critical understandings of globalization and have used it as a source of inspiration for a just world. Through their community work or student activism, the participants in this research demonstrate the power that historical memories can have on peoples' everyday lives. They show that historical memory and oral history, beyond an academic method or tool, are sources of motivation, inspiration, resistance, and dignity (See Hernández in this volume).

MIGRATION OF SALVADORANS AND MEXICANS TO LOS ANGELES

The mass migration of Salvadoran and Mexicans to the United States in the last three decades coincides with structural changes in the global, regional, and local political economies (Robinson 2008). Through neoliberal reforms, civil war, and an increase in economic inequality, many Mexicans and Salvadorans have sought better living and working conditions in the United States, thus intensifying the migration in the late twentieth and early twenty-first century (Hamilton and Stoltz Chinchilla 2001; Menjívar 2000; Booth, Wade, and Walker 2006; Gonzalez and Fernandez 2003). During this current epoch, the transnationalization of capital has in turn induced and exacerbated the transnational circulation of labor. In 2005, about 30 percent of Salvadorans were living outside of El Salvador, while 15 to 20 percent of Mexicans were living outside of Mexico (Robinson 2008, 312). Many of these migrants who come from El Salvador and Mexico make up the lower rungs of the service-sector economy of Los Angeles and the surrounding region. They serve as all of the labor in the agricultural industry, hotels and restaurants, domestic work and landscaping, food processing, light manufacturing, and so on (Robinson 2008, 314). Although they come for better living and working conditions, and most find it, many more migrants are exploited and face a racist Los Angeles landscape (Ochoa and Ochoa 2005).

As urban historian Eric Avila (2006) argues, Los Angeles has historically been the southwestern outpost of white supremacy and capitalist exploitation. California, and Los Angeles in particular, has had a deep-rooted legacy of white supremacy, with racial segregation and oppression as an everyday experience for many people of color (Almaguer 1994; Pulido 2006; Molina 2006; Smith 2013). The racialized hierarchies produced through white supremacy have created differential racialization that George Lipsitz argues creates "alliances and antagonisms, conflicts and coalitions" and "characterizes the complex dynamics of white supremacy within and across group lines" (2006, 58). Salvadoran and Mexican communities in Los Angeles, like other racialized communities, are confronted with such conditions that spotlight their legal status. Tensions between these communities emerge, yet solidarity forms between them as well (Osuna 2015). Even within the unitary pan-ethnic category of Latina/o, Salvadorans and Mexicans, like other ethnic groups within this category, experience an uneven racialization process complicated by a regime of illegality (Gutiérrez 1995; Rúa 2001; De Genova and Ramos-Zayas 2003; Bedolla 2005; Alvarado 2013). This modality structures the lives of many Salvadoran and Mexican migrants as well as their families. It determines their relationship to the state and regulates their behavior. As a result of these material conditions, access to resources for many is scarce, which then shapes their appraisals of each other in competitive ways. The contradictions of racialized capitalism produces group-differentiated vulnerabilities that complicate relationships between and among oppressed communities. In the last three decades Salvadorans and Mexicans in Los Angeles have worked through these contradictions in myriad ways.

Living and working through the contradictions of racialized capitalism, the participants in this research showed the commonalities as well as the differences between Salvadoran and Mexican communities. They recognized that they are part of a heterogeneous (yet often collapsed as a singular) racialized group that faces many forms of oppression and exploitation in the United States, such as racism, capitalist exploitation, and the "legal violence" of immigration and criminal law (Menjívar and Abrego 2012). Their perspectives offer a window into the potentiality of multiple forms of solidarity that can emerge in Salvadoran and Mexican working-class communities in Los Angeles.

INFINITY OF TRACES

According to Italian communist intellectual and strategist Antonio Gramsci, we are all intellectuals since we can all analyze the social formation we inhabit (Gramsci 1971, 9). "[T]he starting point of critical elaboration is the consciousness of what one really is," he states, "and is 'knowing thyself' as a product of the historical process to date which has deposited in you an infinity of traces, without leaving an inventory" (Gramsci 1971, 324). Indeed the participants and I tackled these "infinity of traces" in the interviews conducted. They all discussed growing up between both Salvadoran and Mexican migrant working-class communities in places such as South Los Angeles, Mid-City, Pico-Union, and East Los Angeles. They shared subjectively how they interpreted and understood their realities. Given Gramsci's starting point of critical elaboration, it is vital to connect these subjectivities to the historical and social processes of forced migration, capitalist exploitation, and institutional racism. Oral historian Alessandro Portelli argues for conceptualizing and studying subjectivity as "the cultural forms and processes by which individuals express their sense of themselves in history" (1991, ix). Learning through peoples' subjectivity is key to explaining the complexities of the social formation and allows scholars, organizers, and members of racialized migrant communities to make larger connections to global processes and power relations.

Most of the participants made connections to larger social structures—namely, to transnational migration and memory. The participants consistently shared stories they heard from their parents and relatives about the sociopolitical experiences in El Salvador and Mexico, and in particular the shared encounters of transnational migration to Los Angeles. These stories and memories shared from parent to child are what Central American literary scholar Ana Patricia Rodríguez calls second-hand stories and memories. "For many children of the Central American diaspora who came to the United States at an early age, or who were born here," she argues, "their knowledge of the homelands is oftentimes a secondhand one, mediated by the stories, memories, and texts transmitted to them by others" (Rodríguez 2003, 2). Portelli similarly suggests that through the knowledge "picked up from overheard snatches of conversations among adults, from chance remarks, from seeing how [their parents] look like after work," the children of working-class families become conscientious of their social position (1991, 274).

The participants of this study learned about themselves and their history through the stories and anecdotes their parents shared with them, as well as their occupations in Los Angeles. José, one of the participants, recalls his mother's job in the garment industry of downtown Los Angeles. "She worked a long time in *costura* (garment industry), when I was 10 I used to go with her. She used to go in at 6 a.m. in the morning and leave at 2 p.m., and we would walk home, the same old thing for a couple of years." José's mother worked as a seamstress for many years, and he distinctly recalls the division of labor within the industry, the swelter of the unventilated sweatshop, and his mother's time-consuming work schedule. Throughout the interview he linked her occupation in the sweatshop with her immigration status and her fleeing the civil war in El Salvador in the early 1980s. Her life story gave José a sense of who he was in the United States. He spoke to the specificity of his mother's experiences, yet he related it to the overall working-class struggles of Latina/os in the United States, especially Mexicans and Salvadorans in Los Angeles. His experience of going to work with his mother also allowed him to connect the struggles of Salvadorans in the United States to historical trauma in El Salvador throughout the 1980s.

The memories and stories that José shared, like those of many of the participants discussed below, were transnational in nature since they circulated across and beyond the borders of the U.S. nation-state. They are transnational memories and stories that come from numerous places and spaces in El Salvador, Mexico, and Los Angeles and are passed down to the participants of this research. And from the conversations we had, I sensed that they were obstinate memories. What do I mean by obstinate memories? These memories are stubborn, persistent, unrelenting, not easily subdued or removed, and have been passed down from their family's history. The obstinacy of these transnational memories guided participants of this research, the second generation of Salvadoran-Mexicans, in linking the realities they face in Los Angeles with the social conditions in Mexico and El Salvador. The realities of gendered forms of undocumented migration, a racist landscape, and capitalist social relations were understood as part of a transnational experience that connects Los Angeles to places and spaces in Mexico and El Salvador.

TRANSNATIONAL OBSTINATE MEMORIES

According to Schiller (2005) migrants produce transnational social fields that cross the boundaries of various nation-states. Although the participants were not part of the migration experience, or born in Mexico or El Salvador, they described their connection to their parents' homeland through this transnational social field. As Robert, a high school teacher and community organizer, argued about his connection to El Salvador, "that's the motherland, although I wasn't born there." Not all participants referred to El Salvador as the motherland; some chose Mexico, or some did not use the phrase at all. Yet what was clear in the participants' discussion of their families was their belonging to places beyond the border of the U.S nation-state. They all identified with their parents' homeland, whether they chose one country or the other. The transnational social field created by their parents and the predominately migrant communities they belong to in Los Angeles creates a cultural, material, and ideological link beyond city limits.

The participants provided descriptive and illustrative narratives about their parents' lives before leaving their homeland and their migration experiences. These narratives not only demonstrated that they knew about their parents' history—it showed their relationship and embrace of them. They went into detail about the gendered and national experiences of migration; reasons for migrating, such as state repression or lack of employment opportunities; and their own feelings about these experiences. When speaking about their mothers' experiences, for example, they emphasized the difficulties they faced when traveling toward the United States. Michelle, a community organizer whose mother is Salvadoran, described that her mother fled El Salvador due to gender violence and state repression.

> My mother is from Mejicanos [San Salvador] . . . she worked as a secretary. She came in 1975. She said she came because there was nothing in El Salvador because of the circumstances, economically and politically. A lot of women were being raped and things like that. . . . My mom was not involved politically, but my grandma was. So that was the dynamic, my grandma did not want to put my mom at risk. The house had been raided a couple times and my uncles had been beaten up.

In the working-class community of Mejicanos, Michelle's mother was in a state of heightened danger and fear. Many who lived in El Salvador during this era were vulnerable to political repression, but being involved in the conflict, or a relative to someone who was, elevated the dangers and consequences of state-sanctioned violence (Zentgraf 2005). Although her mother was employed as a secretary, Michelle described that her mother's life was threatened if she remained in El Salvador. While traveling through Mexico, her mother's experience "was a pretty hard one," having to deal with mistreatment by the "coyote" who crossed her over the Mexico-U.S. border. As Arregui and Roman (2005) note, the most common experience of Central American migrants through Mexico has been one of exploitation and abuse.

Robert's mother, who is from San Marcos, El Salvador, left in 1976. She first left El Salvador at the age of seventeen. Robert was not completely sure why she left the first time but was aware that she returned to El Salvador. Her second trip is the one he remembered.

> I guess back in those days the *migra* was not as tough as they are today. I know that . . . I actually was almost born in El Salvador. She was pregnant of me in 1981. She went to El Salvador, she was undocumented, pregnant, and she went back to get my great-grandmother. So it was two women, one older woman and one pregnant woman, and keep in mind the revolution had already started. That was a hell of a journey. So somehow, some way, part of the trip was through land. They said that they caught a cruise ship and that brought them through most of Mexico. And then they passed through cars over the [U.S.] border.

His mother, like many of the participants' mothers who were from El Salvador, went back and forth prior to acquiring residency or citizenship in the United States. They would often return for relatives and loved ones. Both Michelle and Robert were proud to know and share the struggles their mothers experienced and survived. They embraced these memories as their own—they provided a critical understanding of why they were here in the United States. They borrowed from these memories the courageousness that their mothers exemplified. In their work with youth and as community organizers, Robert and Michelle kept these memories close to them as a form of encouragement, as a reminder to continue the struggle. Robert organized with a community organization against police brutality and migrant repression, while Michelle worked with a nonprofit organization focused on violence prevention among young adults. Both argued that their mothers' migration experiences and displacement due to the political repression in El Salvador was an initial motivation for their involvement in struggling for better living conditions in Los Angeles for the many Latina/o migrants and their children.

Like the mothers, many of the fathers also shared their memories of the journey and hardships. Transnational migration is a gendered process that produces and shapes distinct opportunities and experiences (Hondagneu-Sotelo 1994; Abrego 2014). The participants' fathers went through various scenarios that differed from the mothers. In her discussion about her father, Monica, a university student, described that her father, who is from Jalisco, Mexico, worked in agriculture and did not earn a wage that could help support his family. She stated that her father came

> [to] find work. He came [undocumented]. And he got caught at the border twice and made it the third time. . . . What happened the second time was that they went through the sewer [system]. He got really sick; he got pneumonia. He was drinking polluted water. He wanted to keep going, but the cops found him. He almost died, but he attempted again.

Monica goes on to discuss that the third time her father attempted to cross the border he lost one of his family members.

> The final time he crossed, his sister died in the sewer. He said that the sewer was really small. She started coughing and had pneumonia. He saw his sister die and no one could do anything. . . . There was no clean air to breathe. And the next exit was a while away. . . . She died there. He said he carried her body. My grandmother took her body back to the town, and he kept going. It's a crazy story.

Her father's experience is not an aberration. Indeed, many migrants lose their lives through the dangerous journey. While sharing this story, Monica remembered her father illustrating the horror of traveling through a sewer. Just as Gregory Nava depicted two young Maya Guatemalan siblings crossing through a sewer in his film *El Norte* (1983), she shared her father's tragedy as a form of keeping the past in the present. It is not an event that happened in the past but rather a reoccurring event that Monica argued continued to happen to many families. Monica called this a "crazy story" to disrupt the taken-for-granted notions of migration as simply a crossing of a border. Its "craziness" derives not from the people who migrate but rather the political and economic policies that produce these conditions. As anthropologist Leo Chavez (2008) illustrates, the dominant narrative of migration obscures these harsh realities and places blame on individual migrants and treats them as an invading force. Monica's ability to retell this story of her father serves as a "disordering narrative" that incorporates "factors such as poverty, employment, family and other aspects of the story that go unheard or unheeded in court and media accounts" (Phillips 2012, 47). Her father's story, like countless others, shows the tragedies that so many face and how it informs their migration counternarratives of systemic inequalities that lead to migration.

Like the violence of transnational migration, the history of political violence in El Salvador and its current manifestations shape the relationship that many have with the country. When sharing her father's story, Erin, who was born in East Hollywood but grew up in the San Fernando Valley, said she does not want her father to return to El Salvador, out of fear that he might be killed.

No. I don't want him to, because they killed his brother. He was on a bus . . . he saw a bunch of people crowded around a woman. And, he went up to see what was going on. And, it was his sister. And, his sister was having a panic attack. And, then she showed him the newspaper with his brother on the front page, shot in the head wearing his T-shirt . . . it was just crazy shock for him. And, after that they were looking for my dad because they thought my dad was part of it, too. So they sent soldiers, I forget what they call it, but there's a mountain in Santa Ana where they take them to kill them. Like, they see dead bodies out there. And, my dad said they took him in a van. And he had gotten out of the van and he had peed himself, he was so scared. And, they started laughing at him. And, then they were like, "alright, we'll give you 5 seconds to run." And my dad went running [but] they never shot him . . . that's when he left.

Erin first heard this story when she was five years old. Her father has not returned since this event. He recently planned on returning to El Salvador, yet after all these years Erin fears for his life. Many Salvadorans and their families who fled the country during the war still have fear of repression if they return. As García notes, many who fled El Salvador were singled out for persecution and were seeking a safe haven outside of their homeland (2006, 85). The story told to Erin at a young age has left her with a violent image of El Salvador. This image of violence is a reoccurring theme and is currently dramatized with images of youth gangs (Zilberg 2011; Fariña, Miller, and Cavallaro 2010). Yet Erin's image of violence does not come from gangs but rather from the paramilitary "death squads"—clandestine groups with ties to state actors and powerful elites that carried out targeted killings of perceived enemies (Fariña, Miller, and Cavallaro 2010).

According to the 1993 United Nations Truth Commission for El Salvador, paramilitary violence terrorized El Salvador and killed, tortured, and disappeared many throughout the civil war (UN Security Council 1993). Erin's father survived his kidnapping and lived to tell about it. Sharing this experience with Erin at a young age left her with a complicated view and relationship to El Salvador. Although it is her father's homeland, it is a place that he fled and fears returning to. Lipsitz notes many migrants around the world no longer feel "at home" in their countries of origin: "they flee the hatred at home to seek a better life someplace else, making displacement, exile, and homelessness common experiences" (2006a, 299). These experiences have a long-lasting effect that the second generation also internalizes.

Remembering and sharing the experiences of their fathers—one of economic necessity, the other of political repression—were difficult for Erin and Monica. Retelling stories that were shared by their parents, stories that told of deadly, serious consequences, was emotionally taxing. These memories have marked many of the participants. Yet they embrace these memories as a shared burden and experience. Although cringing when sharing these stories with me, Monica and Erin shared them as part of their family's histories and their outlook in social justice work. The transmission of family stories, I argue, has shaped this second generation from mixed nationalities and/or ethnicities to embody their parents' migration experiences into their evolving praxis. There is much specificity that must be taken into consideration when understanding migration, whether it's national or gendered, or fleeing economic insecurity or political violence such as the ones shared by the participants.

In the words of Gramsci (1971), their parents' experiences "deposit" historical events and processes that influence how the participants see the world around them. The shared memories became a way to connect to the experiences of migration, exile, and survival, although the participants did not live them. It gave them a sense of what kind of struggles their parents endured. On the other hand, a few of the participants did not know too many details about their parents' experiences. One participant, Alex, whose father is from El Salvador and mother from Mexico, said his parents never described their experiences. He was aware when they left and their potential reasons for leaving but was not sure of what they experienced. He felt his parents did not seem to think it was important to share these experiences:

> Either that or probably like just to protect us. Just like the thought about it, you know? Probably, like they don't want to traumatize us, if they went through some traumatizing stuff. But, like you know what? We're already here, let's make the most of it.

State violence, war, displacement, sexual assault, and many other experiences that migrants face are not easy to share with others (Abrego 2014). Alex might not have known about the details of his parents' experiences, but that is not because he did not care; rather, he was never told about them. This, perhaps in his parents' rationale, allowed him to make the most of living in Los Angeles. His father and mother are employed as an auto mechanic and domestic worker in the city, and he attends a state university. Alex's parents have chosen, for their own particular reasons, not to share what happened. This can possibly be their way of creating a better life—by moving forward and silencing the traumatic past. Displacement, migration, and navigating a new terrain bring about numerous strategies of survival. Silence, moving forward, and not looking back is one of them. This must be understood as a survival strategy.

Being told at a young age about certain experiences, such as migration, can leave an imprint of the serious high stakes that a loved one has endured, as Erin and Monica discussed. It can lead to a critical perception of migration as an expression of moments of emergency, precarity, and danger, such as many of the other participants shared. Alex is aware that his parents left their homeland for better life chances, but he prefers to think of it as something in the past. This is also a common story in the lives of second-generation Latina/os and may be more the case among children of Central Americans because of the histories of violent political repression. Many do not know the experiences of their parents, whether it is because the parents choose not to share for many different reasons or the second generation might be uninterested. There can be many reasons, but a third of the participants of this research did know about their parents' memories of migration and displacement. This in turn inspired them to do more than simply share their family's memories. Some sought to research the art, culture, and histories of Mexico and El Salvador while others were part of student and community-based organizations that either focused on Mexican and Central American issues or struggled for the political and economic rights of migrants. The oral histories of migration shared by their parents were a node in the development of their political consciousness and ongoing organic praxis.

POLITICIZING THE TRANSNATIONAL MEMORIES

The participants who heard or knew about their parents' transnational migration experiences were left with a strong sense of who they are in the United States. Many have visited El Salvador and Mexico with their families and on their own and have kept close ties with family and friends abroad. More so, the majority of the participants linked the experiences of their parents to other migrants, and those involved in building the social justice movement politicized their parents' migration experiences and memories. Robert illustrated that he identifies as both Salvadoran and Mexican because of the rich history of struggle that both communities have endured. The material conditions of his communities have created the condition of his identification.

> Today, politically, I identify of course as Salvadoran cuz that's who I am, but also I politically identify as a Mexican because of our peoples' struggle here and on this particular piece of the land as it relates to the usurpation of the land by U.S. imperialists. And that really was concretized in my understanding by the struggle of the Salvadorans and the FMLN [Farabundo Martí National Liberation Front]. And even though the FMLN was fighting in El Salvador, the analysis to me made total sense because of . . . anti-capitalist, anti-imperialist politics.

Michelle, like Robert, also argued that knowing the histories of both sides of her family has shaped her political consciousness. She has combined both histories of struggles within the Mexican and Salvadoran communities in Los Angeles.

> It definitely shaped my political consciousness, especially my Salvadoran side. My grandmother was very leftist . . . that understanding of society, economy, and culture . . . and when I learned more about my Mexican culture and history I was like wow . . . its similar struggles that they went through, especially with the Mexican Revolution. And also artistically both have influenced me . . . and even how I talk . . . I talk both Salvadoran and Mexican Spanish.

She embraced not only both political histories of struggle but also the distinct cultural expressions of both ethnic communities. Michelle created what American studies scholar Gaye T. Johnson (2008) refers to as a "constellation of struggle" in which she connected the distinct experiences of two diverse communities to demonstrate the shared and intersecting histories of struggle active in the contemporary context. She also noted how the experience of Salvadoran women throughout the civil war and the reality they face in the United States inspired her own sense of being.

> The gender roles in El Salvador changed during the civil war. The role of women changed. My grandmother was very strong. She was a single woman. My mom

came here, and she was strong in some senses. My mom handled a household and still worked. I see those roles and I have to be like them too. As a woman I have to identify more with my Salvadoran culture. A lot of women I know that are in the "movement" are Salvadoran.

Monica shared this sense of being influenced by Salvadoran women. Although she identified as both Mexican and Salvadoran, and has been heavily influenced by both, the political activism of women during the civil war and the struggles of migration genuinely inspired her political consciousness in her activism in student and political organizations in Los Angeles.

The participants used the transnational memories of their parents to connect their personal biographies to the diverse Mexican and Salvadoran communities in Los Angeles as well as Latinas/os in the United States. One participant linked the experiences of Latina/os in the United States, such as struggling with racism and discrimination in the workplace, to larger structural processes. Elias shared his father's stories of the workplace and his advice: "He always told me that as Latinos we have a negative 10 on our foreheads, so we have to work ten times as hard as anybody else just to have the same recognition. He has always talked about . . . the things he's had to overcome, like the challenges you know . . . dealing with it and turning the other way and doing what you have to do." He related these stories his father told him to the realities of migration for Salvadorans:

> The reason I really exist is because of what happened in El Salvador. Like the reason why everything that formed me as a person has to do with what happened in El Salvador. My father's migration was something that was forced. The fact that all my uncles are here was forced. So it's like, to recognize my true history, I need to realize that I'm Salvadoran.

While acknowledging his Mexican ancestry, Elias sees his father's forced migration from El Salvador as the origin of his existence. According to Elias, to recognize where he comes from, to comprehend the reality that his Salvadoran family has faced, he first must "realize" that he is Salvadoran. For him, part of his identity is linked to the struggles that occurred in El Salvador. Instead of collapsing his identity to a homogenous Latina/o one, Elias expressed the specificities, distinctions, and complexities that exist within this category. Salvadoran forced migration and exile, for him, was the root cause of why he was in the United States in the first place. Like Elias, other participants moved beyond the dominant conception of migration as simply seeking better life chances, and instead understood migration as struggle for survival against the many forms of exploitation and oppression brought by the forces of transnational capitalism. They insisted that their history did not begin in Los Angeles but through the displacement that their parents experienced. These shared memories became obstinate and veritably informed their political identities and social imaginations. They illustrated that identities can be formed by politics, rather than politics formed by identities (Lipsitz 2006b, 67).

In her discussion of utopian thinking, Herbert Marcuse's critical theory, and radical scholarship, sociologist Avery Gordon (2004) argues that obstinacy is necessary in preventing utopian and radical thought from being disqualified or discredited. Obstinacy in critical theory allows radical scholars and utopian thinkers to engage taken-for-granted appearances as misleading and question the social order. Like obstinacy for radical scholars and utopian thinkers, the obstinacy in the transnational memories of the participants provided them with a critical view of migration, of the experiences of Latina/os in the United States, and of their connections to Latin America. In particular, the transnational memories linked the participants to faraway places and events that occurred throughout El Salvador, Central America, Mexico, and Los Angeles. The obstinacy in these transnational memories allows the participants, and contemporary scholars who study Central Americans, Mexicans, and Latina/os in the United States and transnational migration, to connect cities such as Los Angeles to the larger political economy of global capitalism and Latin America and thus excavate emergent forms of social and political possibilities (Ochoa and Ochoa 2005, 5).

CONCLUSION

The struggles of transnational migrants are a living archive interacting with the past and present. They not only communicate historical memory that is then passed down to the next generation but also inspire them to action. As some of the participants illustrated, the numerous struggles of their parents in Mexico and El Salvador and their process of migration shape how they see themselves in Los Angeles and the United States. The memories and experiences shared by their parents were reminders and a source of inspiration for the community organizers and student activists who were part of this research. Those who were not involved in any activism or organizing made important links between the memories shared by their parents to the many immigrant experiences in their communities. Individual experiences of their parents were being transformed into collective community experiences. Histories of migration shared with the participants were part of their development of critical consciousness as Gramsci (1971) describes.

The transnational obstinate memories examined provide an alternative narrative to the actual conditions of the participants' existence—a source of resistance and dignity. This chapter explored how young adult Salvadoran-Mexicans accessed and retrieved their families' stories in the context of mass migration, racism, exploitation, and state violence. For the participants who live in Los Angeles, the obstinate transnational memories have not only helped them achieve this but have also allowed them to be open and aware of other peoples' struggles. Brenda, who was raised in Inglewood, illustrated that growing up in between and learning from the histories of both Mexican and Salvadoran communities had made her more aware of others' struggles: "growing up, it's made me very open minded and it made me who I am . . . I'm just very open."

Illuminating the obstinate transnational memories emerging through the transnational social fields of migration cannot be understated. Oral history provides a wealth of knowledge of the everyday struggles of the transnational Latina/o working classes of Los Angeles. Although distinct, the histories and genealogies of migration of Salvadoran and Mexican communities provide a space to initiate a discussion of the intersections of solidarities between heterogeneous subaltern communities. Scholarship and organizing that seriously engages transnational migration must interrogate the operative memories of migration, not just from the person telling the narrative but also from those who carry those narratives with them. The Salvadoran-Mexicans in this study are examples of those who have been shaped by the memories and narratives of transnational migration. They politicized their view of migration. It is not coincidental that many of these transnational young adults are more inclined to engage and participate in building the social justice movement. In her study of black and Chicana/o coalition building in Los Angeles, Johnson (2012) reminds us that the future has a past, and we must look to it to illuminate the present. By naming and exploring these transnational obstinate memories shared between generations, parents and children, and two distinct national groups, this chapter contributes to an ongoing dialogue that requires presence of mind of the trials and tribulations of the Salvadoran and Mexican working classes of Los Angeles.

ACKNOWLEDGMENTS

I would like to thank the research participants and their families. Their struggles for dignity and social justice are not in vain. Thanks to Roxanna Curiel and Daniel Olmos for their helpful suggestions on prior drafts of this chapter. Much appreciation and gratitude goes to the editors and reviewers of this volume for their thoughtful and generative feedback and suggestions.

REFERENCES

Abrego, Leisy J. 2014. *Sacrificing Families: Navigating Laws, Labor, and Love Across Borders*. Stanford: Stanford University Press.

Almaguer, Tomás. 1994. *Racial Fault Lines: The Historical Origins of White Supremacy in California*. Berkeley: University of California Press.

Alvarado, Karina O. 2013. "An Interdisciplinary Reading of Chicana/o and (US) Central American Cross Cultural Narrations." *Latino Studies* 11 (3): 366–87.

Arregui, Edur Velasco, and Richard Roman. 2005. "Perilous Passage: Central American Migration Through Mexico." In *Latino Los Angeles: Transformations, Communities, and Activism*, edited by Enrique Ochoa and Gilda L. Ochoa, 38–62. Tucson: University of Arizona Press.

Avila, Eric. 2006. *Popular Culture in the Age of White Flight: Fear and Fantasy in Suburban Los Angeles*. Berkeley: University of California Press.

Barrera, Mario. 1979. *Race and Class in the Southwest: A Theory of Racial Inequality*. Notre Dame: University of Notre Dame Press.

Basch, Linda, Nina Glick Schiller, and Cristina Szanton-Blanc. 1994. *Nations Unbound: Transnational Projects, Postcolonial Predicaments and Deterritorialized Nation-States*. Amsterdam: Gordon and Breach Publishers.

Bedolla, Lisa. 2005. *Fluid Borders: Latino Power, Identity, and Politics in Los Angeles*. 1st ed. Berkeley: University of California Press.

Booth, John A., Christine J. Wade, and Thomas W. Walker. 2006. *Understanding Central America: Global Forces, Rebellion, and Change*. 4th ed. Boulder, CO: Westview Press.

Chavez, Leo R. 2008. *The Latino Threat: Constructing Immigrants, Citizens, and the Nation*. Stanford: Stanford University Press.

De Genova, Nicholas, and Ana Y. Ramos-Zayas. 2003. *Latino Crossings: Mexicans, Puerto Ricans, and the Politics of Race and Citizenship*. New York: Routledge.

Ek, Lucila D. 2009. "'Allá en Guatemala': Transnationalism, Language, and Identity of a Pentecostal Guatemalan-American Young Woman." *High School Journal* 92 (4): 67–81.

Fanon, Frantz. 2004. *The Wretched of the Earth.* New York: Grove Press.

Fariña, Laura Pedraza, Spring Miller, and James L. Cavallaro. 2010. *No Place to Hide: Gang, State, and Clandestine Violence in El Salvador.* Cambridge, MA: Harvard University Press.

García, María Cristina. 2006. *Seeking Refuge: Central American Migration to Mexico, the United States, and Canada.* Berkeley: University of California Press.

Garni, Alisa, and L. Frank Weyher. 2013. "Dollars, 'Free Trade,' and Migration: The Combined Forces of Alienation in Postwar El Salvador." *Latin American Perspectives* 40 (5): 62–77.

Gonzalez, Gilbert G., and Raul A. Fernandez. 2003. *A Century of Chicano History: Empire, Nations, and Migration.* New York and London: Routledge.

Gordon, Avery F. 2004. *Keeping Good Time: Reflections on Knowledge, Power, and People.* Boulder, CO: Paradigm Publishers.

Gramsci, Antonio. 1971. *Selections from the Prison Notebooks,* edited by Quintin Hoare and Geoffrey Nowell Smith. New York: International Publisher.

Gutiérrez, David G. 1995. *Walls and Mirrors: Mexican Americans, Mexican Immigrants, and the Politics of Ethnicity.* Berkeley: University of California Press.

Hall, Stuart. 1986. "The Problem with Ideology-Marxism without Guarantees." *Journal of Communication Inquiry* 10 (28): 28–44.

Hamilton, Nora, and Norma Stoltz Chinchilla. 2001. *Seeking Community in a Global City: Guatemalans and Salvadorans in Los Angeles.* Philadelphia: Temple University Press.

Hernández, Ester. 2006. "Confronting Exclusion in the Latino Metropolis: Central American Transnational Communities in the Los Angeles Area, 1980s–2006." *Journal of the West,* 45 (4): 48–56.

Hondagneu-Sotelo, Pierrette. 1994. *Gendered Transitions: Mexican Experiences of Immigration.* Berkeley: University of California Press.

Johnson, Gaye Theresa. 2008. "Constellations of Struggle: Luisa Moreno, Charlotta Bass, and the Legacy of Ethnic Studies." *Aztlan: A Journal of Chicano Studies* 33 (1): 155–72.

———. 2012. *Spaces of Conflict, Sounds of Solidarity: Music, Race, and Spatial Entitlement in Los Angeles.* Berkeley: University of California Press.

Levitt, Peggy, and Mary C. Waters. 2002. *The Changing Face of Home: The Transnational Lives of the Second Generation.* New York: Russell Sage Foundation.

Lipsitz, George. 1999. "World Cities and World Beat: Low-Wage Labor and Transnational Culture." *Pacific Historical Review* 68 (2): 213–31.

———. 2006a. "'Home Is Where the Hatred Is': Work, Music, and the Transnational Economy." In *The Chicana/o Cultural Studies Reader*, edited by Angie Chabram-Dernersesian, 299–313. New York: Routledge.

———. 2006b. *The Possessive Investment in Whiteness: How White People Benefit from Identity Politics*. Philadelphia: Temple University Press.

Menjívar, Cecilia. 2000. *Fragmented Ties: Salvadoran Immigrant Networks in America*. Berkeley: University of California Press.

Menjívar, Cecilia, and Leisy J. Abrego. 2012. "Legal Violence: Immigration Law and the Lives of Central American Immigrants." *American Journal of Sociology* 117 (5): 1380–1421.

Molina, Natalia. 2006. *Fit to Be Citizens? Public Health and Race in Los Angeles, 1879–1939*. American Crossroads. Berkeley: University of California Press.

Nava, Gregory. 1983. *El Norte*. American Playhouse.

Ochoa, Enrique, and Gilda L. Ochoa. 2005. *Latino Los Angeles: Transformations, Communities, and Activism*. Tucson: University of Arizona Press.

Osuna, Steven. 2015. "Intra-Latina/o Encounters: Salvadoran and Mexican Struggles and Salvadoran-Mexican Subjectivities in Los Angeles." Special Issue of *Ethnicities. Latino Formation in the U.S.: Laboring Classes, Migration & Identities* 15 (2): 234–54.

Phillips, Susan A. 2012. *Operation Fly Trap: L.A. Gangs, Drugs, and the Law*. Chicago: University of Chicago Press.

Portelli, Alessandro. 1991. *The Death of Luigi Trastulli and Other Stories: Form and Meaning in Oral History*. New York: State University of New York Press.

Pulido, Laura. 2006. *Black, Brown, Yellow, and Left: Radical Activism in Los Angeles*. Berkeley: University of California Press.

Robinson, William I. 2008. *Latin America and Global Capitalism: A Critical Globalization Perspective*. Baltimore: Johns Hopkins University Press.

Rodríguez, Ana Patricia. 2003. "Second Hand Identities: The Autoethnographic Performances of Quique Avilés and Leticia Hernández-Linares." *Istmo: Revista virtual de estudios literarios y culturales Centroamericanos* 8. Retrieved July 10, 2013. http://istmo.denison.edu/no8/articulos/second.html.

Rúa, Mérida M. 2001. "Colao Subjectivities: PortoMex and MexiRican Perspectives on Language and Identity." *Centro: Journal of the Center for Puerto Rican Studies*. Special Issue on Puerto Rican Chicago 13 (2): 117–33.

Schiller, Nina Glick. 2005. "Transnational Social Fields and Imperialism: Bringing a Theory of Power to Transnational Studies." *Anthropological Theory* 5 (4): 439–461.

Smith, Michael Peter, and Luis Eduardo Guarnizo. 1998. *Transnationalism from Below*. New Brunswick, NJ: Transaction Publishers.

Smith, Stacey L. 2013. *Freedom's Frontier: California and the Struggle over Unfree Labor, Emancipation, and Reconstruction*. Chapel Hill: University of North Carolina Press.

UN Security Council. 1993. "'From Madness to Hope': The 12-year war in El Salvador: Report of the Commission on the Truth for El Salvador." Retrieved December 5, 2014. http://www.usip.org/sites/default/files/file/ElSalvador-Report.pdf.

Valadez Torres, Martin. 2005. "Indispensable Migrants: Mexican Workers and the Making of Twentieth Century Los Angeles." In *Latino Los Angeles: Transformations, Communities, and Activism*, edited by Enrique Ochoa and Gilda L. Ochoa, 23–37. Tucson: University of Arizona Press.

Zentgraf, Kristine M. 2005. "Why Women Migrate: Salvadoran and Guatemalan Women in Los Angeles." In *Latino Los Angeles: Transformations, Communities, and Activism*, edited by Enrique Ochoa and Gilda L. Ochoa, 63–82. Tucson: University of Arizona Press.

Zilberg, Elana. 2011. *Space of Detention: The Making of a Transnational Gang Crisis Between Los Angeles and San Salvador*. Durham, NC: Duke University Press.

4

A GYNEALOGY OF CIGUA RESISTANCE

La Ciguanaba, Prudencia Ayala, and
Leticia Hernández-Linares in Conversation

KARINA O. ALVARADO

VIOLENCE AGAINST WOMEN in Central America and the United States
replicates linkages long established by coloniality, where resistance connects women across borders of time and space, breaking the constrictive
function of nations. The legend of la Ciguanaba, the biography of 1930s Salvadoran suffragette Prudencia Ayala, and her depiction in a poem by Salvadoran
North American poet Leticia Hernández-Linares constitute a trifold analysis in
this chapter. As conjoined narratives of Salvadoran-Salví[1] memory, their stories
travel, crossing and unbounding borders while signifying diasporic narratives
marked by gender and sexuality. La Ciguanaba, for example, connotes meanings of colonization, colonialism, gendered violence, gendered exile, and dehumanization particularly targeted onto female and indigenous-mestiza bodies.
However, the legend can also signal a continuity of resistance retold in the most
common of settings, such as around a dinner table, thus transmitting messages
of insurgency and survival through the signifier of woman as a gendered shape-
shifter. A narrative that may seem to replicate patriarchal hegemony and the
dominant cultural regime can actually serve a counterhegemonic function that
bridges eras and countries while disrupting scripts of gender/racial submission.

How can violent and tragic archetypal narratives in the context of coloniality
and displacement also be resistant and heroic? La Ciguanaba was once a mythic

young woman desired by a plantation master who, when rejected, sends his men to torture and kill her in a cave by a river. From then on, la Ciguanaba, made to exist in permanent exile, embodies beauty and horror. She is beautiful when she seduces men and frightening when she shapeshifts into the form of la Ciguanaba. There are many versions of the tale of la Ciguanaba, both pre-Columbian[2] and postconquest,[3] yet all versions contain four characteristics: la Ciguanaba as a beautiful and desirable woman, her experience of exile, her persistent presence as she haunts the river ways, and her mocking and frightening men when she transmutes herself as the haggard woman. Since all signifiers are inherently ambivalent, la Ciguanaba can replicate heterosexist and hegemonic codes of female domesticity and morality (explored later in the chapter) while also reproducing messages of female resistance and resilience.

The life and times of Prudencia Ayala also show multiple levels of exile and ridicule onto her person for attempting to become president of El Salvador in 1930. Her in-your-face resistance and insistence on gender equality was almost erased from Salvadoran history throughout the twentieth century. She was not forgotten nor completely removed from a mostly male Salvadoran history because of acclaimed Salvadoran writer Alberto Masferrer's influence and the work by women organizations like la Concertación Feminista Prudencia Ayala. North American–born Salvadorans such as Hernández-Linares continue to recuperate Ayala as part of diasporic cultural memory. Similar to Chicanas' reclamation of poet and heroine Sor Juana Inés de la Cruz, mythic/historic figure Malintzin (Malinche), and la Llorona, U.S. Central American writers, poets, artists, and academics are actively recuperating and resignifying the signs, symbols, and narratives of Central America to draw connections and find meaning to Central American gendered lives within the U.S. diaspora.

The project of recuperation plus resignification for U.S. Central Americans connects to the Popular Cultural Movement begun in El Salvador and Guatemala. Novelist and poet Claribel Alegría situates this movement as a response to the ongoing historical erasure by the dominant classes onto the rural and labor masses. She explains, "these groups developed repertoires stemming from popular traditions. . . . They breathed new life into the archetypal figures of El Salvador's ancient folklore" (1986, 498), which included making the legends and traditions "class conscious" (498). U.S. Central Americans, in this case a Salvadoran American poet, continue to revise the repertoires and oral memories but with significant emphasis on gender consciousness. Central American diasporic and 1.5+ revisions can be compared to Chicana revisions of la Llorona or Coatlicue

(Editors 1997 Chabram-Dernersesian 1992; García 1997; Lara 2008), and African American resignification of Afro-based lore exemplified in *The Signifying Monkey* (1988) by Henry Louis Gates Jr. While comparisons and parallelisms can be drawn to other U.S. Latina/o and ethnic revisionist practices, U.S. Salvadoran as U.S. Central American lore must be understood in its own right. Distinctions and clarifications must be drawn among Mesoamerican cultural lore so as not to overstate differences among Latinas/os but to honor our ancestors or the prior generations who passed down these stories from individual to individual, within families, and among specific and regionally located communities. Rewriting and rearticulating a class-conscious and feminist Ciguanaba-in-diaspora fundamentally restores projects begun in Central America. Hernández-Linares clearly draws these rebuilt bridges for us by connecting la Ciguanaba to Ayala's feminist writings and movement. In other words, la Ciguanaba is not just another Llorona. U.S. Central American revisions emerge from cultural memory practices that return to the isthmus but loop back to the United States.

While the transnational *Departamento 15*[4] may be considered derooted or uprooted, it also shows signs of rooting (in North America) and rerooting (in Central America). The U.S. Central American diaspora embodies and extolls a trans-site of cultural memory that, for the purpose of this chapter, returns to El Salvador as a tangible environment and the referent place of cultural memory/origin precisely because of its affective, symbolic, real, and shifting absence in the United States. For example, U.S. Central Americanist Robin DeLugan's work explicates transnational cultural memory against forgetting. Her work explores the linkages occurring between El Salvador and its U.S. diaspora around recuperation of indigeneity (2013). Both collective and communicative memory reconstruct the past to give meaning to the present. As it is remembered, commemorated, signified, and retold through performance, festivals, essays, artworks, and poems, collective and communicative memory become formalized within cultural memory. Astrid Erll explains, "'Cultural Memory' does therefore *not* describe all manifestations of 'memory in culture'; rather it represents a subset of this: the societal construction of normative and formative versions of the past" (2011, 30). Hernández-Linares's poem—in the retelling of the legend of la Ciguanaba, the remembrance of Prudencia Ayala, the exploration of their intersections, and the meaning offered in this chapter—resituate memory in both time and space.

This chapter explores Hernández-Linares's poem ("The Sybil, the Cigua, and the Poetess [Conversations]," my translation) as an opportunity to remember la Ciguanaba and Prudencia Ayala as women and symbols of gendered cultural memory of resistance reenacted transnationally and transculturally. The essay first establishes my methodological lens, followed by Hernández-Linares's critical biography. The focus then shifts to exploring the life and times of Prudencia Ayala. The next section familiarizes readers with the legend of la Ciguanaba, giving her greater historical and material context to the past and present and to El Salvador and U.S. Central America. The sections are laid out as such in recognition that some readers may be completely unfamiliar with the Salvadoran women and legend and their significance for the U.S. Central American diaspora. This framework informs readers with all the elements needed to understand the last section, which close reads my translation of Hernández-Linares's poem. The essay redeploys the word *Cigua* throughout as a term for U.S. Central American and Latina resistance that founds and supports a hemispheric consciousness of gendered resistance.

HEMISPHERIC THEORIZING: RECUPERATING CIGUA GYNEALOGIES

Cigua, Siwat, Cegua, Cihuatl, and Ciwuat are Mesoamerican Nahuat/Nawat[5] (El Salvador, Honduras, and Nicaragua) and Nahuatl (Mexico) terms for women. Putting the Cigua signifier in use (re)members indigenous-mestiza women within a nexus of residual and emergent cultures, memory, and discourses. In the face of major economic and gendered violence, Cigua narratives are recovered, acknowledged, and contemporized within the long struggle of female resistance as a historical continuum in and of the Americas. Exploring the lives and works of Ciguas represents an opportunity for conscientization that centers and sutures Latina, U.S. Central American, and indigenous resistance against female displacement from her own body, voice, and civil rights. In situating our subjects within Cigua discourses and practices, I highlight the Salvadoran and Salví gendered struggles, but as part of collective narratives being told and renarrativized by the U.S. Central American diaspora.

For the purpose of this chapter, Cigua especially demarcates a U.S. and Central American space that overflows the boundaries of nation. Cigua constitutes an act of self-naming and reclamation within our communities and movements as an important process of self and transcultural empowerment. For example, feminism scholar Shira Tarrant explains that terms like *womanist* are typically viewed as "eccentric." Yet, as Chicana scholar Laura Pulido proposes, self-naming is an absolute necessity in the act of agency and re-empowerment (Pulido 1996; Oquendo 2010). It includes the proposal of a feminine language that could explain lived female experiences (Irigaray 1985; Kristeva 1984) that cannot be divorced from race, ethnicity, and culture (Moraga 1983; Anzaldúa 1987).

New terms proposed by scholars of color are deemed "eccentric" because they are nonhegemonic and noncomplying as they locate their own spatial and cultural meanings. I apply the term *Cigua* to remember indigenous-mestiza women as peoples indigenous to the Americas and to re-center U.S. *centroamericanas*, who in absence of their own space must often employ feminist discourses from other area women's studies and cultural locations in the United States. Moreover, Cigua disaligns us from Anglo or European feminist movements that may maintain white or Eurocentric privilege, as it realigns indigenous-mestiza female resistance with the various heterogeneous communities, discourses, and movements of liberation throughout the hemisphere. U.S. *centroamericanas*, Latinas, Boricuas, and Chicanas have been instrumental in disseminating Cigua stories of resilience to future generations. They have literally walked them across borders while older immigrant generations continue to share cultural knowledge through oral traditions. Strategies for survival embed these narratives passed to younger generations as a growing and hemispheric mobile people that, regardless of where they migrate within the Americas, remain within a continental and historical homeland.

Collectively, or relationally, all Cigua signifiers, symbols, and discourses at work in the poem presented in this chapter, including the poet, create what Norma Alarcón deems "a feminist reinscription of gynetics" (1993–1994, 150).[6] Alarcón suggests a type of orientalism in the proposed knowing of women through clinical study that correlates every aspect of their lives to their reproductive organs and stages. Where Alarcón rewrites gyniatrics or the gynecological study of women into gynetics as a rewriting of women into history, I in turn have transmuted genealogy to gynealogy. Genealogy has served Western history as the study of generations within the power-laden term: civilization that in Western societies is linear, male-centric, and written through the erasure of women. Alegría critiques this type of historicizing (as discussed earlier in this chapter) as representative of "official," elitist, male, dominant remembrance constituted as culture and knowledge. I offer the concept and process of gynealogy to emphasize a long continuum of presence throughout the Americas that records Cigua women back into our collective stories and cultural memories. These narratives are not simply Salvadoran/American, nor only female, but highlight integrated struggles of indigenous, mestiza/o, Afro-descendent, civil, and human rights. This chapter employs gynealogies alongside and at times instead of history/ies, especially when discussing Cigua and U.S. Central American movements, versus when I speak on Salvadoran-nationalist and masculinist-constructed histories.

HERNÁNDEZ-LINARES WRITING WOMEN IN CONVERSATION

Each woman's biography must be explained to expand on their personal stories and to highlight why it is important that we recover or record each one into a hemispheric gynealogy. Born in Los Angeles, Hernández-Linares is the daughter of Salvadoran parents. An established performance artist and poet from the U.S. Central American community, in 1996 she was awarded the William Carlos Williams Prize from the Academy of American Poets. Calaca Press published her first poetry chapbook, *Razor Edges of My Tongue* in 2002. *Mucha Muchacha, Too Much Girl* was published in book and CD format in 2010. Hernández-Linares has worked with various well-established Latina/o and Chicana/o poets, especially through live performance.

Her collaborative acts, written work, and repertoire reveal an ideal that art should decolonize and cross "genre boundaries and geopolitical borders." Her body of work includes "digital media, audience interaction and costume and props."[7] She has opened on stage with Danza Mexica. An altar to Lukumi gods may be included in her performance. Her work is performative in that she shares with her audience her daily indigenous-based beliefs and rituals. Counter to performance as a temporary and artificial staging or role playing, performativity means that these acts constitute an integral sense of being and making (Butler 1990). Hernández-Linares puts into practice what Gloria Anzaldúa calls the "wild tongue," as strategies that break Spanish, because as spoken by Chicanas/os, Spanish stops being a "pure" tongue (1987, 75–76). If language symbolizes and manifests our subjectivities and identifications, both Anzaldúa and Hernández-Linares emphasize multiplicity, where the very existence of the multiple Other's sexuality, gender, and willful acts of transgression challenge the supposed authenticity of the dominant order. This is how I define hybridity, as a dialectic of noncompliance and as a way of cultural resilience. Hernández-Linares incorporates, juxtaposes, and transposes Salvadoran, Salví,

Chicana, Latina, Latino, American, and Caribbean traditions because, as she explains, "When nationalism arises between the Mexican/Chicana/o and Salvadoran sides of the room, I have no desire to pick sides" (2002b, 113). This decision is not apathetic or apolitical. Her performativity crosses borders that confine and segregate and that do not acknowledge her historical location or the processes by which she became interpolated into various discourses and life practices that produced a transcultural subjectivity.

On stage, she uses poetry and "performance antics" to address gender violence and silencing and migrant and female labor, among other social issues, while engaging the seeming contradictions of being a transcultural Salví. For example, by calling herself "tecpatl, artista, poet, vieja, los angelina, maestro, performer, salvadoreña, chicana, guide, gitana, bruja, bard, tierra, water, música, fire, hopeful" (2002a, 597), she refuses to be typecast within a singular identity even as she claims particular though various national, of color, female, sexed (both the gendered *a* and *o* in Spanish), and Nawat locations such as *tecpatl*. As the flint, or obsidian, knife (the razor edges of her tongue), she claims the role of sage embodied as an organic intellectual. Choosing to leave a doctoral program in the English Department in the University of Pennsylvania because of the alienation she experienced as the only Latina Salvadoran in the program, she has since been an active educator in the Latina/o San Francisco community. She assists migrant Latina/o families and youth through various organizations for which she has worked. She defies intellectual intimidation that denies her indigenous-based mestiza spiritual practices and perspectives and instead connects art, activism, and all her locations of knowledge as part of her trans- and pluri-cultural memory work.

Hernández-Linares purposely uses the stage to strategically question forms of restriction on one's identity and relations. She explains,

In college, I was . . . frustrated by the pointless, ridiculous authenticity game in which those around me engaged. Worse yet, beyond college campuses, similar kinds of power struggles impede the education and liberation of disempowered communities, young girls in particular. When people of color who have not yet challenged and healed themselves try to help youth, they perpetuate misogyny, homophobia, and prejudice. (2000b, 114–115)

Decolonizing projects heal on gendered, personal, and communal levels. As her poetry shows, being multiple does not exclude her from contributing to the cultural memory work of North American Salvadorans. Being Salví does not exclude her from making transcultural alliances.

Hernández-Linares promotes "multiplicity, without the loss of specificity" (2000b, 116) to underscore the need for dialogue within and across ethnonational identified groups. In the poem presented, she chooses to have the conversation fully in Spanish. With two poems in Spanish, the rest of *Razor Edges of My Tongue* is either bilingual and/or in Spanglish. By removing English from the equation, she heightens the critique of national-enforced identities. This move emphasizes gender solidarity that crosses off national lines (signified through language) to open up a space where various cultural memories converge, diverge, and dialogue. As memory scholar Marianne Hirsch reminds us, "For them [the 1.5 and second generation], the past is located in objects, images, and documents, in fragments and traces barely noticeable. . . . Standing outside the family, the narrator receives the story . . . and affiliates with it, thus illustrating the relationship between familial and affiliative postmemory" (2012, 41). Within the diasporic, memory praxis can create an affective solidarity that transcends U.S. Central American populations within and across to non-Central Americans.

PRUDENCIA AYALA: HERSTORICAL CIGUA FIGURE OF LIBERATION POETICS

Who is Prudencia Ayala besides Hernández-Linares's muse? An indigenous woman, Ayala was born on April 15, 1885, in an autochthonous community in Sonzacate, Sonsonate, and raised in Santa Ana, El Salvador. Ayala describes her father as a "Mexican indio" and her mother as "una indígena," proudly laying claims to her indigeneity.[8] By age twelve, she was known as a psychic. By 1914, newspapers in Santa Ana began publishing her prophecies under the heading of *Sibila Santaneca* (Santaneca Sybil).[9] She is said to have prophesied the fall of Germany's kaiser and the United States' entry into World War I. In other words, she had to present her political analysis as psychic in order for it to be printed by newspapers. Though Ayala attained a limited education, she managed to transition to publishing her feminist, anti-imperialist, and antidictatorial politics, which included supporting the Nicaraguan fight led by César Augusto Sandino. She was viewed as a *loca* (a crazy woman) by sexist political conservatives. In 1919, city officials jailed her for her open criticism of a Salvadoran mayor of

Atiquizaya, Ahuachapán. Newspapers were concurrently publishing her social political poems that caused significant unrest. She continued to disturb social conventions, shown, for example, by her willingness to include in her political platform the rights of illegitimate children.

She was persecuted for her public criticism of gender and social inequality. Like other revolutionaries exiled into adjoining Central American nations, Ayala fled to Guatemala. She was imprisoned there, charged for conspiring against the dictator Manuel Estrada Cabrera. She returned to El Salvador and subsequently published a book detailing her experiences as a prisoner: *Aventuras de un viaje a Guatemala* (*Adventures of a Journey to Guatemala*, 1919). In 1925, she founded her own newspaper, *Redención feminista* (*Feminist Redeemer*). In 1930, as a representative of el Partido Unionista (the Unionist Party), Ayala ran for the presidency, unheard of at the time, especially for a single mother. In response, several local newspapers such as *La Epoca* printed satirical commentaries and mocking illustrations that exaggerated her physical features as an indigenous (and possibly afro-indigenous) woman. However, university students and Salvadoran author and intellectual Alberto Masferrer wrote in her defense in the newspaper *Patria*. Ayala published two books of poems: *Immortal: Loves of a Madwoman* (1925) and *Literary Clown in Combat* (1928)[10] (my translations). She died June 11, 1936, at forty-nine years of age. Salvadoran women were given the right to vote and to hold political office until 1950. Exemplifying hemispheric Cigua gynealogies, Ayala challenged her intersectional marginalization as both female and indigenous, defying an identity and stratification of silent subaltern.

Walking a fine line between acknowledgment and tokenization, official Salvadoran history continues to marginalize her even as she gains greater recognition within Salvadoran collective memory. In 2014, the presidency posthumously awarded her the Grand Cross with Silver Star under the National Order of José Matías Delgado for her fight for women's rights.[11] The distinction was handed to Ayala's granddaughter, Carmen de los Angeles Barra Escalante.[12] As Ima Guirola from the Center of Women's Studies (Centro de Estudios de la Mujer "Norma Virginia Guirola de Herrera,"[13] within la Concertación Feminista Prudencia Ayala)[14] stated in a recent interview, the life and struggle of Prudencia Ayala is never formally taught in school.[15] The women's organizations attempt to redress women's absence in judicial and historical memory and representation. El Salvador's Museum of Word and Image (MUPI) and its claim to the "weaving of memory" remains key for preserving her legacy.[16]

THE CIGUA LEGEND

The myth of la Ciguanaba is a story that has been passed down for centuries and is found in mediums other than oral culture. For example, renown author Manlio Argueta depicts her story in his book *Siglo de O(g)ro* (translates to Age of the Ogre/Age of Gold, 1997). I draw from his novels to establish the context of violence at the foundation of la Ciguanaba. A worldwide published author, Argueta proclaimed his own writing for the purpose of historicizing Salvadoran culture. His novels are internationally assigned in translation on college campuses. He was fundamental to the movement called *generación comprometida* (the committed generation) that used art and poetry as part of a cultural front to the civil war (1979–1992). As director of art and culture for the national library, he is an expert on Salvadoran history and cultural narratives. In continuing to write or fictionalize la Ciguanaba, he fleshes out her narrative, connecting a continuum of violence from colonization to the Salvadoran civil war.

Contrary to popular versions that begin la Ciguanaba's narrative with her physical encounter with a Don Juan–type of man, in *Siglo de O(g)ro* Argueta narrates her origin story. La Ciguanaba[17] was originally named Sihuehuet, which means beautiful woman in Nawat. She was married to prince Cipitl. It is said they, like the Pipil people, had eternal life. However, when the Spanish conquistadors arrived, Sihuehuet, Cipitl, and their son, Cipitillo, were forcibly separated. Argueta narrates, "Cuando vino la conquista a unos les tocó salir huyendo y a otros hacer la guerra. . . . Con todo, los indígenas fueron vencidos por los españoles, y en una batallas más cruentas, en Acaxual, Cipitl quedó aislado. . . . la Siguanaba se había extraviado entre los ríos y lagunas . . . y para subsistir en las condiciones difíciles también se había separado de su hijo, el Cipitillo, para defenderse cada quien a como diese lugar" (When the conquest came, some had to flee and others had to make war. . . . Along with everything, the indigenous people were conquered by the Spanish, and in the cruelest battles, in Acaxual, Cipitl was left stranded. . . . la Siguanaba was lost among the rivers and lakes . . . and to subsist in those difficult conditions, she also separated from her son, Cipitillo, each having to defend themselves in whichever way they could [my translation]) (1997, 139). Argueta simultaneously signifies the mythical and historical as he reenacts memory. Sihuehuet's transformation to la Ciguanaba through the violence of conquest and the dissolution of family resonates with modern Salvadorans in their re-experience of family separation, exile, and forced migration. Before separating, Cipitl warns Sihuehuet to protect herself from colonial male assault or rape by never showing her true beauty. Heeding his warning, she hides her appearance and changes into a haggard woman roaming the rivers searching for her husband and son. After two hundred years of fidelity and mourning, she decides to accompany herself with a man again, as Argueta explains, out of need rather than to replace the love of Cipitl: "pero si quería encontrar compañero no debía rehuir el asedio, por contrario buscaría a los hombres, con su arma lista para la burla: hacerse fea a su discreción para defenderse de un abuso.... la Siguanaba nunca encuentra amor, la desean para satisfacer caprichos animales" (but if she wanted to find a mate, she would not shun their pursuit, in the contrary, she would pursue men armed and ready to mock them: to become hideous at her discretion to defend herself from being abused. . . . la Siguanaba never finds love, they desire her only to satisfy their animalistic cravings [my translation]) (147). Once Othered, Sihuehuet refuses revictimization and chooses to mock the men who will attempt to seduce or abuse her. The narrative thus inverts the gendered script of female sexual submission. The assumption that she can be used only for sex violates her physical body and psyche but also her body of memory as once having belonged to an indigenous or rural community where she lived safely and securely.

No longer Sihuehuet but now la Ciguanaba, she is said to appear young, beautiful, and sometimes naked by the rivers, most often washing clothes. The men see her as a vulnerable and gullible woman easily seduced. Fooled by their desire, at the moment of sexual contact la Ciguanaba turns into a monstrous figure. Argueta describes how her nails grow into long claws dragging to the ground (148). The imagery represents the disfiguring weight of the hundreds of years gone by since the conquest. All versions told include the men's reactions, which involve one or all of the following: the man defecates himself, faints, or enters a feverish coma. "El hombre cagado y hediondo se desmaya agonizante. Ya no será el mismo. Si se salva quedará convertido en bobo e idiota"[18] (Argueta 148). According to Argueta, la Ciguanaba will continue to haunt men until she finds another prince with hawk wings like those of her dead husband, where Cipitl represents the binary opposite to men who use women as flesh. Argueta's narration suggests that it is the structural and social condition of coloniality that created la Ciguanaba.

There are variations to the legend. Argueta dedicates a whole chapter to her in his novel about El Salvador's civil war, *One Day of Life/Un día en la vida*, which was banned during the war. The story centralizes indigeneity through the elders Chepe and Josefina. Their granddaughter, Adolfina, symbolizes their hope for a just and equitable future. Adolfina defies the guards' attempt to make her cower. She voices her identity by stating who she is and by naming the tortures her family endured. In the midst of the civil and decolonial struggle, Argueta embeds and encodes the legend of la Ciguanaba in the book with defiance to the military state represented through abusive men. His work suggests that we consider la Ciguanaba a mythic woman, like his character Adolfina, who carries with her a long history and cultural memory that needs to be retold for transformational meaning.

However, within a hegemonic reading, the myth represents maintenance of female domesticity, punishment of adultery, and corrupt motherhood. Popular versions on the Internet[19] fashion her as an adulteress who neglects her son, reproducing the idea that she merits punishment á la Llorona. She also echoes the Kekchi-Mopan tale of the "promiscuous young Moon Goddess" (Vail and Stone 2002, 223). Anthropologists Vail and Stone explain,

> Another threatening stereotype of women's sexuality. . . . stem[s] from the rejection of the values of the nurturing female role. Unlike the young and sexually attractive woman portrayed in the codices, this female figure is frightening in appearance and is usually endowed with bestial characteristics. . . . In the codices she can be identified as the bestial aspect of Chak Chel, shown with her serpent head tie, clawed hands and feet, and costume of bones. (223)

Depictions of bad motherhood as monstrosity were constructed as part of a "larger pattern in which female sexuality is seen as a threat to men and in need of control" (222). Through this argument, la Ciguanaba resembles Mexico's and Guatemala's la Llorona, where la Ciguanaba serves as a cautionary tale of infidelity and bad domesticity. However, as I proposed in prior work, the colonial version of la Ciguanaba also served the purpose of social control on the rural populations since the story contained a curfew and warning: Do not travel alone, especially at night.[20] Violations of curfews justified violence and incarceration onto the rural population. For these communities, transmitting a story of la Ciguanaba could literally save lives if it stopped men and women from traveling alone and entering the woods at night.

Vital distinctions need to be considered in counterhegemonic versus hegemonic versions of la Ciguanaba and in relation to la Llorona. "Typically Mexican, [la Llorona] has been reported from the city of Los Angeles and as far south as Panama" (Bierhorst 1990, 173). While la Ciguanaba roams in exile, she is not caught in (Catholic) limbo like la Llorona, who is "condemned to wander for eternity, crying and repenting" (Castro 2001, 141). Chicana folklore scholar Rafaela Castro explains, "Contemporary texts of La Llorona in Mexico assert that the original Llorona was La Malinche, the mistress of Cortés" (141), an association that is not present in Central America. Moreover, la Ciguanaba shapeshifts from one female form to another female form; she is not a ghost. She haunts only men, though women and children tell that they saw or heard la Ciguanaba. As I have explained, Ciguanaba's personal, communal, and histori-cal memory encode the narratives of those who come in contact with her with a particular lieux or cultural region. While she resonates with other Cigua myths (the horse-headed Cegua of Guatemala, for example), distinctions should not be blurred, to avoid cultural erasures, especially in the greater context of global consumerism as a culture that reproduces mass identities. Cultural groups should not give up the narratives passed down to us through so much life and death. In other words, we have to remember who we are and from where we emerge.

However, within the counterhegemonic, la Ciguanaba similarly symbolizes feminist resistance to the Chicana project of recuperating or "renam[ing] the much misunderstood Malinche, Malintzin," which includes resignifying la Llorona (Chabram-Dernersesian 1992, 84). These recuperations empower la Llorona's negotiations of motherhood, marriage, and Christian salvation that talks back to oppressive situations: colonial Mexico, gendered ideologies within the Catholic Church, and sexism within the Chicano Movement (83). While Ciguanaba's specific cultural location and narrative must be considered and not subsumed under la Llorona, they can be placed in conversation without mar-ginalizing one culture to another.

It remains vital that we explore how Salvadorans, U.S. Salvadorans, Cen-tral Americans, and U.S. Central Americans articulate antisexist resistance in writing our gynealogies. In the counterhegemonic versions, la Ciguanaba does not marry the colonizer nor the plantation owner. She abandons her son because of the structural context of exile and coloniality. She does not haunt by wailing. She does not kill her children though she abandons Cipitillo. The cry, "Mis hijos!" (My children!) is not associated to her. La Ciguanaba does not seek Catholic redemption and is not in mortal sin. She attracts men with her silence and domestic work (washing clothes in the river) or when stranded alone, a stage setting that functions similarly to a Venus flytrap. Rather than representing the punishment of women, she is a punisher of male promiscuity and adultery. Significantly, when she turns into la Ciguanaba, the distortion of her feminine youthful beauty is not what makes her a monster. On the contrary, all the attributes that become ugly (hair, nails, breasts) are the signs that mark or are used to fetishize and Otherize women. Her "monstrosity" is that she destroys these signs. She determines when she will reveal herself as la Ciguanaba, and though she initially depicts a silent object of the male gaze, she speaks throughout the encounter. Her voice vociferates with loud cackling once she has fooled her seducer.

Whichever version we prefer, la Ciguanaba remains a woman who defies her colonization and mocks her seducers or colonizers. The fact that she haunts the rivers of memory, and our gatherings, is representative of a signifier that refuses erasure. She remains alive for a greater purpose than mere entertainment. A good sense of who Prudencia Ayala and la Ciguanaba are allows a more informed reading of Hernández-Linares's poem within the context of Cigua gynealogies.

A CLOSE READING IN CONVERSATION

Hernández-Linares tactically interweaves her own voice with the symbolic voice of Prudencia Ayala. Ayala in turn is guided by the spirit of the Ciguanaba. When we take all three Ciguas into account, a gynealogy of Salvadoran Cigua resistance emerges, now migrated to San Francisco.

Her poem gives the three women voice. Hernández-Linares actually quotes from Ayala's poem titled "Lamentation." This direct intertextual inclusion creates a doubling of voice as if both women speak simultaneously:

> Hey destiny, my complaint and lamentation [is]
> That I can no longer fulfill this hard sentence
> In case you'd like to challenge my emotions
> Try me, yes, but without placing me in chains

By personifying her own destiny, Ayala renders her despair and isolation. However, while Ayala did endure exile and imprisonment multiple times, at least symbolically in the life of the poem, she is no longer alone since Hernández-Linares melds their voices together by including part of Ayala's poem.

The conversation is not just between Ayala and Hernández-Linares since it includes the convocation of a third Cigua—where la Ciguanaba symbolizes the intersected space of the sacred and the political. The poem continues:

Prudencia, in order to dance better,
built a cane
so entertained was she in her project
she didn't notice that something had burned
and in the ashes, visions of water appeared

Spirit of the water
Mocking spirit

Cigua-naaaa-baaaa

Just as Hernández-Linares incorporates Ayala's voice through Ayala's poem, in this instance, she creates a voice and presence for la Ciguanaba. The mythic woman emerges after Ayala constructs a fire and after she creates her own cane. Photographs of Ayala often depict her posing with a cane, mimicking the use of the cane by elite plantation dons of the early 1900s. The cane can be considered a symbol of classed masculinity (don/sir), phallic institutional power, access to language, and as a racialized symbol of Spanish settler privilege. Ayala calls la Ciguanaba into being after constructing her public emblem: the cane. La Ciguanaba is conjured and made to speak:

La Ciguanaba arrived in support:
    what's up sister
    you gotta give it all you got
    don't worry because we all get punished
    but with our persistence, we'll keep on being chingonas!

The "we" within the narrative is female and indigenous-mestiza and not just Salvadoran since la Ciguanaba/Ayala come to archetypically represent anti-colonial patriarchal resistance. The term *chingonas*, which loosely translates to *badasses*, reinforces the movement of resistance since the term connotes, and thus aligns with, Chicana praxis.[21]

The women symbolize these very real, corporeal punishments of confinement and exile. Though Ayala and la Ciguanaba are having a conversation, at this point a third voice interjects the poetic narrative. Hernández-Linares personifies grammar itself. Grammar's words are signaled by the colons that follow it. When Hernández-Linares performs the poem, she gives grammar a voice. In this way, grammar literally speaks, and it says, "¡¿Bueno, qué pasa aquí, estas palabras no son salvadoreñas?!"meaning, "Well, what's going on here? These words aren't Salvadoran!" (36). Recall Hernández-Linares's own claim to an identity of multiplicity; this line shows this very critical self-reflection of transgression.

Hernández-Linares incorporates grammar as a regulatory system of tongue used to internalize social-national norms that can silence vernacular and gendered voices. Grammar becomes a linguistic form of punishment and imprisonment. The poet reflects on her own linguistic transgression as a Salví-in-solidarity-Chicana.[22] Her self-reflection exposes that her Spanish will be judged as not Salvadoran enough. The transgression purposefully highlights noncompliance. The interjection demands a response where Hernández-Linares as narrator makes her own political statement:

Ahhh, get out of here grammar of shit, this mestiza poet

doesn't swallow nor burp

not one tongue, not one nation

Thus, Hernández-Linares critiques the mechanisms of linguistic identification through "forms of spatial thinking that naively equate people, territory and nation" (Howes 2000, 61). She literally tells grammar to "go to hell," since this is the connotation in Spanish. The poet refuses to embody the colonial-initiated projects that restrict how one must act and how one must sound to be considered part of a cultural group. Her claim that she doesn't "burp" language means her language is cognizant and purposeful as she lays claim to language agency. Moreover, there was a time when "Salvadoran" words did not exist in Cuscatán.[23] Implicit in the name of the nation-state and its citizens are histories of colonization and colonialism, systemically and fundamentally gendered projects.

The poem creates a useful conversation that simultaneously critiques and disrupts neocolonial dominations through the symbol of the mouth. Representing the relationship of the self with society, the mouth as an instrument consumes and internalizes the stories, narratives, and conversations that replicate and pass down collective and cultural memory. The mouth represents structural, physical, and discursive freedoms. Thus, the right to speak freely is paralleled by women's right to their own bodies, a life without violence, full voice in the governance of society, and a say in shaping their cultures. As a neocolonial nation with a very strong conservative and Catholic faction, El Salvador, like other Central American countries, continues to deny women full civil and cultural rights. Freedom of speech and expression must build on sexual and gender freedom.[24]

Hernández-Linares conjures and imagines multiple female indigenous "voices" (Ayala and la Ciguanaba) that globalize and give greater historical context to women's rights as human rights. Her poem suggests that Ayala and Ciguanaba's narratives are part of global gendered memory. She accomplishes this by integrating another cultural intertext through Totó la Momposina's song "Mohana." The singer's glorious voice narrates a story of love, loss, and migration using Colombia's own legendary *mami wata* (water woman).[25] In the music clip, Totó la Momposina laughs upon hearing her voice echo in the river. One can conceive of these echoes as conversations among the Mesoamerican women water spirits. To illustrate, Hernández-Linares describes a ritual that takes place before Ayala leaves to walk to city hall to demand her citizenship rights. She breaks and buries pieces of squash for "Sihuán," who she describes as "mujer, espiritu del agua" (34). All three terms—"woman," "spirit," and "water"— become synonymous with one another. Water is conjured to remind the reader of the convergence of bodies of water in the Americas that have no borders. Moreover, Ayala feeding seeds of squash to the woman water spirit who waits "with open mouth" (34) signifies the social political struggle that must be internalized or fed, and therefore planted. Ayala feeding Sihuán suggests a different form of impregnation and dissemination where women feed each other the seeds of social change.

IN CLOSING: HEMISPHERIC QUEST
FOR CIGUA HUMAN RIGHTS

The poem closes with the lyrics of Argentinean Atalhualpa Yupanqui, an acclaimed musician who centralized indigenous knowledge, practices, and experiences of political exile. I turn to his lyrics because Hernández-Linares embeds them into her poem. This intertext forces readers and listeners to ask why she ends her poem with the words of a male musician.

His poignant voice must be heard, especially to understand the broader context in which Hernández-Linares is placing women-of-color liberation.[26] Yupanqui exemplifies acts of global solidarity. In 1989 when the University of

Nanterre in France asked him to commemorate the French Revolution by writing a cantata, he in turn wrote the song titled "The Sacred Word," dedicated to all oppressed countries. In doing so, he decentered Europe's French Revolution. His lyrics (within the poem) are: "Sometimes I'm like the river / I arrive singing / and without anyone ever knowing / life / I leave crying." By closing the conversation with him, the poet connects the Southern Cone to Colombia's Totó la Momposina, through Central America, and into Mexico since Yupanqui's lyrics echo forward to women water spirits throughout Mesoamerica, now located within the United States. The poem begins with Ayala marching to city hall to claim in "high voice" her enfranchisement and ends with Yupanqui's haunting lyrics of the "peregrine" leaving his native land for the beautiful dream in the horizon. By ending with migration, Hernández-Linares does not foreclose gender solidarity to women only, or human and indigenous rights for Salvadorans only, but connects these as long historical migratory movements. This understanding coincides with memory-studies praxis, which Alon Confino explains, "have been transnational and international in their scope, interests, origins, and historiographical foundation" (2010, 79). What may seemingly have been read as a poem dealing with Salvadoran-located memories, myths, histories, and iconographies were already decentered as such by the fact that Hernández-Linares remembered, wrote, and performed these within California. Moreover, she created linkages for U.S.-based Latina/o identities through differences, specificities, and commonalities. As I attempted to show, she purposely created a space of gendered memory to tell the entwined stories of la Ciguanaba, Prudencia Ayala, and women of the Salvadoran and U.S. Central American diasporas. Lastly, intergenerational memory holds the potential to create an affective solidarity that binds and transcends the U.S. Central American population within and across to non-Central Americans. Cigua legacies show that a poem, a song, and a cultural legend can bring light to social issues as they also continue to give us courage, *ganas*, memory, and a blueprint for hemispheric gendered/racial equality and justice.

NOTES

1. Refers to 1.5 and subsequent generations of North American Salvadorans who through this self-appellation invert their liminal and contested positions to Salvadoran, American, and other Latinidades. The internal self-referent calls on one's sense of inclusion and presence within a Salví difference. I consider

Salvís' spectrum subjectivities in/formed through their urban, multicultural, and transnational socialization and contradictions (2013, 378–383). While *Salví* emerged as a self-appellation within U.S.-raised and U.S.-born Salvadoran youth, *Salvadoran American* differs in several ways. *Salvadoran American* functions as an official term, marking those born or raised in the United States as (cultural or documented) citizens and/or their identification with Americanness. *Salvadoran American* claims ethnicity within the U.S. American nation. It involves the shift from immigrant rights visibility to minority politics as a cultural and lobbying group within the United States. *Salví* is distinctive as *Chicana/o* compares to *Mexican American*. Salvís claim and mark their own third space as historically and culturally distinctive yet informed in relationship to Salvadoran and American influences.

2. There are no records of la Ciguanaba nor Siguanaba mentioned in the Mayan nor Mexican codices, or the Mayan *Popul Wuj*. According to Tedlock, in the *Popul Wuj*, Xtaj (Lust woman) and Xpuch' (Wailing woman) are sent out to wash clothes by a river in order to tempt and destroy the three god-boys Tohil, Auilix, and Hacauitz. Tedlock believes the women "become the first prostitutes" (1996, 49) and are "the first pre-Columbian predecessors of the figure known as La Llorona in the Hispanic folklore of Mesoamerica" (310).

3. A Google search yields numerous sites with differing versions. *Siguanaba: Sigueguet* (2012) written in the United States by M. Orellano contemporizes her by having a group of men attempt to document her existence by capturing her in film. All the men end up mentally broken, sick, or dead. Author E. Jurado's *The Life and Times of El Cipitio* (2015) rewrites her as an ex-prostitute who feels remorse for having attempted to kill her son, thus modeling her after la Llorona. In the United States, la Ciguanaba becomes a successful owner of a laundromat chain.

4. Fourteen departments comprise El Salvador. The fifteenth signifies the one outside its borders; its diasporas.

5. Nawat is the popular name of the most prominent indigenous peoples (other than Lenca) and their language in El Salvador. Also as Nahuat, it is said to be a dialect of Nahuatl (Tilley 2005, 35).

6. Showalter in "Towards a Feminist Poetics" introduces vital innovations in literary analysis. Showalter is interested in feminist meaning making and introduces the term *gynocritics*, which she explains is more "self contained and experimental" (Showalter 1997, 1377), where women concern themselves as writers and meaning makers. Gynocritics creates a conversation that is no

longer "male orientated" (Showalter 1997, 1378). Gynocritics engages female culture, and this means the commonalities that may be experienced as women who have experienced similar types of struggles within society that "generates a sisterly solidarity" (Showalter 1997, 1379). However, the three (historical) phases that she discusses of the feminine (1840–1880), feminist (1880–1920), and female (1920 forward), as all having contributed to the development of a gynocritique, focused solely on Anglo-European women overlooking Latina and women of color writers such as Prudencia Ayala, thus limiting "sisterhood" and solidarity within Eurocentrism.

7. See CiguanabaInk, Hernández-Linrares's website, at http://www.ciguanabaink .com/CiguanabaInk/About.html.

8. El Salvador's Museum of Word and Image offers her biography. See http:// museo.com.sv/2010/11/biografia-prudencia-ayala-la-hija-de-la-centella/; and http://issuu.com/mupi/docs/exposicio__n_prudencia_ayala.

9. A female soothsayer who is guided by a god or goddess to foresee the future.

10. *Inmortal, amores de loca: Payaso literario en combate.*

11. See "Palabras del Ministro de Relaciones Exteriores, Jaime Miranda, durante la condecoración póstuma de la orden José Matías Delgado en el Grado de Cruz Placa de Plata a la Sra. Prudencia Ayala," http://www.rree.gob.sv/index .php?option=com_k2&view=item&id=3392:palabras-del-ministro-de -relaciones-exteriores-jaime-miranda-durante-la-condecoracion-postuma -de-la-orden-jose-matias-delgado-en-el-grado-de-cruz-placa-de-plata-a-la -sra-prudencia-ayala&Itemid=942.

12. Gobierno de El Salvador realiza condecoración póstuma a Prudencia Ayala, published May 5, 2014, https://youtu.be/FoTGGWPEqKg.

13. See the official CEMUJER website at http://cemujer.com/.

14. See the official website of Concertación Feminista Prudencia Ayala at http:// www.concertacionfeministaprudenciaayala.org/. Twenty-one Salvadoran organizations are part of this female collective symbolized by Prudencia Ayala.

15. See Michelle Rabimirios, "Prudencia Ayala y su legado por los derechos de las mujeres sigue vivo en las nuevas generaciones," July 12, 2013, http://voces.org .sv/2013/07/12/prudencia-ayala-y-su-legado-por-los-derechos-de-las-mujeres -sigue-vivo-en-las-nuevas-generaciones/.

16. MUPI and the University of Texas at Austin are now part of a transnational effort to maintain cultural memory. See the audio link Tejiendo la Memoria 04: Prudencia Ayala, la hija de la Centella, at http://av.lib.utexas.edu/index.php ?title=Mupi-tlm-00004.

17. In the novel her name is spelled Siguanaba.

18. "The man, crapped on himself and stinking, faints with agony. He won't ever be the same. If he does survive, he remains feeble-minded, an idiot" (my translation).

19. For a brief explanation of the legends of el Cipitillo and la Siguanaba, see http://dunlapsinsansalvador.blogspot.com/2008/11/legends-of-el-cipitillo -and-la.html; and a brief film directed by Brenda Vanegas at https://www .youtube.com/watch?v=JGPsjnweL3M.

20. See Oliva Alvarado (2007).

21. For elaboration of the Hernández-Linares poem in context to *chingonas* as countermasculinist to *la chingada*, see Oliva Alvarado (2013).

22. In Hernández-Linares's article, she claims a Chicana identity among other identities.

23. Nawat name for the region that is now the nation-state of El Salvador.

24. Since 1997, El Salvador passed an anti-abortion amendment that does not allow abortions under any circumstance. See Jack Hitt, "Pro-Life Nation," *New York Times*, April 9, 2006, http://www.nytimes.com/2006/04/09/magazine/ 09abortion.html?pagewanted=all&_r=1&. Since 1998, 628 women have been imprisoned for abortion, with some facing first-degree murder, carrying a sentence of thirty to fifty years (http://mic.com/articles/41771/beatriz-el-salvador -woman-in-need-of-an-abortion-fighting-for-her-life). In 2012, sixty women died because of health complications due to pregnancy, which can be understood as a form of femicide. The case of Beatriz in 2013 galvanized the nation, where feminist groups in El Salvador condemned the criminalization of women seeking abortions as a form of torture. See Claire Provost, "El Salvador: Meet the Women who Dare to Challenge the Anti-abortion State," *Guardian*, April 17, 2014, http://www.theguardian.com/global-development/2014/apr/17/ beatriz-case-resistance-el-salvador-abortion-law. Unfortunately, this law places Salvadoran women as pre-positioned for incarceration in cases related to the Zika virus in that the virus attacks children in vitro. While the Zika virus can have mild effects for an adult, it is dangerous for pregnant women because of the fetus's susceptibility to be born with microcephaly when carried to full term. Pregnant Salvadoran women do not have the option, nor right, to abort, for example, if she or the fetus is infected with Zika. Striking images of women (pro-choice and anti-mining) protestors with their naked, youthful torsos painted a ghastly white and blue (for the Salvadoran flag and to symbolize death) conjure modern-day Ciguanabas. The vociferous protestors become

specters of women killed—ghosts of past, present, and future—through state-sponsored gendered violence.

25. See "La Mohana," also known as "Espíritu del Agua" (Espiritu del agua, espiritu Burlón!), sung by Totó la Momposina at https://youtu.be/fHBE6Bf7F4Y.

26. See "Piedra y Camino" written and sung by Atahualpa Yupanqui at http://youtu.be/gWQOeF9fiqQ?t=2m14s.

REFERENCES

Alarcón, Norma. 1993–1994. "Anzaldúa's Frontera: Inscribing Gynetics." *Anuario de Letras Modernas* (6): 143–59. Colegio de Letras, Facultad de Filosofía y Letras. Mexico City: UNAM.

Alegría, Claribel. 1986. "The Two Cultures of El Salvador." *The Massachusetts Review* 27 (3/4) Latin America (Fall-Winter): 493–502.

Alvarado, Karina O. 2007. *Transnational Lives and Texts: Writing and Theorizing US/Central American Subjectivities.* PhD diss., University of California, Berkeley.

———. 2013. "An Interdisciplinary Reading of Chicana/o and (U.S.) Central American Internarrations." *Latino Studies Journal* 11 (3): 366–87.

Anzaldúa, Gloria. 1987. *Borderlands/La Frontera: The New Mestiza.* 1st ed. San Francisco: Aunt Lute Books.

Argueta, Manlio. 1983. *One Day of Life.* Translated by Bill Brow. New York: Vintage Books.

———. 1997. *Siglo de O(g)ro.* San Salvador: Direccíon General De Publicaciones.

Bierhorst, John. 1990. *The Mythology of Mexico and Central America.* New York: William Morrow and Company.

Butler, Judith. 1990. *Gender Trouble: Feminism and the Subversion of Identity.* New York: Routledge.

Castro, Rafaela G. 2001. *Chicano Folklore: A Guide to the Folktales, Traditions, Rituals and Religious Practices of Mexican Americans.* New York: Oxford University Press.

Chabram-Dernersesian, Angie. 1992. "I Throw Punches for My Race, but I Don't Want to Be a Man: Writing US—Chica-nos (Girl, Us)/Chicanas—into the Movement Script." *Cultural Studies*: 81–95.

Confino, Alon. 2010. "Memory and the History of Mentalities." In *A Companion to Cultural Memory Studies*, edited by Astrid Erll and Ansgar Nünning, 77–84. Berlin: Walter de Gruyter GmbH and Co.

DeLugan, Robin. 2013. "Commemorating from the Margins of the Nation: El Salvador 1932, Indigeneity, and Transnational Belonging." *Anthropological Quarterly* 86 (4): 965–94.

Editors, The. 1997. "Introduction to Encuentro Femenil." In *Chicana Feminist Thought: The Basic Historical Writings*, edited by Alma M. García, 113–16. New York: Routledge.

Erll, Astrid. 2011. *Memory in Culture.* Translated by Sara B. Young. New York: Palgrave Macmillan.

Ertll, Randy Jurado. 2014. *The Lives and Times of El Cipitio.* Los Angeles: Ertll Publishers.

García, Alma M. 1997. "Introduction." In *Chicana Feminist Thought: The Basic Historical Writings*, edited by Alma M García, 1–16. New York: Routledge.

Gates, Henry L. 1988. *The Signifying Monkey: A Theory of African-American Literary Criticism.* Oxford: Oxford University Press.

Hernández-Linares, Leticia. 2002a. *Razor Edges of My Tongue.* San Diego, CA: Calaca Press.

———. 2002b. "Gallina Ciega: Turning the Game on Itself." In *This Bridge We Call Home: Radical Visions for Transformation*, edited by Gloria Anzaldúa and Analouise Keating, 110–16. New York: Routledge.

Hirsch, Marianne. 2012. *The Generation of Postmemory: Writing and Visual Culture after the Holocaust.* New York: Columbia University Press.

Howes, Marjorie. 2000. "'Goodbye Ireland I'm Going to Gort': Geography, Scale, and Narrating the Nation." In *Semicolonial Joyce*, edited by Derek Attridge and Marjorie Howes, 58–77. New York: Cambridge University Press.

Irigaray, Luce. 1985. *Speculum of the Other Woman.* Ithaca, NY: Cornell University Press.

Kristeva, Julia. 1984. *Revolution in Poetic Language.* New York: Columbia University Press.

Lara, Irene. 2008. "Goddess of the Americas in the Decolonial Imaginary: Beyond the Virtuous Virgin/Pagan Puta Dichotomy." *Feminist Studies* 34 (1/2): 99–127. Spring/Summer.

Moraga, Cherríe. 1983. *Loving in the War Years: Lo que nunca pasó por sus labios.* Boston: South End Press.

Oquendo, Angel. 2010. "Re-imagining the Latino Race." In *The Latina/o Condition: A Critical Reader*, 2nd ed., edited by Richard Delgado and Jean Stefancic, 34–41. New York: New York University Press.

Orellano, Mario. 2012. *La Siguanaba: Sigueguet.* Bloomington, IN: Palibrio.

Pulido, L. 1996. *Environmentalism and Economic Justice.* Tucson: University of Arizona Press.

Showalter, Elaine. 1997. "Towards a Feminist Poetics." In *The Critical Tradition: Classic Texts and Contemporary Trends*, edited by David Richter, 1375–86. 2nd ed. New York: Bedford Books.

Tarrant, Shira. 2013. "Womanism." In *The Encyclopedia of Political Science*, edited by George Thomas Kurian. October 22, 2013. DOI: http://dx.doi.org/10.4135/9781608712434.

Tedlock, Dennis. 1996. *Popol Vuh: The Mayan Book of the Dawn of Life.* Translated by Dennis Tedlock. New York: Touchstone.

Tilley, Virginia Q. 2005. *Seeing Indians: A Study of Race, Nation, and Power in El Salvador.* Albuquerque: University of New Mexico Press.

Vail, Gabrielle, and Andrea Stone. 2002. "Representations of Women in Postclassic and Colonial Maya Literature and Art." In *Ancient Maya Women*, edited by Traci Ardren, 203–28. New York: Altamira Press.

PART II

DIVERSITY AND MEMORY

Creating Counterhegemonic Spaces and
Practices in Public Places

D URING THE PAST three decades, Central Americans and their descendants have transformed Los Angeles. Part 2 explores the public spaces in which Central Americans have made their mark in the city. Rather than viewing Central Americans through the lens of invisibility, the chapters promote visibility and presence in establishing counter discourses and spaces.

The section opens with Maritza E. Cárdenas's "Performing *Centralaméricanismo*: Isthmian Identities at the COFECA Independence Day Parade," which explains yet problematizes the Central American *Fiestas Patrias* celebration of independence tradition in the isthmus as transposed and represented in the pan–Central American parade in Los Angeles. The parade underscores that this is a location recognized by U.S. Central Americans as a homing beacon. She examines how Central Americans perform their identities and insist on recognition in a context that she argues typically depicts their "American" and "Latina/o" experiences as homogenous and ahistorical. Analyzing gender and class within the parade floats, she notes how they signal particular understandings of national identity. Visual rhetorics of class, indigenousness, and *mestizaje* are deployed in the parade to mark notions of authenticity. Cárdenas maps how the Confederacion Centroamericana (COFECA) organizes independence celebrations originating from regional state-sponsored projects, which are reinvented and reinterpreted within the U.S. diasporic, multicultural context to counter Central Americans' invisibility. If discourses of Latinidad fail to capture Central Americans, the annual celebration performs and deploys *centralamericanismo*.

She interrogates how this pan-ethnic identity ends up producing ongoing erasures in terms of class, gender, and race as indigenous people's histories and Afro-descent communities continue to be displaced.

Aside from the parade, the Los Angeles area houses critical centers of information and legal assistance for Central Americans. CARECEN, El Rescate, and Clinica Romero have served the Central American communities in Los Angeles since the early 1980s and continue to adapt to serve evolving needs. Ester E. Hernández argues that creating political consciousness through the promotion of social memory and art promotes and solidifies a quest for social justice. In "Remembering Through Cultural Interventions: Mapping Central Americans in L.A. Public Spaces," Hernández explores the transmission of cultural memory in the Westlake/MacArthur Park area. She pays particular attention to the mural "The Migration of the Golden People" located at the Central American Resource Center (CARECEN) and the construction of the new Central American Plaza that illustrate a counterhegemonic dynamic and visual discourse. She argues that public Central American identity symbols provide a mnemonic cue and foundation to individual, collective, and intergenerational past and present Angeleno/Salvadoran/Central American sensibilities embedded in social justice struggles. Therefore, these public visual displays of cultural memory establish a Central American presence as a way to ensure their remembrance in perpetuity. The act of public memory is given space and meaning not only to preserve a past but to safeguard the future generations' memory of the Central American diasporas. In constructing these pan–Central American spaces and places, Hernández considers how these heterogeneous communities and identities are themselves reshaped as they in turn transform Latina/o, urban, migrant, and diasporic Los Angeles.

Alicia Ivonne Estrada, in "(Re)Claiming Public Space and Place: Maya Community Formation in Westlake/MacArthur Park," similarly explores Westlake/MacArthur Park, a residential and commercial area approximately two miles west of downtown Los Angeles that historically has been an initial site of residence for many Guatemalan immigrants. Since the late 1970s, the park itself became a space for U.S. Central American activism on issues ranging from the Central American civil wars, solidarity, and immigrant rights. In the past two decades, the Westlake/MacArthur Park neighborhood has become one of the most vibrant Maya communities outside of Mesoamerica. The chapter examines the ways in which Mayas living in the area have altered the city's landscape through the re-creation of a weekend *mercado*, or public street market, located on the city sidewalks between Sixth Street and Union Avenue.

In this way, Mayas that reside in Westlake/MacArthur Park not only create a sense of community within this global city but also maintain transnational links to their communities of origin. The existence of the *mercado* makes visible the types of cultural and economic survival strategies Mayas employ in a labor market that limits their participation and a city that criminalizes and erases their existence. This is particularly evident in the ways city authorities through often-violent regulations of public space continuously challenge the cultural and social dynamics re-created by Mayas in and around Westlake/MacArthur Park and the strategies Mayas use to counter their repression. Her contribution provides an important discussion on the Maya diaspora, indigenous studies, cultural activism, public space, and state violence.

Estrada's contribution also provides context to Floridalma Boj Lopez's chapter, in which she challenges the stereotypical reading of Maya women as submissive subalterns. "Weavings That Rupture: The Possibility of Contesting Settler Colonialism Through Cultural Retention Among the Maya Diaspora" explores the politicization of Maya dress through the self-representation of the female indigenous body, thus making a statement through Maya textiles. She analyzes the wearing of traditional regional Maya clothing as a purposeful act that intersects the cultural and political in order to bring visibility and counter marginalization of Maya migrants from Guatemala. Just as significant is the way in which Maya youth integrate yet adapt the *traje* tradition to voice their own historical location in Los Angeles as the youth negotiate their identities and circumstances. As part of a Guatemalan (but also and primarily a Maya) diaspora, the youth's rearticulations of clothing and textiles become an opportunity to highlight their exclusions and inclusions to nation (U.S./Guatemala), to ethnicity (Central American/Latina/o), indigeneity (Maya/Native American), and gender. Boj Lopez's personal and interviewee accounts help in beginning to comprehend just how complexly woven the cloth of their self/community expressions are in reshaping generational and diasporic meanings to long-traditional practices of clothing and Maya values. Boj Lopez and Estrada remind us that identities are mobile and portable through cultural markers like Maya regional dress, *traje*, and embodied practices. The *traje* highlights the fabric and mobility of identities and culture through links that tell of land-based belongings that enter in dialogue with native identities contending with displacement and settler colonialism.

The section ends with Yajaira Padilla's "Illegal Chickens: The Art of Branding Poultry in Central American Los Angeles," which critically examines the work produced by street artist and muralist Cache as an intervention in current immigration debates. She examines the specific venues in which the art is featured and the "illegality" of street art. Padilla notes that murals constitute a physical and imagined interface for discourses of illegality regarding undocumented migration to be contested and reconstituted, ironically by similar discourses of illegality. These exciting images coded with Guatemalan/ Central American symbols are blasted on walls throughout Southern California, engaging viewers—bus riders, walkers, tourists, and residents—on a visual level as they are compelled to ponder the significance of Cache's political and cultural chickens. Moreover, Padilla examines the globalizing logic that draws and ensnares the U.S. Central American workforce into the Midwest and in jobs such as poultry processing. Migrants caught in the undocumented labor racket where factories exploit their labor and bypass immigration laws are punished when caught in spectacular raids by the U.S. Immigration and Customs Enforcement (ICE). They are caught up in a literal chicken coop, but their stories cannot be constrained by their dire location in the labor force. Guatemalan Angeleno artist Cache's graffiti chickens speak back and insert themselves in the visual spheres as if to say "the liberation struggle continues."

In re-creating homeland narratives, imagery, and practices, U.S. Central Americans find themselves interpellated between a Latina/o identity and a pan-Latina/o-identity, yet they also insist on their Maya, Lenca, Garifuna, and Pipil identities beyond folkloric gestures. Part 1 focuses on the meaning and memories of 1.5 prior and current generations and on U.S. Central American women's narratives, bodies, well-being, and social movements as the contributors employ and highlight ethnographies, biographies, and stories whose intimacy testifies to resilience across temporal and spatial terrain. Similarly, part 2 uses space and (dis)locations to frame Central American presence in Los Angeles. The chapters in this section explore the ways in which Central Americans have visually marked and transformed the Westlake/MacArthur and Pico-Union regions known as "Little Central America" in ways that contest the reification of Central Americans as U.S.-born, migrant, and diasporic. These chapters on the institutions that serve the community, the *mercado* that sustains their culture, and parades that reinforce identity highlight how cultural practices rooted in Central America are *Centralamericanizing* spaces in Los Angeles and beyond. Cárdenas, Hernández, Estrada, Boj Lopez, and Padilla implicitly engage cultural citizenship in showing Central American claim to U.S. spaces (sidewalks, murals, *mercados*, *trajes*) and in transcending its tangible meaning to an intangible one that references cultural memory while simultaneously morphing it to Central American Angeleno experiences.

5

PERFORMING *CENTRALAMÉRICANISMO*

Isthmian Identities at the COFECA Independence Day Parade

MARITZA E. CÁRDENAS

"This is the best date to remember our national identity as Central Americans and as part of each nation that was integral to this federal republic [Central America]."[1]
—WALTER DURÁN, LOS ANGELES SALVADORAN CONSULATE

FOR THE LAST thirty-two years, residents of the city of Los Angeles have transformed that urban landscape into an extended parcel of Central America. Every second weekend of September the streets of the Pico-Union district, an area colloquially referred to as *pequeña Centroamérica* (Little Central America) are crowded with an average 200,000 spectators as they partake in the Central American Independence Parade sponsored by La Confederación Centroamericana (COFECA).[2] These participants symbolically reproduce the isthmus not only by importing a transnational cultural practice found in several of the countries of Central America but also by visually invoking this geophysical space as the sidewalks are covered in waves of light blue (in the form of flags, banners, and clothing), mimicking the Pacific and Atlantic waters, while the street resembles a land bridge. Although such cultural events foster the growing trend of using "ethnic" festivals to expand the heritage and tourism industry by selling the idea of Los Angeles as a "multicultural" city, the work of Latina/o scholars (Sommers 1991; Cadaval 1998; Rivas 2014) also reveals them to be vital sites of identity making, becoming dynamic arenas "where interrelationships and identities are generated, experienced, communicated and altered" (Cadaval 11). This chapter explores how cultural performances, specifically ethnic festivals known as *las fiestas patrias*, and its most prominent visual spectacle—the COFECA Central American Independence Parade—enable different subjects to imagine themselves as part of a Central American community. Using data collected from Los Angeles and gathered in 2006, I illuminate the ways in which the COFECA parade becomes a space of interpellation for mostly mestiza/o subjects of the isthmus—one that shapes ideas of Central American belonging. It is important to stress that this process of interpellation operates unevenly among different subjects. As Central American scholars have noted (Hamilton and Stoltz Chinchilla 2001; Alvarado 2013), many mestiza/os, as well as black and indigenous communities like Mayas and Garifunas,[3] do not necessarily "ascribe to a pan-Central American identity" (Alvarado 369); still, they are often nevertheless read or framed as "Central American."

Moreover, though a parade is a multimodal and polyphonic social text containing a myriad of interpretations, for this chapter I focus on the cultural history behind this COFECA event, as well as the structure of the parade itself, in order to highlight how this festive form facilitates (1) *Centralaméricanismo*; although I explain this term in greater detail below, this nomenclature describes the sociodiscursive processes that foster Central American identification, often (though not exclusively) by promoting the belief that subjects from the isthmus share a common history and social location. (2) A prominent space of self-definition where Central American identity is both constituted and publicly performed. The title "Performing *Centralaméricanismo*" therefore illuminates the important need to see how the dual concepts of performativity (seen here as "unconscious iteration" of discourse) and performance (understood as "conscious knowing display") function within these cultural practices whereby subjects are not only constructed by such discourse but also position themselves within it (Bettie 2014, xxix). It is in these signifying practices, like parades, that social actors learn to both internalize and "display" predetermined scripts about matters such as gender, nation, and race in their articulation of Central American identity. (3) A "heterotopic" space—an effect of the displacement Central American experiences occupy within discourses of Latinidad circulated in Los Angeles. As such, the COFECA parade is symptomatic of Central American cultural productions in the U.S. diaspora that seek to make visible this community's presence and contest their social marginalization within U.S. and Latina/o imaginaries (Arias 2003; Alvarado 2013; Padilla 2013).

CENTRALAMÉRICANISMO

While Latina/o scholarship (Padilla 1985; Sommers 1991; Oboler 1995; Flores 2000; De Genova and Ramos-Zayas 2003) has described several contributing factors for the production of this group identity formation, one of the earliest and most enduring theories emerges from Felix Padilla, who claimed that social conditions along with the belief of shared cultural elements fostered unity among disparate peoples. In his study of Mexicans and Puerto Ricans, Padilla (1985) contends that these groups forged a pan-ethnic identity, one he terms as "Latinismo," due to their need to address structural inequalities as well as their sentimental identification with the Spanish language (Padilla 1985, 61). This myth of a common culture galvanized both groups into forming a "situational alliance" over particular sociopolitical issues that were deemed important to both communities. Laurie Sommers, who examines how festive forms create symbols of pan-ethnic culture, further builds on Padilla's theories, positing that a "successful pan-ethnic strategy requires both a *common interest* (some kind of need of unity, often political) and a *common identity*, solidified and expressed by an overarching symbol or cultural umbrella" (Padilla 1985, 35).

As Sommers's (1991) work illustrates, Padilla's theories have been seminal to the field of Latina/o studies, particularly his notion that Latina/o pan-ethnicity is a "situational" identity. Nevertheless, by conceiving of these Latin American national communities as solely "Spanish-speaking groups," he problematically renders Latina/o as synonymous with mestiza/o. The process of identification often requires discursive enunciative strategies that mark and bind symbolic boundaries of what and who belongs in that identity (Du Gay and Hall 1996, 3). Relying on "common" symbols or culture to foster identification often excludes other groups (like indigenous and black diasporic populations) that may share the same political concerns or who are equally disenfranchised by the same broader sociopolitical forces, but may not be "Spanish-speaking," and who experience marginalization by nonindigenous U.S. Central Americans/Latina/os, as noted by Alicia Ivonne Estrada's work on the Maya diaspora in this anthology. Subsequently, recent Latina/o scholars have critiqued utilizing "cultural elements" like language, which reproduce cultural essentialism, and propose viewing Latina/o unity and identity as emerging from a shared historicity among peoples who have been marginalized by colonialism, imperialism, and the sociopolitical order of white supremacy (De Genova and Ramos-Zayas 2003, 21).

With this in mind, it is important to foreground the possibilities and limitations present in Central American identification. In trying to theorize the deployment of Central American as an identity category, I offer the term *centralaméricanismo* to refer to the ways discursive structures, along with macro and micro sociopolitical forces (i.e., migration, racism, imperialism, etc.), enable subjects from both on and off the isthmus to see themselves or be seen as "Central American." Centralaméricanismo differs from Latinismo since I view the former as both a conscious and unconscious process, while Padilla theorized the latter as a form of "ethnic consciousness." In contrast, centralaméricanismo not only describes acts that explicitly attempt to foster and link Central American group identification and solidarity, it also delineates those larger structural mechanisms that "hail" subjects into becoming Central American. As a form of interpellation, centralaméricanismo acknowledges the power of discourse in creating a social position for all subjects, including those that may not explicitly identify as Central American. For even if subjects consciously reject seeing themselves as Central American, it is within institutions and cultural practices (like the COFECA parade) where these same subjects become discursively framed as "Central American."

In its more conscious manifestation, centralaméricanismo parallels the way that Latinismo functions, as an "ethnic principle of organization"—one emerging from a myth of common origins and broader social conditions (Padilla 1985, 5). In this context, Central American identification develops from the mostly mestiza/o *belief* that people from the isthmus share a common history and also from the need to create a strategic alliance to contest their marginal social location within U.S. American and Latina/o imaginaries. When the mass migrations from Central America took place in the early 1970s and 1980s, over a million Central Americans (mostly Guatemalans and Salvadorans) who previously lived independently of one another in their respective nation-states found themselves living in closer proximity in the U.S. diaspora. This form of cohabitation is exemplified in the city of Los Angeles, where currently one in five Central Americans in the United States reside (Terrazas 2011). Living in this new context provided these immigrants with opportunities to engage with one another in everyday spaces and learn how larger sociopolitical processes like the civil wars, displacement, and the homogenizing racialization they experienced in the United States similarly affected them. The latter proved to be a vital catalyst in fermenting group identification since Central American immigrants were not only viewed as racial Others within the U.S. American imaginary but were also invisible within the local Los Angeles landscape. Discourse about the greater metropolitan area of Los Angeles, for instance, has made Latina/o coterminous with Mexican American. Scholar Earl Shorris (1992) claims that "Los Angeles belongs to Mexicans and Mexican-Americans" (243) while Rodolfo Acuña (1996) has labeled Los Angeles as "Chicano LA" and at times refers to non-white people in Los Angeles as "Mexican-looking"(Acuña 1996, 6).[4] In doing so, the urbanscape of Los Angeles has been discursively marked as Mexican/Mexican American and, by extension, so have the bodies—especially racialized brown bodies—inhabiting this place. This social unrecognition from Latinidad in turn propels the conditions for centralaméricanismo since many subjects come to believe they share the same space of invisibility.

This notion that Central Americans are displaced within the broader Latina/o imaginary is one component that encourages this explicit form of centralaméricanismo. The other is the presumption that Central Americans (mostly mestiza/os) share common symbolic attachments like language and history. This ideology of mythic cohesion is one that does not emerge in the diaspora; historical narratives and cultural practices on the isthmus routinely promote the idea that five countries (Guatemala, El Salvador, Nicaragua, Honduras, and Costa Rica) share a common history and culture. Such discourse contributes to an isthmian-based identification by establishing a Central American imaginary—a notion of shared memory, congruent histories of misery and struggle, and intertwining utopias (Flores 2000, 198). In this context, the "intertwining utopias" manifest by conceiving of Central America as a *patria grande*—an "imagined community" that is predicated on ignoring political tensions and factions within and among various Central American states. A primary vehicle for promoting this ideology of isthmian-based unity can be found in the (re)production of *las fiestas patrias*, which views colonial independence (September 15, 1821) as a "Central American" holiday.

COFECA: TRANSPLANTING *LAS FIESTAS PATRIAS*

The first COFECA event took place on September 15, 1983, when "thousands of Central American pacifists along with U.S. Americans protested for peace and against military intervention in Central America" (Confederación Centro Americana 2015). That this initial protest took place in the early 1980s is not surprising since scholars have marked this era as the time period when isthmian immigrants began to forge political coalitions and deploy the pan-ethnic term *Central American* to obtain sociocultural visibility (Coutin 2000; Alvarado 2013, 370). Exemplifying centralaméricanismo, this first event illuminates how "situational alliances," coupled with the assumption of a shared history, propelled a Central American cultural institution like COFECA to emerge. According to COFECA, September 15th was selected to "convene the Central American people" because that day is a "national" holiday celebrated in most Central American countries (Confederación Centroamericana 2015). As such, this public performance of Central American solidarity became a way to suture the historical memory of a particular past (Central American independence) with then current historical events (the civil wars in Central America). This process in turn propagates the notion of a common history (present and past) between Central American subjects. In fact, a year after this first political manifestation, the organization COFECA was created to "unify the Central American community" by preserving its "roots, identity and patrimony" (Confederación Centroamericana). At present COFECA is responsible for the biggest Central American civic events in Los Angeles like the Central American Independence parade, the Central American Independence festival, and the crowning of Miss COFECA. Inspired by cultural festivals on the isthmus known as *las fiestas patrias*, these cultural institutions, attended by many Central American residents in Los Angeles, have proved to be instrumental in constructing centralaméricanismo.

Las fiestas patrias, which are celebrated throughout Central America, embody Eric Hobsbawm's notion of how "invented traditions" rely on "accepted rules and ritual of symbolic nature, which seek to inculcate certain values and norms of behavior by repetition," creating "continuity with a suitable historic past" (1983, 1). Emerging in the nineteenth century, these fiestas patrias were enacted by several states to create a tradition that privileges the historical period of postindependence when the Kingdom of Guatemala became transformed into a "united" Central America. The annual independence parades of the countries of Guatemala, El Salvador, Nicaragua, Honduras, and Costa Rica further promote this notion of a Central American "imagined community" since regardless of the nation-state they inhabit, subjects within these five countries know that every year their fellow compatriots celebrate the same holiday in their own respective countries.

This display of nation and memory is also contingent on forgetting; for September 15, 1821, is the day that only Guatemala declared itself independent. Not only did the other provinces declare themselves independent on a different date but some opted to separate from Guatemala over Spain. Despite the fact that this dominant narrative of "unity" is not sustained by the political documents or events that transpired in that historical era, via repetition, narrative, and performance this idea of shared independence is generally assumed by most mestiza/o subjects on the isthmus. While manifestations of this civic celebration differ from state to state within Central America, it is important to note how these various performances share particular racial, gender, and sexualized meanings by positioning whiteness and heteropatriarchy as central to the national narrative. For instance, often at these events speeches celebrate *criollo* men of the nineteenth century, referring to them as *padres de la patria* (founding fathers). By presenting white men as national "saviors," such renderings minimize the contributions of other ethnoracial communities to this process as well as obfuscate how these *criollo* "liberators" were equally responsible for the construction and enforcement of sociopolitical codes that enabled racial and class stratifications. Moreover, within parade performances, gender roles are fervently enforced as men are often represented as active agents of history via their association as war heroes (such as when military men perform their drills in the parade) whereas female participants are often relegated to passive roles such as beauty queens— an embodied reminder of the "spoils of war."

But these cultural festivities (and their respective ideologies of race, class, gender, and sexuality) are not limited to the isthmus, as they have been transplanted onto U.S. soil. The adoption of these festive forms in the U.S. diaspora is significant since it signals how Central Americans are increasingly seeing themselves as a part of a transnational (Padilla 2013; Rivas 2014) or "transisthmus" *collective* (Rodríguez 2009). For Rodríguez, the trope of the "transisthmus" provides an alternative to current understandings of Central America, which do not take into account the multiple and ever-shifting terrain of this space and often ignore "locally inflected" iterations of this term (2009, 3). Consequently, even though the COFECA celebration of las fiestas patrias takes place in the Westlake/Pico-Union area of Los Angeles, the cultural impact exceeds the confines of this urban locale as it joins the larger sphere of the transisthmus.

Technology and media have proven to be a valuable tool in fostering this transnationalism by allowing Central Americans from around the world to be virtual participants. Most of the COFECA events, including web video of the parade as well as the crowning ceremony of Miss COFECA, can be found on free websites like YouTube. This twenty-four-hour access enables Central Americans both on and off the isthmus to partake in these festivities and in the process expand the territorial parameters of the Central American imaginary. In her work on Salvadoran immigrants, Cecilia Rivas (2014) argues that it is through media images that emigrants are linked with a "transnational migrant space" as they become "reclaimed" by their home countries (Rivas 2014, 31). Arguably, this transpires via the media dissemination of las fiestas patrias as media consumers on the isthmus reclaim Central Americans. Subsequently, COFECA's celebration of cultural nationalism is transformed into a larger communal event, where regardless of location, subjects of different countries and racial, gender, and social strata can conceive of themselves (albeit unevenly) as Central Americans. Thus, just as early nineteenth-century technological media such as print capitalism helped to create "imagined communities," these new technological devices have enabled the formation of decentered transnational imagined spaces.

Accordingly, the COFECA parade has been touted as "the largest sociocultural expression of Central America in the world" ("COFECA Carnaval y Desfile por Independencia" 2013, 17). Indeed this annual celebration has attracted crowds as large as 450,000 participants (*COFECA Corporate Sponsorship Package* 2009); only the Rose Parade, which attracts 700,000 spectators (Rose Parade Statistics 2014), and the Cinco de Mayo celebrations, which host 500,000 participants (Tatum 2014, 259), yield larger attendees, suggesting that this isthmian-based celebration is a mainstream cultural phenomenon. Moreover, it is estimated that more than a million Central Americans see it worldwide. Transnational television networks like Univision, Telemundo, Centroamérica TV, as well as emerging technological media like Latinotv.com and CXCA not only are part of the process of displaying transnational Central American culture but also seek to capitalize on the term *Central American* since, as Arlene Dávila reminds us, "culture is never free from economic and political determination" (2001, xix).

In fact, despite COFECA's proclamation of being a "nonprofit" organization, one should be mindful that both international and local corporations are active sponsors that provide the majority of financial support for these fiestas patrias. In their marketing materials, COFECA appeals to businesses by telling them that their sponsorship will "turn 450,000 into loyal customers." For those that opt for the "title sponsor package" of $100,000, COFECA promises to "coordinate efforts together with [the] president of COFECA to ensure successful public presentations" (*COFECA Corporate Sponsorship Package* 2009). Moreover, given the fact that the cost to have a float participate in the parade ranges from $500 to $3,000, it becomes evident that both international and local businesses are central figures in deciding what gets to be presented as Central American culture.

THE COFECA PARADE

Though the COFECA parade is an inherited cultural tradition from the isthmus, there are important distinctions that emerge in the U.S. diaspora. Unlike independence parades hosted in the isthmus, which are sponsored by the nation-state and celebrated on the same day by five countries but independently of each other, in Los Angeles the parade and festival is hosted in a physical space that enables Central American immigrants to celebrate together. Further, whereas in the isthmus independence parades emphasize their individual respective national culture, in the diaspora this cultural event is composed of various nations (e.g., Salvadoran, Honduran). The structure of the parade itself, which has not changed much in its thirty years, also reveals how immigrants have altered this performance. The parade always takes place in "Little Central America" (the area that contains the most Central American businesses), has an annual theme generally tied to political issues, showcases a "grand marshal," and contains floats from seven countries on the isthmus.[5] Usually a banner designating a national country will precede the floats, which are often sponsored by hometown associations, locally based transnational community organizations, and local businesses that cater to those populations. The inclusions of "themes" and of a "grand marshal" are both elements that are uniquely diasporic contributions. The themes in the COFECA parade, such as the one chosen in 2006, "Today We March, Tomorrow We Vote," are usually connected to a sociopolitical issue salient within the United States. In this instance we see how the title creates a teleology for this community's narrative of identity politics: We have to first perform our cultural identity so we can have a political one (or political visibility). Therefore, its inclusion (along with a grand marshal) indicates the beginnings of a cultural fusion between cultural practices of the isthmus with those of U.S. culture.

Another important distinction is the insertion of countries that have been discursively marked as falling outside of the Central American imaginary. Central America as a national formation has self-ascribed borders that typically contain only peoples and cultures that were originally part of the Kingdom of Guatemala. Most scholarship on Central American history and culture rarely if ever includes discussion of Panama or Belize. However, in the COFECA parade and in the organization itself, Belize and Panama are positioned as equally Central American.[6] It is then notable that in the U.S. diaspora these two nations, which have no direct relationship to this date of independence, and in the case of Belize has had its own sovereignty constantly threatened by Guatemala, become symbolically incorporated into this collectivity. It signals a moment where diasporic subjects are (re)articulating what they deem as Central American. Public performances like COFECA are important to this process, employing iconic symbols like banners to reconfigure the borders of the Central American nation. Still, this incorporation into the Central American imaginary has its limits. For instance, the parade floats of Belize and Panama, which are mostly composed of Afro–Central Americans, stand out as "exceptional" from the other Central American countries whose floats showcase predominantly mestiza/o subjects.

In fact, like las fiestas patrias on the isthmus, the COFECA parade promotes a mythic and utopian vision of cohesion and unity among Central Americans by minimizing the contentious relations that permeate within national and ethnoracial populations. The year I attended (2006), for instance, two of the most popular floats (as determined by the amount of applause and cheers given by the spectators) were those that represented the indigenous groups of the Garifuna and the Maya. Ironically, these communities have been marginalized, physically and culturally, by both individual national and the larger Central American imaginaries, which via its choice to privilege a particular historical moment, erases other diasporic histories and undermines the political claims of sovereignty enacted by these two groups. Therefore, rather than reading these moments of celebration by the spectators as signs of cultural inclusion and acceptance, they should be viewed as an example of how marginalized ethnoracial groups are utilized as authenticating measures. For example, several floats that represented the country of Honduras often played *punta* music—a musical style developed by Garifunas. However, most of these Honduran floats were composed of mestiza/os, and there were no floats linked with Honduras explicitly devoted to Garifuna culture. Such displays reinscribe the dominant location of *mestizaje* via the visual presence of "brown" bodies, which obfuscates blackness within Honduran culture. This act of cultural appropriation by the local Honduran constituency affirms that what is valued in this arena are commodified, unembodied notions of Garifuna culture.

Similarly, several local vendors often used images of gendered indigenous culture to sell their products as authentic of the region. In 2006 a local business, Restaurante y Panaderia Ilobasco, prominently displayed the painted image of an indigenous woman on the side of its float. An autochthonous and gendered representation emerges of the municipality of Ilobasco, El Salvador, in this portrait of a dark-skinned, dark-haired woman holding clay pots and wearing textile-based clothing. This portrait of an indigenous woman, who is at the forefront of the image, is surrounded by a vast and empty natural landscape void of any markers of modern culture. Race, class, and gender ideologies converge in the marketing of this product, for this female figure is not only linked with domesticity (kitchen) but is also deployed to appeal to a mestiza/o class fantasy of having your own indigenous servant making your food. The float therefore re-entrenches class and racial hierarchies as indigenous women are often utilized as cheap domestic labor within the United States and Central America.

In addition, by framing indigenous subjects as "native," but largely atavistic, to the land one loves, the image reifies indigenous culture as outside the current contemporary cityscape. Two problematic tropes are yielded in this float as feminized corporeality is presented as the "conservative repository of the national archaic" in a permanently anterior time within the modern nation (McClintock 1993, 67). In this aforementioned image both the land and the female body are framed as passive subjects—the recipients of the modern gaze that views them at a distance, as "inert, backward-looking and natural" (McClintock 1993, 66). The painted woman here appears static and seems out of time when contrasted with the animated physical bodies on the float dressed in industrial-made clothing like white T-shirts and denim jeans. Rarely are there floats that combine physically embodied indigenous (female) subjects with "modern" mestiza/o subjects. Instead, indigenous floats are often solely composed of members from that community, furthering the notion that indigenous peoples belong to the "national archaic." Furthermore, in linking a female body with the natural landscape, the float circulates a common national association not only of landscape as feminized body (e.g., motherland) but also about the role of women within the nation, which sees their use-value in their ability to biologically and culturally (re)produce. In doing so, the parade serves to relegate and cement gender roles within national identities as different racialized female bodies are placed on display during this performance.

Like las fiestas patrias on the isthmus, in the use of symbolic markers like racialized, gendered, and classed bodies to sustain certain ideologies, the parade reveals some of its most prevalent contradictions about the role marginalized subjectivities occupy within the Central American imaginary. As previously indicated, female bodies are constantly on display in these floats, often wearing sexually revealing attire, suggesting that one's patriotic duty is to be as fecund as the motherland. The virile female sexual body, however, is lauded only in this nationalist context, for in the quotidian lives of everyday women on the isthmus juridical policies limit their autonomy over their own body. Thus, every year, for only one day, marginalized populations are viewed as integral to Central America culture, even if their lives and political aspirations are not.

These ethnoracial gendered and class tensions notwithstanding, the COFECA parade occupies an important function in the United States: It offers an opportunity for Central Americans to perform their cultural difference from other Latina/o groups. The term *Central American*, like Latina/o, is not a racial category but an ethnic category that, as the parade shows, becomes symbolically linked via gendered corporeal representations with mestiza/o. Therefore, self-identified Central Americans in the diaspora have no "visible" markers to differentiate themselves from other racialized groups, specifically from other Latina/o groups. Using this event to self-narrate and perform a particular ethnic identity is especially significant given the fact that U.S. culture tends to read "brown bodies" in Los Angeles as always already Mexican. The COFECA parade then becomes not only a prominent site of self-fashioning but also a vehicle to undermine racist and homogenizing tropes that fail to recognize Latina/o heterogeneity.

One way in which the parade provides a space of self-definition is by including and allowing non–Central American nations to participate in this event. Like the process of identity formation, which is relational and requires a subject to construct itself on the premise of "difference" from another subject, the parade includes other national communities as a way to assert their distance from them. In the parade the participation of other national groups serves to visually demarcate "Central American" from other non-isthmian communities. Countries identified as Central American are clearly characterized by blue-and-white banners that contain their name and their respective coat of arms, which resemble one another. On the other hand, countries and cultures that are viewed as external to this collectivity are clearly defined by having banners that claim to "salute" Central America (e.g., Ecuador salutes Central America), while those that are viewed as Central American are not required to make that distinction. Further, none of the non-isthmic countries are allotted the same privileges that Central American countries receive, like selecting the grand marshal or leading the parade. Their seemingly sole purpose is to display their own individual national cultures, which is then used to highlight their "difference" from the other Central American countries. Although such gestures of inclusion replicate facile notions of multiculturalism, they are equally important in their demonstration of how this local community delineates what and who qualifies as Central American.

Indeed, as an act of identity politics—a self-conscious attempt by this Central American community to claim a space within Latina/o cultural politics—the COFECA parade also provides Central Americans a means to publicly contest dominant U.S. narratives of cultural assimilation, especially for spectators of the performance. Routinely, spectators of the event will wear the "national" colors of blue and white or bring with them national flags in order to identify themselves as Central American, and, perhaps implicitly, as a way to challenge the idea that immigrants need to or should "melt" into a larger U.S. American culture. In 2006, for instance, I observed a brown-skinned man wearing a dark-blue T-shirt with white printing stating "100% Guatemalan" and a white barcode underneath the printed text. The production and public displaying of this material object exposes an anxiety regarding Central American identity in the diaspora—it is one that constantly needs to be performed and visibly articulated in order to prevent being collapsed with other Latina/o identities. It also reveals the problematic nature of performing this identity; to pronounce that there is a 100 percent Guatemalan subject is a troubling affirmation, especially in light of the fact that the nation-state of Guatemala has engaged in its own violent military campaign to preserve and maintain a national identity that has been defined by the abjection—culturally and physically—of its indigenous peoples. This spectator provides us with a key ambivalence for some Central American subjects, for it speaks to the ways in which this cultural event allows Central American immigrants a moment to visibly protest the idea of inevitable assimilation, even as it as serves as a powerful reminder of the manner in which nationalism, both at the macro (regional) and micro (national) level are sustained by a fiction of homogenization (a different melting pot). In other words, to privilege a certain implied citizen-subject as Guatemalan is to rely on a national identity that was formed via the exclusion of other diverse ethnoracial populations within the nation-state.

Nevertheless, this spectator's choice of wearing this T-shirt needs to be read within its specific context of an ethnoracial minority subject in the United States visibly asserting a type of resistance toward the dominant narrative of assimilation and accommodation. This is particularly significant since the year I attended the COFECA parade, just four months prior on May 1, 2006, Los Angeles hosted one of the largest protests regarding immigrant rights.[7] The political climate in the nation, and especially in spaces like Los Angeles in the last three decades, beginning with such policies as Proposition 187, has been hostile toward immigrants, especially Latina/o immigrants. Thus, for this spectator to wear a shirt that states that he is "100% Guatemalan," with a barcode on it, as if to suggest that his body and labor are merely a disposable form of commodity within U.S. culture, needs to be recognized as a moment of agency. It also calls attention to the contradictory position U.S. American culture has toward its immigrants; on the one hand it resents immigrants like this spectator for their ethnoracial difference and resistance toward assimilation, and on the other hand it needs this population as a cheap source of labor to sustain its economy.[8]

In this sense the COFECA event becomes a radical site of critique—a manipulation of space in order to cast light on those "other [discursive] spaces" that continually position Central Americans as racialized Others and outsiders (Foucault 1986, 22). Michel Foucault has labeled such spaces as "heterotopias" that operate as "counter-sites" whereby "all other real sites that can be found within the culture, are simultaneously represented, contested and inverted" (1986, 24). According to Foucault, this is achieved because these heterotopias expose those spaces that produce their own conditions of possibility and act as mirrors where "I see myself where I am not . . . a sort of shadow that gives my own visibility to myself, that enables me to see myself there where I am absent" (24). Foucault posits that these Other spaces emerge from an act of recognizing one's displacement. Thus, we may need to start thinking about the production of the COFECA parade and a diasporic Central American identity itself as heterotopian texts—as remnants discarded during the constructions of other identities like "American" or "Latina/o," which seldom link those categories with the experiences of Central Americans (Arias 2003, 3). Conceived under this lens, the construction of this parade as a heterotopia becomes a powerful form of critique; it acts as a "mirror" from which its mere presence or existence challenges totalizing discourses from the isthmus, the United States, and Latinidad that claim to be inclusive of all peoples and cultures.

CONCLUSION

The cultural institution of COFECA and its sponsored parade is a complex site where dominant notions of Central American belonging converge with the material realties faced by immigrants in the United States. While the parade and fiestas patrias are vestiges of isthmian state-sponsored projects of national cohesion, in the diaspora they become the critical terrain where Central Americans can contest their marginalization from U.S. American and Latina/o imaginaries. They also provide isthmian subjects sites from which to articulate their identities and foster notions of a shared culture and history. This type of centralaméricanismo, in turn, allows these subjects to "claim a spot within the array of nationalities that make up immigrant America" (Coutin 2000, 157). The fact that Central Americans have opted to construct their own celebrations, in relation to but distinct from other Latina/o festivities in California, also signals that Latinidad has not been able to interpellate all of its supposed members. Thus, every year that Central Americans march down the streets of "Little Central America," they become metaphoric mirrors to a Latina/o discourse that simultaneously speaks for their traditions and social experiences but also renders them invisible.[9] Consequently, the COFECA parade—as catalyst, embodiment, and vehicle of centralaméricanismo—needs to be viewed as a heterotopian space that serves to not only undermine racist and homogenizing tropes in circulation in the United States that fail to recognize Latina/o heterogeneity but also allows Central Americans to produce and perform a cultural identity.

NOTES

1. See Marvelia Alpizar, "Centroamérica esta de fiesta," *La Opinión*, September 12, 2014. Accessed April 24, 2015. http://www.laopinion.com/2014/09/12/centroamerica-esta-de-fiesta/. All Spanish quotes have been translated by the author unless stated otherwise.
2. Attendance figure obtained from COFECA website.
3. Mayas are one of the many Mesoamerican indigenous groups found on the isthmus; they currently reside in parts of Mexico, Guatemala, and Belize. Garifunas are a black indigenous community (descendants of Carib Indians and black slaves) who reside mostly on the Caribbean coast of the isthmus.
4. These national assumptions and ascriptions are historically based since up until 1848 California was Mexican territory and, to date, houses the largest Mexican population outside of Mexico.
5. Previous themes include "No Human Being Is Illegal" (2008) and "United for Immigration Reform" (2010).

6. In 2012 Belize was declared the "host" country and was allowed to lead the parade floats and choose the grand marshal for that year.

7. On May 1, 2006, 200,000 protestors marched the streets of city hall, and 400,000 protested along the Wilshire Corridor during the national protest titled "A Day Without an Immigrant."

8. For more information regarding Central Americans and job occupations in the United States, see *Seeking Community in a Global City* (Hamilton and Stoltz Chinchilla 2001) and *Waiting on Washington* (Repak 1995).

9. To explore how other Central American celebrations have been utilized as a counterresponse to marginalization, see "Confronting Exclusion in the Latino Metropolis" by Ester Hernández (2006).

REFERENCES

Acuña, Rodolfo. 1996. *Anything but Mexican: Chicanos in Contemporary Los Angeles*. London: Verso.

Alvarado, Karina O. 2013. "An Interdisciplinary Reading of Chicana/o and (US) Central American Cross-Cultural Narrations." *Latino Studies* 11 (3): 366–87.

Arias, Arturo. 2003. "Central American-Americans: Invisibility, Power and Representation in the US Latino World." *Latino Studies* 1 (1): 168–87.

Bettie, Julie. 2014. *Women Without Class: Girls, Race and Identity*. Berkeley: University of California Press.

Cadaval, Olivia. 1998. *Creating a Latino Identity in the Nation's Capital: The Latino Festival*. New York: Garland Publishing.

"COFECA Carnaval y Desfile por Independencia." *Día a Día*, Los Angeles edition. September 13, 2013, p. 17. https://issuu.com/diaadianews/docs/1209/17.

COFECA Corporate Sponsorship Package. 2009. http://wilfredolinks.com/DOC/COFECA2009.pdf.

Confederación Centroamericana. 2015. http://www.cofeca.org/

Coutin, Susan Bibler. 2000. *Legalizing Moves: Salvadoran Immigrants' Struggle for U.S. Residency*. Ann Arbor: University of Michigan Press.

Dávila, Arlene. 2001. *Latinos, Inc: The Marketing and Making of a People*. Berkeley: University of California Press.

De Genova N., and Ana Y. Ramos-Zayas. 2003. *Latino Crossings: Mexicans, Puerto Ricans, and the Politics of Race and Citizenship*. New York: Routledge.

Du Gay, P., and Stuart Hall. 1996. *Questions of Cultural Identity*. Los Angeles: Sage.

Flores, Juan. 2000. *From Bomba to Hip-Hop: Puerto Rican Culture and Latino Identity*. New York: Columbia University Press.

Foucault, Michel. 1986. "Of Other Spaces." *Diacritics* 16 (1): 22–27.

Hamilton, Nora, and Norma Stoltz Chinchilla. 2001. *Seeking Community in a Global City: Guatemalans and Salvadorans in Los Angeles*. Philadelphia: Temple University Press.

Hernández, Ester. 2006. "Confronting Exclusion in the Latino Metropolis: Central American Transnational Communities in the Los Angeles Area, 1980s–2006." *Journal of the West* 45 (4): 48–56.

Hobsbawm, Eric. 1983. *The Invention of Tradition*. Cambridge: Cambridge University Press.

McClintock, Anne. 1993. "Family Feuds: Gender, Nationalism and the Family." *Feminist Review* (44): 61–80.

Oboler, Suzanne. 1995. *Ethnic Labels, Latino Lives: Identity and the Politics of (Re)presentation in the United States*. Minneapolis: University of Minnesota Press.

Padilla, Felix M. 1985. *Latino Ethnic Consciousness: The Case of Mexican Americans and Puerto Ricans in Chicago*. Notre Dame: University of Notre Dame Press.

Padilla, Yajaira. 2013. "The Central American Transnational Imaginary: Defining the Transnational and Gendered Contours of Central American Immigrant Experience." *Latino Studies* 11 (2): 150–66.

Repak, Terry. 1995. *Waiting on Washington: Central American Workers in the Nation's Capital*. Philadelphia: Temple University Press.

Rivas, Cecilia. 2014. *Salvadoran Imaginaries: Mediated Identities and Cultures of Consumption*. New Brunswick, NJ: Rutgers University Press.

Rodríguez, Ana Patricia. 2009. *Dividing the Isthmus: Central American Transnational Histories, Literatures, and Cultures*. Austin: University of Texas Press.

Shorris, Earl. 1992. *Latinos: A Biography of the People*. New York: W.W. Norton and Co.

Sommers, Laurie. 1991. "Inventing Latinismo." *Journal of American Folklore* 104 (411): 32–53.

Tatum, Chuck. 2014. *Encyclopedia of Latino Culture*. Santa Barbara, CA: Greenwood.

Terrazas, Aaron. 2011. "Migration Information Source—Central American Immigrants in the United States." *The Migration Information Source*. Migration Policy Institute, January 10. http://www.migrationpolicy.org/article/central-american-immigrants-united-states-0

"Tournament of Roses." 2015. *Tournament of Roses*. June 13. http://www.tournamentofroses.com/.

6

REMEMBERING THROUGH CULTURAL INTERVENTIONS

Mapping Central Americans in L.A. Public Spaces

ESTER E. HERNÁNDEZ

ASIDE FROM NEGOTIATING legal and economic concerns in the process of settling in the United States, Central Americans of multiple generations have also searched for strategies of belonging and remembering. These strategies are particularly evident in the cultural production by and about Central Americans. Community organizations and activists have recreated rituals of their homeland through religious festivals and civic commemorations, like those of Central American independence. Importantly, the process of transmitting cultural memory brings to light the history of diaspora. Using the concept of working memory, I examine how through film, murals, and performances, Central Americans revisit painful histories of migration and war, often through complex and contradictory narratives. Within Los Angeles public space, Central American identity symbols provide mnemonic cues to individual, collective, and intergenerational pasts of Angeleno/Salvadoran/Central American social justice struggles. Hence, the chapter calls for an urgent discussion on alternative forms of memory that go beyond the transmission of culture and the learning of history to situate Central American experiences as lived experiences.

VOLCANIC ERUPTIONS FROM THE EPICENTER OF CENTRAL AMERICA

Central American migration stories do not begin or end at arrival in Los Angeles. Migrants become embedded in a larger struggle for justice; they create community and provide a historical context for the following generations. This chapter examines Central American stories, commemorations, and cultural production such as documentaries, memoirs, novels, poetry, and mural art by and about Central Americans. I analyze this active process through community events and key sites of engagement to demonstrate that beyond a subjective experience, cultural memory is constructed and embedded in social spaces that communities create and inhabit. I rely on cultural theorist Ann Rigney's concept of "working memory" for understanding how Central Americans reconstruct their past "through various forms of memorial activity" (2005, 17). This concept best highlights an open-ended, contested, ongoing process replenished by new information and events.

My interest in memory and cultural production about Central Americans began in 2001 when I volunteered at the Central American Resource Center, Los Angeles (CARECEN-LA) and learned about a community archival project to promote intergenerational discussions about migration from Central America and the conditions of the community in Los Angeles, California. These conversations were among Central Americans of primarily Salvadoran descent, but the space itself brought together multiple nationalities and ethnicities as well. These groups were creating their unique spatial imaginaries on the urban cityscape of Los Angeles.

The archival project at CARECEN-LA collected various odds, ends, and new beginnings that mark Central American experiences; it even contained political buttons dating to the Central American civil wars in the 1970s and 1980s. The technology and education coordinator for the center from 1999 to 2002, Leda Ramos, curated a collection of posters and photographs of the Central American solidarity movement donated by community members.[1] Ramos, a second-generation Salvadoran, explained to me that the archive fomented through exchanges between activists at CARECEN-LA and their counterparts in El Salvador and was informed by the work of El Museo de La Palabra y la Imágen (a video, audio, and photographic archive museum) and Equipo Maíz[2] (a popular education group in El Salvador), who have published remarkable images of wartime El Salvador (*Imágenes para no Olvidar 1999/Images to Never Forget*). The archival material in the collection documented the devastating raw violence in Central America and also brought to the foreground faces and bodies commonly erased in abstract descriptions of violence linked to civil wars, through posters, photographs, and Truth Commission Reports.[3] College students and young residents in local high schools participated in discussion and confronted these images.[4]

The library archive of political art and ephemera were integral to the production of a digital mural project spearheaded by the Social and Public Art Resource Center (SPARC) to promote dialogue about the origins and reasons for migration among families; it was eventually named "The Migration of the Golden People,"[5] or simply the CARECEN mural. Using as its backdrop a Central American volcanic landscape, the CARECEN mural depicts deeply buried histories poised to bubble forward. The mural includes prominent and ordinary people in Central American history; their presence spills into the visual space of Los Angeles. The mural depicts loaded images of militarized territories; religious figures such as Salvadoran Monseñor Romero, whose assassination while delivering mass turned him into a martyr of the people in 1980; and known political figures and activists like Maya Guatemalan Rigoberta Menchú. It conveys state violence prevalent in the region from the late 1970s to the mid-1990s but also those who opposed it (See Menjívar and Rodríguez 2005). Carlos Rogel, a student at UCLA who was part of the mural project, noted that it helped him discuss difficult topics with his parents about painful events in their shared family history (histories) (Calfund.org, 7).

The mural greets viewers with the spectral image of a woman running with her child, and a woman raises her fist behind a group of mourners and/or evacuated refugees carrying Monseñor Romero's portrait. Another woman walks in front of riot police holding her child at her breast. Chicana artist Judy Baca, who was in charge of the CARECEN mural, says that the image represents a slain teacher activist from El Salvador (n.d., 24). Teachers, like clergy, were front and center in the struggle for social justice as leaders, witnesses, and martyrs. As Chela Sandoval and Guisela Latorre explain, Baca engages her student artists, parents, and various community voices "to testify and witness on behalf of their communities" (2008, 81). Baca's projects acknowledge origins and foundations of people in their land, their deep roots and connections to the Americas. The use of a mountain/volcano reinforces and encourages physical, spatial, and temporal connections to Central America. The mural conveys social histories in the struggle against globalization and neoliberal agendas that diminish sovereignty, land reform, education, and social safety nets. Furthermore, its subject matter may elicit a discussion of those memories, as mentioned previously by Rogel, or encourage viewers to engage in a search for their own family stories.

The archive room as such no longer exists. When I first learned about the Memoria Histórica archive, it was in its conceptual stages. The mural was finished long after my participation as a volunteer. However, the "archive" room and library closed down, and material was packed away. Nonetheless, the mural was finished and rises from the center of CARECEN-LA's building.

Ramos coordinated a cultural night called "Post-dramatic Stress" at CARECEN that brought together contributors from an anthology of Salvadoran youth, *Izote Vos*, and members of the Epicentro collective for spoken-word performances of Salvadoran, Honduran, and Guatemalan youth (December 20, 2001). These young people participated in telling their own stories in passionate, funny, and emotional words in an act of "post-dramatic stress" release to author(ize) their "working memory" and embodied experiences. These youth artists, many college students and college graduates, represented multiple voices from diverse backgrounds and experiences. In 2007, their poetry was featured in a chapbook titled *Desde el Epicentro* (2007), edited by Karina O. Alvarado in collaboration with author Maya Chinchilla. The cover of the chapbook, designed by Raquel Gutiérrez, who was the emcee at the 2001 poetry night, reads: "Get Lifted. See poets spit testimony, resurrect memory, inspire action, laugh loudly and heal wounds." This chapbook description reinforces a U.S. Central American identity doing deep, emotional memory work and constructing solidarities for the present and future.

Their performance at "Post-dramatic Stress" on that December night in 2001 juxtaposed the static nature of the CARECEN archive with the second generation's desire to author their own stories as U.S.- born and/or raised U.S. Central Americans. They revealed a fissure that challenged the nonprofit priority to not engage their distinct histories, as the literal packing away of the "archive" room suggests. In addition, their efforts were linked to broader social justice struggles in the city of Los Angeles, such as advocacy for extensions of Temporary Protected Status (TPS) and the Nicaraguan Adjustment and Central American Relief Act (NACARA).[6] At the performance, the poetry collective—through spoken-word poetry like Maya Chinchilla's "Solidarity Baby," Leticia Hernández-Linares's "Prudencia Ayala," and Gustavo Guerra Vásquez's "Hybridities"—highlighted a spectrum of refugee, immigrant, and Central American identities, a politicized "working memory" contending for inclusion in ongoing local struggles for immigrant rights and visibility and historically situated within distinct national and ethnic transnational communities (Hamilton and Stoltz Chinchilla 2000).

Thus, CARECEN and the mural represented a public site and type of documentation of the past and the working memory of community making. It is a space where Central Americans and their children use poetry and documentary to explain the context of the struggle for visibility and rights. However, rather than bring people to a spatial commemoration as with the mural, young documentarians, artists, and intellectuals create and weave compelling narratives to/ for Central American and general audiences, adding their powerful voice to the constellation of voices working on representing U.S. Central American issues.

REFUSING TO FORGET

Working memory, I argue, provides a way to deal and interact with turbulent histories and come to terms with what Avery Gordon (1997) calls "ghostly matters." Ghostly matters allude to and go beyond the visible effects of state violence or warfare. For Salvadorans this includes remembering the dead and the "disappeared" in various public sites, thus disrupting the logic of "covert" wars and complicating the ends to state violence. Seen in this light, the ghosts (of memory) left behind by violent repression reappear. The very presence of Central Americans in Los Angeles disrupts suppressed knowledge about said wars.

U.S. Central Americans piecing their family histories and ethnonational heritage must confront deep layers of meaning encoded in sites like the mural. Containing references to persecution and repression, it leaves open-ended who belonged to which camp in the conflict. These new public sites of memory allow for intergenerational dialogue and also invite multiple voices to intervene in the content of emerging U.S. Central American public memory. Blurring the lines between literature, art, history, and social science, these projects present a way to deal with the unspoken, the hidden. Murals, photographic archives, documentation, and mechanical reproduction of art (computer-aided graphics), institutions, and documentaries are producing what Chela Sandoval refers to as "differential consciousness," as "the convergences between creative expression, social activism and self-empowerment" (Sandoval and Latorre 2008, 82).

Unfortunately, it is difficult to assess how the projects are embraced collectively. For example, there have been many organized events that frustrated organizers and activists with low turnout, which might be due to geographical logistics—the event location versus the residential areas of potential attendees. As the community grew larger, their residential patterns became more diffused throughout the metropolitan region (Segura 2010, 125).[7] Political worldviews are also not uniform. Whereas there is a strong presence of leftist views institutionally, divisions are deep and are reflected in the Salvadoran election campaign of

2014, where the Farabundo Martí National Liberation Front (FMLN) candidate won by less than 1 percent of the vote. This is also the second time that the FMLN won the presidency in two consecutive elections. These divisions could be the reason that cultural and historical projects are not wholly embraced by the diaspora. It is also important to consider that when people are engaged in a struggle to survive, as working-class people are in our city, they may not have the resources to engage in a discussion of their histories, let alone political divisions or classed differences in public manifestations.

DOCUMENTED TRANSNATIONAL LIVES: BEYOND LATINA/O SUBMARKETS

Salvadoran and/or Central American spaces are created against a greater Latina/o imaginary in the city. For example, in the culturally hybrid space of Pico-Union, Central Americans become intelligible as a difference within a difference. This section highlights how various city spaces discursively construct Salvadorans and other Central Americans as Latinas/os and immigrants seeking inclusion, although their experiences are vast and diverse. Salvadoran and other Central American cultural and social spaces reveal nuanced community formation against a totalizing racialization of Latina/o in Los Angeles and the tension of producing neoliberal interpretations of their history as an untapped submarket. To understand how Central Americans insist on historical memory, I begin by discussing Jennifer Cárcamo's *Children of the Diaspora: For Peace and Democracy* (2013), a documentary film about youth who seek a connection to their roots through a 2009 electoral delegation organized by Unión Salvadoreña de Estudiantes Universitarios (USEU), a college-based organization that started in El Salvador in 2007 and established various chapters in U.S. college campuses, predominately in California. Then, I connect the film to working memory and representation.

In the summer of 2013, I walked up to a house smack in the middle of the Pico-Union/Westlake region. I joined a diverse group of people—children, parents, activists, artists, students, and professors—who gathered to watch Cárcamo's *Children of the Diaspora*. The house was old. It was not a typical site to hold a film screening. But the location could not have been more perfect since the house was the first location of CARECEN in the early 1980s, then known as the Central American Refugee Center.

As I entered the building I could not help but notice an exposed wooden frame awaiting a drywall treatment, perhaps from the labor of Central American or Mexican laborers. The event organizers resourcefully turned one of the rooms into a theater by using black plastic to cover up walls from floor to ceiling. It was a remarkable scene to see the children of the refugees who might have entered that building in the early 1980s now embracing the struggle for economic and social justice both in El Salvador and in Los Angeles as they prepared to watch the documentary.

The film was exacting when discussing the experience of those who suffered the effects of state violence. As observers of the 2009 Salvadoran elections, they also explored key events and visited monuments and sites of the Salvadoran conflict. The film focused on the narratives of children recollecting their parents' exodus and how what they heard from their parents differed from what they learned on the delegation. One young woman in the film mentions her mother would disapprove of her taking part in the delegation to observe the elections.[8] "My mom doesn't know anything because she is against me getting involved politically. Even worse if she knows that it's about El Salvador." Another analyzes their parents' deliberate silences: "Some of our parents that were involved in the war, they try to pass that knowledge on but those who weren't involved live in fear [and don't want to talk about what happened] and thus deny [us] a connection to their culture." Here, this youth connects the parental silence to the huge gaps in the children's understanding of their culture and history.

Fear of reviving conflict from the civil war period that produced the two contending parties, Alianza Republicana Nacionalista (ARENA, representing the right) and FMLN (representing the left), permeates the elections and preoccupies the participants in the trip. The son of a captain in the armed forces says, "All I ever knew of the FMLN, that they were terrorists, that's all they were branded as. But coming here and learning what that shit is really about and having it broken down ... and just seeing how systematic it all is and how systematically oppressive it is." This is a critical insight that suggests that youth not only pursue their histories but also wish to participate in promoting a peaceful future as a result of what they have learned.

The students learn about the role of the Church during the civil war and the story of Salvadoran Archbishop Romero, known popularly as "Monseñor Romero," who, slain while delivering mass, is considered the people's martyr. They visit his dwelling, listen to his speeches, and learn about how the Catholic Church documented disappearances, killings, torture, and imprisonment through its human rights office Tutela Legal and through the Church's radio. They visit the 1989 massacre site of six Jesuit priests: killings perpetrated by the military that have enjoyed immunity for over twenty-six years. Only two soldiers served prison sentences, but they were released based on the country's 1993 amnesty law. These prominent cases were examples of the repression that was prevalent in the country and the impunity that followed and remains to be addressed. Highlighting the cases of impunity for crimes deemed to be crimes against humanity, these visits reveal incomplete histories yet to be "closed." In effect, as reported by Cooper and Hodge (2016), Spain wants to bring them to trial, and four of the perpetrators out of the twelve indicted by Spanish courts have been arrested as of February 8, 2016. This further illustrates that these histories are still being worked out; they are unresolved and erupt into the present. Regionally, Guatemala leads efforts to prosecute war crimes as crimes against humanity. Amnesty laws passed by the right-wing governments in power have been obstacles to prosecution.

Part of the film also spotlights the resistance of two communities that faced intense repression. Among these is El Mozote[9] in the Morazán Department, which was the site of a series of military operations that led to the massacre of an estimated 900 to 1,000 people, mostly women and children, in 1981. The incident was reported in the news, but both the Salvadoran government and the U.S. embassy and government denied it. It was not officially confirmed until the 1990s when forensic anthropologists unearthed the bodies. Another site they visit was in the Bajo Río Lempa in the Usúlutan Department, where notorious massacres were attributed to the government military forces during the civil war period (1980–1992).

Aside from silence due to painful memories, some of the students note that their parents expressed views that were very much pro-government. Several students explain in the film that their parents were not sympathetic to the guerrillas. One says that his parents always referred to the guerrillas as *los malvados* (the bad guys), and another one says that her family was "super right wing," so that she only got a positive perspective of the right-wing party before her trip. All of these histories come to a head in the election campaigns, where the rhetoric of good guys and bad guys and the threat of external communist influence were rehashed by the right-wing party in power. The students eventually participated in a media campaign where they made their message clear: "If you are voting in fear, *that* is not democracy." The FMLN won the 2009 election.

The filmmaker and organizers emphasized that the goal of their trip was to understand their parents' silences, pain, and suffering of leaving home. Through

activist student organizations like USEU, this re-vision of the past is deliberate, unflinching, and purposeful and is one of the many ways in which young
people of different political backgrounds are connecting to the past through
historical memory projects. It is also one view of young college-aged students
who returned home to acquaint themselves with the history of social struggle
in El Salvador.

This *re-encuentro con la historia* (acquainting themselves with history) could
be rather different for the generation of young people who returned home invol-
untarily as deportees (Zilberg 2011). Whether seeking haptic or visual engagement with their history through an archive or taking a trip home to interpret
their present, the second generation's efforts to recover history are never apolitical. For example, Coutin notes that in seeking to connect biographies to
histories, the narratives of individuals differ from narratives arising from government entities. She argues that the Salvadoran government deploys stories
that erase the civil war and transform refugees into emigrants and their children
into heroic nationals helping to rebuild the nation, while young people in search
of "roots" use their stories to critique, find and reveal truth, and call for social
justice (Coutin 2011). As I have argued previously, the government discourse
on development repackaged the separation of families through migration and
the concomitant remittances as a benefit to El Salvador while ignoring the dire
conditions and lack of status that Salvadorans faced in the United States as
unauthorized workers. In so doing, they ignored the in-limbo status of Temporary Protected Status (TPS) programs of most migrants and recast them as
heroes to the nation (see Baker-Cristales 2004; Hernández 2006a; Hernández
and Coutin 2006; Menjívar 2010).

Cárcamo's documentary engages in postconflict dialogue, adding emigrant
and second-generation voices that relate historical facts but also insist on
a social conscience. Through witnessing the historical context that produced
emigration, we see that an exodus also gives context to Salvadoran and other
Central Americans' legal status in the United States. Central Americans have
been predominately and primarily relegated to undocumented status when they
would have benefited from recognition as refugees (Menjívar 2010; Hamilton
and Stoltz Chinchilla 2000; Hernández 2006a; Coutin 2000). As is well documented, this was a political decision by the U.S. government not to acknowledge that state violence clearly produced the exodus of Central Americans
(García 2006).

MULTIPLE DISPLACEMENTS:
SEEKING SANCTUARY IN LOS ANGELES

While prominent in the public space of cities like Los Angeles, Central Americans' very visibility and association with informal economies in locations like MacArthur Park often indexes an overexposure to the gaze of the state: as vendors, as day laborers, as invisible service workers who may be subject to an unfair share of traffic stops, fines, and arrests that could eventually devolve into a deportation order.[10] This, like Padilla's discussion of the 2007 raids in this volume, and current deportations targeting Central American women and children, is linked to ongoing displacement of the 1980s civil wars.

Many refugees became active in "the solidarity movement" to stop U.S. intervention in Central America and to support the people's struggle in El Salvador and their integration as unrecognized refugees in cities like Los Angeles. For example, Maria Guardado, who was a union organizer for Salvadoran teachers, had to flee the country after being tortured and left for dead. She joined the Central American sanctuary movement, which supported people fleeing political persecution and seeking entry into the United States. Her testimony highlights the connection between refugee rights and immigrant rights in *The Maria Guardado Story* (2002). The Sanctuary Movement of the 1980s was a political and religious initiative to provide safe haven for Central Americans fleeing their countries while, for the most part, they were denied asylum in the United States (Stoltz Chinchilla, Hamilton, and Loucky 2009). Sharing her story with human rights activists, Maria was able to connect to the sanctuary movement and remained involved in mobilizing support for the sanctuary and Central American peace movement (Perla 2008).

After the United States granted her political asylum in 1983, Guardado continued to be a vocal activist in ongoing struggles for justice for immigrants—for example, in campaigns for health care, education, dignified employment and wages, and housing. In one of the scenes in the film, she reads a poem dedicated to the mothers looking for their disappeared children for hundreds of Belmont High students. The poem is about the agony of looking at hundreds of bodies in search of a disappeared *hijo* (son) or *hija* (daughter). In the beginning of the film, there is a discussion of the campaign of terror whereby tortured bodies would be dumped in the street as a way to demonstrate the fate of those willing to join the guerrillas. The film makes the historical context of violence in El Salvador painfully clear.

The filmmaker, Randy Vasquez, began to work on the documentary after attending a meeting of a group called "Crack the CIA" in South Los Angeles, where activists wanted to expose the connection between foreign policy and the crack cocaine epidemic. At one demonstration, Guardado refused to move and turns to the police and says in Spanish, "I was tortured by the CIA and the death squads in El Salvador."[11] She, bluntly, stands in testimony and evocatively joins her memory work that recalls death squads with ongoing U.S. police brutality.

Both documentaries contextualize the status of Central Americans and how deportation and separation affected them. Various gaps exist in family relationships connected to migration at a time of great political repression where families may have had members in both camps. Families have also been forced to remain apart for whole life cycles as they struggle to survive family separation through migration, deportation, and living in economically dire conditions in the United States.[12] Moreover, since 1996, as the immigration system became more restrictive and less amenable to family unification, El Salvador, Honduras, and Guatemala each account for more than 20,000 deportees per year (see Abrego, Estrada, and Padilla in this volume). By comparison, deportations from all nationalities other than Mexico and Central America account for 24,000 per year (Golash-Boza 2012). Thus, migration, unauthorized status, repression, and deportation have shaped the parameters of working memory.

Murals and films connect youth to their family and cultural roots, foster cross-coalitional work between Central Americans, and produce a Central American spatial presence. For example, Arturo Zepeda,[13] a Chicano coordinator for CARECEN-LA's day laborer site, shared with me his interpretation of the CARECEN mural. For him it reinforced the links between the stories of workers he saw daily. He linked the larger issues of political repression to the struggles laborers face in the city of Los Angeles, as well as the conditions that spurred their migration. He explained how in his interactions with day laborers, he often visualized their struggles as a load that migrants carry with them. It gave him a better appreciation of the sociopolitical reality of different nationalities and ethnic groups. In the midst of trying to help Central Americans deal with a neoliberal climate in the city that criminalized their work, excluded them from most social services, and made them subject to deportation simply for seeking work, the mural made him aware of how Maya stories differed from those of Guatemalan ladinas/os, Salvadorans, and Hondurans.

Thus, he observed that workers become vulnerable to other labels coming from state institutions and from each other as a hierarchy emerges between groups based on language, nationality, ethnicity, and age. This exchange reminds me that working memory must tell stories that insist on historical connections. In a sense, these visual stories emplace Central Americans, however tenuously, in their current space within a dominant Latina/o immigrant identity that tends to repackage their past and present political struggles into immigrant narratives.

Local organizations have led efforts to confront the precarious situation of immigrants and have been at the forefront of organizing day laborers, vendors, domestic workers, and janitors in various economic justice campaigns. Crucial institutions serving the legal and health needs of Central Americans such as CARECEN, El Rescate, and Clínica Romero also symbolize the critical struggles and demands for human rights. The commemoration of the March 24, 1980, anniversary of Archbishop Oscar Romero's assassination has been important to historical memory for Salvadorans and their children as his life and death have been interpreted by the Church and secular sectors. Despite the struggle for inclusion, Central Americans have been actively developing connections to the city throughout four decades in spatializing their presence. For example, celebrations such as those of the Cristo Negro from Guatemala and El Salvador's Salvador del Mundo establish continuity between the homeland and Los Angeles, creating chronotopic and synchronic connections between generations (Hernández 2006b). The statue of Monseñor Romero at MacArthur Park and the newly created Plaza Morazán (April 20, 2013) are also establishing a historically specific U.S. Central American experience in the city that different generations can learn from and continue to share long after they move out of the area.

Combined with the annual festivals and events, these public spaces and institutions reinforce Central American presence and political participation. Although the Pico-Union and Westlake areas have always been multiethnic environments, in 2013 Salvadoran business leaders have succeeded in naming a twelve-block area as the Salvadoran Community Corridor but have been unsuccessful in getting a larger area named Central America Town or Little Central America. However, since this is primarily a Salvadoran corridor there are similar moves to name other areas more specifically, such as the Guatemalan Corridor along 6th Street and Alvarado (Bermudez 2014).

Activists linked to organizations such as El Rescate, CARECEN, and SANA (Salvadoran American Network Association) saw learning the national anthem and traditional folklore and dance customs as key for youth to be interested in visiting their or their parents' homelands and knowing their origins so that they would be aware and proud of their Central American identities and histories. As part of this mobilizing of cultural memory, the city of Los Angeles now celebrates Monseñor Romero Day (March 24), Garifuna Day (April 12), Salvadoran Day (August 6),[14] and many more festivals and parades in relation to those dates. Religious celebrations include Guatemalans' Black Christ procession in South Central and Salvador del Mundo in the month of August. These celebrations encourage participants to strengthen ties with the homeland and at the same time transform Los Angeles into a transnational space of belonging (Hernández 2006b). Here efforts between promotion of ethnicity and economic development potentially open an opportunity for critical consciousness.

Promoting a sense of community among second-generation Central Americans grapples with a larger struggle to be global citizens with progressive, historically situated agendas while contending with the same risks of invisibility to which other Latina/os are subject. As Dávila explores in *Barrio Dreams*, Latina/os (and Central Americans now being a submarket) must contend with the potential of being reduced to consumers "depoliticized from history and struggle" at festivals sponsored by big corporate sponsors (2004, 95).

BREAKING SILENCE THROUGH SOCIAL MEMORY

The militarization of life in Central America has circulated in the world stage through news coverage, film, and testimonials,[15] contesting both the official Central American governments' and U.S. denial of the veracity of the devastation and death in the isthmus and outright dismissals of human rights abuses as communist propaganda. Martín-Baró (1994) suggests that the persistence of violence in society and the transmission of traumas persists beyond those who experienced them in El Salvador, and thus efforts to disclose these histories publicly and generationally are significant moves with the potential to transform societies in Central America and here in the United States. Therefore, cultural memory projects have implications beyond individuals and could address current events. "Unaccompanied children" are now fleeing Honduras, Guatemala, and El Salvador, this time supposedly fleeing generalized violence. Of course, this idea of generalized violence itself encourages assessment of current social conditions as unrelated and discontinuous from the state-sponsored violence of the 1980s and delinks it from U.S. policies in the isthmus and their impact in shaping U.S. Central Americans.

Within El Salvador, silence about repressive conditions promoted the burial of emotions both in public settings and in the privacy of the home. According to Salvadoran psychologist Martín-Baró, theorists of memory note that some memories are easily talked about while others involving trauma or conflict are not easily commemorated. He grounded his studies on the notion of psychosocial trauma and questions about how imposed silence orders memory of certain events. His work contextualized the injuries to childhood (hence social memory) within the theater of governmental forces fighting against a guerrilla movement (1994). This polarized context meant that individuals witnessing the ensuing violence could not talk about or critique it without exposing themselves to either camp. Adding to this, Ricardo Falla-Sánchez (2013) notes that the violence unleashed on indigenous Guatemalans was intended to root out the generation of life itself—"acabarlos hasta la semilla . . . (los niños), un acto genocida" (the killing [of children] to stop the generation of life. Genocide).[16] Falla-Sánchez's point about genocidal campaigns gets to the larger issue of how globalization agendas sought to displace indigenous populations in the way of capitalist projects; the military executed an extermination campaign that would dislodge indigenous communities from their lands and push Maya populations to become migrant wage workers in Guatemala and North America (2011).

A U.S. Central American identity in Los Angeles engaged in public memory engages issues of power and debate in culture. For young people, time-related and place-related efforts to remember may include reading the Truth Commission Reports, looking at photographs of demonstrations dispersed violently, and reading about the migration stories of men and women. These processes allow new generations to "witness" and old generations to comment on the disconcerting violence and destruction of civil war.

In this context, the archival project at CARECEN raised politically charged questions about positionality. To examine the archival record is an intensely political act. Utilizing visual and textual material chronicling the violent events in the region provided a public forum from which to construct a public memory. It involved key questions such as, Would the archive jog or confront the memories of government soldiers? Who would want to look at the atrocities recorded and stored in it? Who remembers? Why? For what purpose? The process of remembering has its counterpart in people's efforts to also forget.[17]

At the archive, Leda Ramos shared with me that one of the images that young students picked for the CARECEN mural was in the end rejected in the process of discussion that preceded its final version. It was the photograph of a Sandinista soldier smelling a flower. The objections focused on how the image could be misunderstood because there was no way to tell that he was a Sandinista soldier. But beyond the photo's ambiguity, I argue, the debate over the photograph illustrates debate about who can speak about suffering and trauma. At the same time, it is well known that both soldiers and guerrillas settled in Los Angeles. There is a blurring/fusion that is quite possible as a result. For example, several notorious members of the *kaibiles*, Guatemala's elite military unit, and Salvadoran generals faced trials on U.S. immigration law violations for crimes against humanity. Some *kaibiles* who participated in crimes against humanity lived for decades in the United States until four were deported and stood trial in Guatemala (Kriel 2012). Two Salvadoran generals who were involved in the assassination of Monseñor Romero; the torture of a surgeon; and the killings of four U.S. nuns and six Jesuit priests, their cook, and her sixteen-year-old daughter have also faced immigration trials, and some were ordered deported in June 2014 after various appeals (Bach 2014; Center for Justice and Accountability). However, among the latter, even when deported, the amnesty laws of 1993[18] protected them from prosecution until recently.

Historically, military states in Central America chose to omit their involvement in the mass murder of their people.[19] This institutional strategy to forget or rewrite memory makes the survival of working cultural memory especially pertinent (See Jelin 1998). For example, in 2013, El Salvador's Catholic Church closed down the archive that tracked deaths and disappearances during the war years. Clearly this was a move toward erasure/burial of the past in Central America. Public debate focused on whether remembering will lead to reconciliation or to resentment and vengeance. Will we be happier/better if we forget? The answer is that people will continue to demand justice. Just in January 2015, the killers of Rigoberta Menchú's father were convicted, and the generals who presided over crimes against humanity have been called to account for their actions in U.S. civil and immigration courts (Grandin 2015). In El Salvador, there have been new arrest orders for the killers of the Jesuits to face trial in Spanish courts; this development reinforces calls to exempt crimes against humanity from amnesty laws. In Guatemala, convictions against military officers accused of subjecting women to sexual slavery have recently occurred.

CONCLUSION

In this chapter, I have looked at documentaries, memory sites, and commemorations that place Central American subjects in a position to recognize themselves, to authorize their own stories, and to chart their own sense of community in dialogue with other communities. Central American histories of massive migration and dislocation continue to emerge.

For the second generation, cultural production has implications for working through political division being passed down through their parents' involvement and noninvolvement in the civil war conflicts of their respective countries. The spaces of dialogue being created, I argue, offer the possibility for U.S. Central Americans to attempt to mediate these very divisions.

As explored, working memory confronts these histories and demands for justice. In representing these stories, reading texts, and engaging in pilgrimage, the dead are remembered, grieved, and mourned, and moreover the retelling, whatever the form, allows for those who have not been allowed to speak to supplement the history of this period—potentially re-membering the community. In adopting this notion of working memory, I acknowledge the work of scholars such as Karina O. Alvarado (Alvarado 2013, 2) who critique how Central Americans have been (mis)represented by other Latina/os and by Central Americans themselves in not considering their complex and hybrid subjectivities. For instance, Alvarado notes that 1.5-generation and second-generation Central Americans have been interpolated into the various discourses found in the communities where they grew up. This interpolation occurred through institutions such as K–12 education, through neighborhood and/or regional demographics, and through cultural contact with other ethnicities in the United States. Rodríguez (n.d.) also critiques the production of an undifferentiated U.S. Central American subject that is inattentive of specific histories and first-hand experiences. Menjívar's (2010) discussion of liminal identities structured around legal status and multiple forms of erasures are also powerful analyses of the cultural production of Central Americans in the United States.

In Los Angeles, a mural, festival, and even a documentary engage with similar questions against forgetting. They allow for rethinking hegemonic stories of the right and left, opening up space for "biographical" interventions in social memory—and contesting official history. Murals, fictional accounts, documentaries, and spoken-word performances bridge the stories of displaced refugees who have become undocumented immigrants, and offer an interpretation of the polarizing and disconcerting effects and aftereffects of violent histories. These interventions can and do reflect the ambiguities and pitfalls of a polarized political environment. Through various forms of representations, it is perhaps possible to go beyond simply retelling violent events in order to allow these events to become meaningful to those who did not live or witness them. According to Bennett's (2002) analysis of artistic renderings of trauma and violence, some artists believe it important to provide a "sense memory" of loss. That is, a sense memory is not just about the abrupt loss of someone's life but also about taking account of the absences that suffuse the everyday lives of those who survive.

The U.S. Central American diasporas will continue to deal with the absences imposed by warfare, migration, and deportation. The testimonial literature, fictionalized histories, and historical archives fill in a lot of gaps because it is impossible to go back in time and recover a complete archival record. Strobel (1999) argues for the importance of keeping archives, notes, photography, and speeches as a way to jog memories that have not been recalled for some time. Similarly, events to remember along with murals, for example, provide opportunities for individuals to incorporate these memories into their lives and produce their own stories. Their individual memories and these archives will inform what constitutes future collective memory, across generations, and the extent to which they include pluralistic, transnational social justice concerns of both the past and present. Estrada (2013) has written about how through radio programming Maya communities from Guatemala are creating community archives that are multilingual and link indigenous communities in Los Angeles and in the hemisphere. As Salvadorans and other Central Americans seek a place in the multicultural metropolis and establish U.S. Central American spaces, they will increasingly participate in discussions about what constitutes social memory and belonging. They will insist on democratic ideals that actually promote genuine democracy and go beyond state projects.

NOTES

1. Hector Perla (2008), "Si Nicaragua Venció, El Salvador Vencerá: Central American Agency in the Creation of the U.S.-Central American Peace and Solidarity Movement," *Latin American Research Review* 43 (2): 136–58.

2. Museo de la palabra y la Imagen (MUPI) is an institution in El Salvador "dedicated to the creation and preservation of historical memory" whose website is located at http://museo.com.sv/en/; Equipo Maiz is a Salvadoran popular education collective whose website is located at http://www.equipomaiz.org.sv.

3. See El Salvador's report, "From Madness to Hope: The 12-year war in El Salvador," UN Security Council, Annex. Report on the Commission of the Truth for El Salvador. Posted by USIP Library on January 26, 2001 http://www .usip.org/sites/default/files/file/ElSalvador-Report.pdf; for Guatemala, the report of the Commission for Historical Clarification was called "Guatemala: Memory of Silence." Its conclusions and recommendations can be accessed at http://www.aaas.org/sites/default/files/migrate/uploads/mos_en.pdf.

4. Two Salvadoran college students during that summer thumbed through visual imagery, historical and literary books, watched documentary films about the conflict, and reflected on that process in a small gathering. Their presentations and discussions with other volunteers underscored the fact that it was not easy to talk about the Central American stories of migration, as one could not do so without bringing up the violence of civil war.

5. Golden people signals indigenous origins and at the same time "new" Golden State residents.

6. NACARA and TPS I and II are two U.S. legal statuses that have been pertinent to Salvadoran, Guatemalan, Honduran, and Nicaraguan nationals, primarily in the 1990s.

7. Pew Research Center "Hispanic Populations in Select Metropolitan Areas, 2011," http://www.pewhispanic.org/2013/08/29/hispanic-population-in-select-u-s -metropolitan-areas-2011/.

8. See Center for Justice and Accountability, "El Salvador: 12 Years of Civil War," http://www.cja.org/article.php?list=type&type=199. Mauricio Funes, the candidate for the FMLN, won the presidential elections in 2009. In 2014, Salvador Sánchez Cerén, the candidate for the FMLN, won the presidential elections in a highly contested second round of voting.

9. El Mozote is a series of massacres that occurred in 1981, where an estimated 900 to 1,000 people died, mostly women and children, in military campaigns by the Atlacatl Batallion. The massacre was denied in the United States, and forensic anthropologists confirmed the only survivors' stories in the early 1990s. El Bajo Rio Lempa was also the scene of such massacres. See Mark Danner, "The Truth of El Mozote," *New Yorker*, December 6, 1993, http://www.markdanner .com/articles/the-truth-of-el-mozote; Leigh Binford, *The El Mozote Massacre:*

Anthropology and Human Rights (Tucson: University of Arizona Press, 1996); and reports by the International Commission on Human Rights.

10. *Por la Vida: Street Vending and the Criminalization of Latinos* (Olea 1994) examines these structural constraints to membership at MacArthur Park, a space where street vendors, who are mostly new immigrants, struggle for their livelihood in the informal economy. They face immigration enforcement and police harassment. It features a group of mothers, primarily from Central America, talking about their struggle to send money back while trying to get work.

11. In the film, Guardado recounts her kidnapping, rape, and torture in 1980. She suffers PTSD, and psychologists with the Program for Torture Victims, Los Angeles talk about her psychological symptoms in the film.

12. PBS aired a documentary in 1994 about the immigrant community and showcased the plight of a Salvadoran child. In *Fear and Learning at Hoover Elementary*, Mayra, a young Salvadoran girl growing up in the Pico-Union neighborhood, confronts urban violence, poverty, and teachers both sympathetic and unsympathetic to the long-term situation of undocumented children or children of the undocumented. It highlights children's fears of being deported along with their families in a context compounded by the crime, gangs, and poverty in the area.

13. He worked for several years with the organizations' *jornaleros* (day laborers) project.

14. The celebration is in its sixteenth year in 2014 and was started by SANA, the Salvadoran American National Association.

15. See, for example, Arias's (2003) writings on the Rigoberta Menchú controversy. She has been vindicated in court. Those responsible for setting the Spanish embassy on fire, with the protestors occupying it, have been convicted by the Guatemalan court system.

16. Falla-Sánchez is the author of the book *Negreaba de Zopilotes: Masacre y Sobrevivencia, Finca San Francisco Nentón, Guatemala 1871–2010*, which can be found online at http://avancsoaudio.org/libro-en-version-digital/.

17. As part of their reflections on their intern project, two college summer interns in the CARECEN archival project expressed their initial ambivalence in participating. For one of them, her mother expressed concern about what she saw as CARECEN's leftist political nature. The other one noted that family members did not want to talk specifically about their memories of the period; however, they did acknowledge to their children the overwhelming number of young people who died and that "*Fueron tiempos terribles. Tristes*" (It was a terrible, sad time.)

18. The Salvadoran Supreme Court overturned amnesty laws on July 13, 2016.

19. For a comparative discussion of state-sponsored violence in the hemisphere, see Menjívar Cecilia and Néstor Rodríguez, eds., *When States Kill: Latin America, The U.S. and Technologies of Terror* (Austin: University of Texas Press, 2005).

REFERENCES

Alvarado, Karina O. 2013. "The Boo of Viramontes's Café: Retelling Ghost Stories, Central American Representing Social Death." *Studies in 20th & 21st Century Literature* 37 (2): 77–99.

Alvarado, Karina O., and Maya Chinchilla, eds. 2007. *Desde el Epicentro: An Anthology of U.S. Central American Poetry*. Los Angeles: Epicentro.

Arias, Arturo. 2003. "Central American Americans: Invisibility, Power and Representation in the U.S. Latino World." *Latino Studies* 1 (1): 168–87.

Baca, Judy. n.d. "La Memoria de Nuestra Tierra, Sites of Public Memory." Foreseeable Futures #8 Position Papers. *Imagining America: Artists and Scholars in Public Life*. Syracuse, NY: Imagining America.

Bach, Trevor. 2014. "Two Salvadoran Generals Ordered Deported for Civil War Torture." *Miami New Times*. June 12.

Baker-Cristales, Beth. 2004. *Salvadoran Migration to Southern California: Redefining El Hermano Lejano*. Gainesville: University Press of Florida.

Bennett, Jill. 2002. "Art, Affect, and the 'Bad Death': Strategies for Communicating the Sense Memory of Loss." *Signs: Journal of Women in Culture and Society* 28 (1): 333–51.

Bermudez, Esmeralda. 2014. "Advocates Seek to Carve Out Official Latin American areas in L.A." *Los Angeles Times*. April 2.

Cárcamo, Jennifer. 2013. *Children of the Diaspora: For Peace and Democracy*. Documentary film. USA. http://childrenofthediaspora.com/.

Center for Justice and Accountability. "Doe vs. Saravia: El Salvador: The Assassination of Archbishop Oscar Arnulfo Romero." http://www.cja.org/article.php?list=type&type=157.

Cooper, Linda, and James Hodge. 2016. "Extradition Order in Jesuit Priest Killings Could Lead to More Arrests." *National Catholic Reporter*. February 8.

Coutin, Susan. 2000. *Legalizing Moves: Salvadoran Immigrants' Struggles for U.S. Residency*. Ann Arbor: University of Michigan Press.

———. 2011. "Re/membering the Nation: Gaps and Reckoning within Biographical Accounts of Salvadoran Émigrés." *Anthropological Quarterly* 84 (4): 809–34.

Dávila, Arlene. 2004. *Barrio Dreams: Puerto Ricans, Latinos, and the Neoliberal City.* Berkeley: University of California Press.

Estrada, Alicia I. 2013. "Ka Tzij: The Maya Diasporic Voices From Contacto Ancestral." *Latino Studies* 11: 208–27.

Falla-Sánchez, Ricardo. 2011. "Presentación de Negreaba de Zopilotes: Masacre y Sobrevivencia (1982) en Finca San Francisco, en Huehuetenango" (interview). Avancso, TV Maya. Guatemala. Minutes 5 to 10. https://www.youtube.com/watch?v=rH-NtfohPso.

———. 2013. "Los Restos del conflicto armado: Como que no hubo genocidio?" *Agencia Latinoamericana de Información. America Latina en Movimiento.* http://alainet.org/active/62995.

García, Maria C. 2006. *Seeking Refuge: Central American Migration to Mexico, the U.S. and Canada.* Berkeley: University of California Press.

Golash-Boza, Tanya. 2012. *Immigration Nation? Raids, Detentions and Deportations in Post-9/11 America.* Boulder, CO: Paradigm Publishers.

Gordon, Avery. 1997. *Ghostly Matters: Haunting and the Sociological Imagination.* Minneapolis: University of Minnesota Press.

Grandin, Greg. 2015. "Rigoberta Menchú Vindicated." *Nation.* January 21.

Hamilton, Nora, and Norma Stoltz Chinchilla. 2000. *Seeking Community in a Global Village: Guatemalans and Salvadorans in Los Angeles.* Philadelphia: Temple University Press.

Hernández, Ester E. 2006a. "Relief Dollars: U.S. Policies toward Central Americans, 1980s to Present." *Journal of American Ethnic History* 25 (2–3) Winter/Spring: 225–42.

———. 2006b. "Confronting Exclusion in the Latino Metropolis: Central American Transnational Communities in the Los Angeles Area, 1980s–2006." *Journal of the West* 45 (4): 48–56.

Hernández, Ester E., and Susan Coutin. 2006. "Remitting Subjects: Money, Migrants and States." *Economy and Society* 35 (2): 185-208.

Jelin, Elizabeth. 1998. "The Minefields of Memory." *NACLA Report on the Americas* 32 (2): 23.

Kriel, Lomi. 2012. "Seeking Justice for Guatemalan Village Where Hundreds Were Raped, Tortured, Killed." *Houston Chronicle.* May 26.

Martín-Baró, Ignacio. 1994. "War and Psychosocial Trauma of Salvadoran Children." In *Writings for a Liberation Psychology*, edited by A. Aron and S. Corne, 122–35. Cambridge, MA: Harvard University Press.

Menjívar, Cecilia. 2010. "Immigrant Art as Liminal Expression: The Case of Central Americans." In *Art in the Lives of Immigrant Communities in the United States*, edited by Paul DiMaggio and Patricia Fernández-Kelly, 176–96. New Brunswick, NJ: Rutgers University Press.

Menjívar, Cecilia, and Nestor Rodríguez, eds. 2005. *When States Kill: Latin America, The U.S. and Technologies of Terror*. Austin: University of Texas Press.

Olea, Olivia. 1994. *Por La Vida: Street Vending and the Criminalization of Latinos*. Riverside, CA: Salsa Films.

Perla, Hector. 2008. "Si Nicaragua Venció, El Salvador Vencerá: Central American Agency in the Creation of the U.S.-Central American Peace and Solidarity Movement." *Latin American Research Review* 43 (2): 136–58.

Rigney, Anne. 2005. "Plenitude, Scarcity and the Circulation of Cultural Memory." *Journal of European Studies* 35 (1): 11–28.

Rodríguez, Ana. P. (n.d). "Second Hand Identities: The Autoethnographic Performances of Quique Avilés and Leticia Hernández-Linares." http://istmo.denison .edu/n08/articulos/second.html.

Romero, Edgar, and Equipo Maíz. 1999. *El Salvador Imágenes para No Olvidar (1900–1999)*. Asociación Equipo Maíz. San Salvador: El Salvador.

Sandoval, Chela, and Guisela Latorre. 2008. "Chicana/o Artivism: Judy Baca's Digital Work With Youth of Color." In *Learning Race and Ethnicity: Youth and Digital Media*, edited by Anna Everett, 81–108. Cambridge, MA: MIT Press.

Segura, Rosamaria. 2010. *Central Americans in Los Angeles*. San Francisco: Arcadia.

Stoltz Chinchilla, Norma, Nora Hamilton, and James Loucky. 2009. "The Sanctuary Movement and Central American Activism in Los Angeles." *Latin American Perspectives* 36 (6): 101–26.

Strobel, Margaret. 1999. "Becoming a Historian, Being an Activist, and Thinking Archivally: Documents and Memory as Sources." *Journal of Women's History* 11 (1): 181.

Tobar, Héctor. 1998. *The Tattooed Soldier*. New York: Penguin Books.

Vasquez, Randy. 2001. *Testimony: The Maria Guardado Story*. West Hollywood, CA: High Valley Productions.

Wilkinson, Tracy. 2013. "Catholic Church Shuts Down Rights and Legal Office." *Los Angeles Times*. October 2.

Zilberg, Elana. 2011. *Space of Detention: The Making of a Trasnational Gang Crisis Between Los Angeles and San Salvador*. Durham, NC: Duke University Press.

7

(RE)CLAIMING PUBLIC SPACE
AND PLACE

Maya Community Formation in
Westlake/MacArthur Park

ALICIA IVONNE ESTRADA

D ATA FROM THE 2010 U.S. census states that there are approximately 1,044,209 Guatemalans living in the United States, with the largest community residing in Los Angeles. However, these statistics are unrepresentative since many undocumented Guatemalans did not fill out census forms, nor were Mayas provided with an ethnic or linguistic category. Maya studies scholars' analysis of the 2010 census statistics state that there are approximately 500,000 Mayas living and working in the United States (Jiménez Mayo 2010; Brown and Odem 2011). An examination of this data suggests that Los Angeles has the largest Guatemalan Maya population outside of their place of origin. The U.S. census's representation of Guatemalans as a homogenous national group erases the existence, contributions, and experiences of Mayas in the United States. In the framework of official counting, and miscounting, the Maya diaspora is marked as illegible and consequently, invisible.

These official discourses and practices of legibility and erasure signal the varied forms of marginalization, criminalization, and disposability that Maya immigrants encounter in the United States. It is in this context of sociopolitical invisibility that Maya immigrants affirm their culture, memory, and knowledge as they navigate within a hostile national environment that needs their labor but rejects their presence. In this chapter, I examine the ways Mayas create a sense of community and place through the construction of a weekend *mercado* on the public sidewalks of the Westlake/MacArthur Park neighborhood where they reside.[1] The informal Maya market in this part of Los Angeles serves as an important survival strategy in a racialized city with growing social inequalities. It is in their performance of market relations that vendors and customers transmit the embodied cultural memory and practices of Mesoamerican mercados.[2] Collectively, vendors as well as their customers and members of the community visually reproduce social mercado relations and networks customary in Guatemala. Thus, the public performativity and reproduction of mercado dynamics function as an important survival strategy as well as "means of remembering and transmitting [embodied] social [and cultural] memory" (Taylor 2003, 209). As performance studies scholar Diana Taylor emphasizes, these embodied practices have historically been fundamental for indigenous peoples as a way of transmitting "communal memories, histories and values from one group/generation to the next" (193). Hence, the weekend mercado in the Westlake/MacArthur Park community continues these practices and survival strategies as the Maya vendors and customers transmit, perform, and reenact their cultural embodied knowledge to multiple generations in Los Angeles.

Following Stuart Hall's scholarship on diaspora, I situate Maya immigrants in Westlake/MacArthur Park in a continuous process of change and transformation (Hall 1997, 209). Therefore, I argue that Maya diasporic identity be understood as constructed, reconstructed, performed, and articulated through various cultural, economic, and symbolic exchanges and movements that occur between the immigrants' place of origin (Guatemala) and their new residence, one of which is Los Angeles. Many of these exchanges and movements often take place within unequal power relations. Geography theorist Doreen Massey's notion of "power-geometry" is useful when considering the connections between power relations and diasporic identities since she highlights that diaspora is not just about "who moves and who does not although that is an important element of it; it is also about power in relation to the flows and movements" (1993b, 61). For this reason, groups and individuals experience social and geographical movements differently (61). She stresses that because of these unequal power relations "space is by its very nature full of power and symbolism, a complex web of relations of domination and subordination of solidarity and co-operation" (Massey 1993a, 156). I employ Massey's framework to suggest that the mercado created by Mayas in Los Angeles is an essential space for this community since it produces the possibilities for solidarity and what she calls "co-operations." Similarly, the recreation of this informal mercado must be understood as existing within violent forms of marginalization, domination, and erasure espoused by city officials and nonindigenous community members. Moreover, it is important to recognize that often Latina/os replicate in their relations with indigenous immigrants' national imaginaries that maintain racist ideologies. Consequently, Maya immigrants experience double forms of marginalization from within dominant U.S. society as well as nonindigenous U.S. Central Americans and Latina/os that reside in the area.[3]

In addition to Hall and Massey's scholarship, I engage and expand work on the Maya diaspora (Hamilton and Stoltz Chinchilla 2001; LeBaron 2012; Loucky and Moors 2000; Popkin 1999, 2005) and street vendors in Los Angeles (Hamilton and Stoltz Chinchilla 1996; Bhimji 2010; Rosales 2013). Most of the studies on the Maya diaspora in Los Angeles have concentrated on the reasons for migration as well as the creation of hometown associations, patron saint festivities, and religious organizations. Less scholarship has focused on community formation through the creation of a historical memory (Estrada 2013) as well as the experiences of the 1.5 and second generation (Boj Lopez in this volume; Batz 2014). Additionally, studies on street vendors in the city have mainly emphasized the gendering of this labor practice, its conditions, and the strategies employed by the mostly Central American and Mexican workers. I engage and expand on both areas of study by examining the ways the Maya mercado in Los Angeles becomes an essential cultural and economic survival strategy for that neighborhood. Furthermore, I note that the Maya mercado serves to create a sense of community through the public affirmation of shared cultural practices and memories. In doing so, the weekend public market emphasizes community relations between generations as well as other Maya linguistic groups, like K'iche', Kaqchikel, and Q'anjob'al speakers.

During the last two decades, I have conducted informal interviews with vendors and residents in Westlake/MacArthur Park. The data used for this chapter are based on ongoing participant observations in Maya organizations as well as research in the community that started in the early 1990s. These ongoing observations and participations stem from my own personal connection to the area. I grew up and lived on Westlake and Sixth Street between 1981 and 1994. Though I no longer reside in the neighborhood I regularly participate in Maya organizations and events.[4] An examination of the ways Mayas publicly recreate community in this part of the city is important given the rise of specifically Maya, and broadly indigenous, immigrations to the United States and, particularly, to

Los Angeles. Thus, an analysis on Maya community dynamics in this historically multigenerational, working-class U.S. Central American neighborhood also expands scholarship on U.S. Central American communities and identities.

I begin by briefly contextualizing and examining Westlake/MacArthur Park as an area in the city that is often referred to as "Little Central America" by scholars, U.S. Central American activists, and city officials since this neighborhood has been an initial site of residence for many Central American immigrants starting in the late 1970s. Secondly, I note that while some of the ladino[5] Central American community dynamics still remain today, during the past two decades Maya immigrants have altered or Mayanized the space. I argue that this is particularly visible through the affirmation of specific Maya cultural and linguistic practices that challenge the national identities articulated by non-indigenous U.S. Central Americans. The reproduction of these Maya cultural practices via the weekend mercado as well as the businesses owned and operated by Mayas not only serve as an essential survival strategy but also create a sense of community and place. Lastly, I argue that unequal power relations between the Maya vendors, residents, and city officials also mark the space reproduced on the streets of Westlake/MacArthur Park. The mercado, therefore, must be understood as taking place within a racialized city, where public areas are envisioned in a particular order that emphasizes and legitimizes national (racialized) conceptualizations of space. Often these community-building efforts by Mayas in Los Angeles take place under and within varied forms of inhumane conditions—like substandard housing, exploitation, exclusion, and criminalization—experienced daily by undocumented indigenous immigrants.

CENTRAL AMERICANIZING LOS ANGELES

Westlake/MacArthur Park is a residential and commercial area approximately two miles west of downtown Los Angeles. Nora Hamilton and Norma Stoltz Chinchilla note that by the late 1970s the area was transformed by Central Americans, particularly Guatemalan, Salvadoran, and Honduran businesses, through the establishment of restaurants, markets, bakeries, and *pupusa* stands[6] (Hamilton and Stoltz Chinchilla 2001, 59). These spaces provided recently arrived Central American immigrants familiar foods and needed resources like travel agencies, express couriers, and newspapers as well as news bulletins that maintained connections to the homeland for immigrants fleeing civil wars and state repression. During this time MacArthur Park started to serve as an important meeting space for rallies against human right abuses in Guatemala, El Salvador, and Honduras as well as calls to end U.S. military aid in those countries. At the same time, Hamilton and Stoltz Chinchilla remind us that by "the early 1970s [Westlake/MacArthur Park] had become a transient neighborhood," initially for Mexican and later Central American immigrants, since the living conditions in the area were substandard and consequently, rent was cheaper (2001, 59). This is because many of the apartment buildings were built in the early 1900s in an era when the neighborhood was conceived as one of the most desirable residential areas in the city. By the mid-1950s when the predominately white middle-class residents left the neighborhood, the abandoned apartment buildings were occupied by Mexican immigrants.

Most Maya immigrants started to arrive to Westlake/MacArthur Park in the 1990s and occupied the same buildings with little to no renovations.[7] Between the years 1990 and 2000, a series of fires engulfed several apartment buildings in the area because the owners did not meet required fire safety codes and the city failed to enforce these regulations in the neighborhood. Regarded by fire department officials and the *Los Angeles Times* as one of the worst fires in Los Angeles history, the 330 Burlington Avenue fire on May 5, 1993, killed eleven Guatemalan and Mexican immigrants and two fetuses as well as injuring over forty residents.[8] The fire and others that followed exposed the substandard and hazardous housing conditions in which many undocumented Central American and Mexican immigrants are forced to live. During the 1990s there were several legal cases convicting landlords in the Westlake district for the slum conditions of the apartments they own. In 1990, a jury convicted landlord Devanand Sharma of twenty-three slum charges for his 737 South Westlake Avenue apartment building.[9] By 2010 the U.S. census estimated that the neighborhood continued to be densely populated. It is the second-densest neighborhood in Los Angeles. This area of the city is made up of 94.9 percent renters and only 5.1 percent homeowners. The median age of residents in the area is twenty-seven years and the median annual household income is $26,757, which is one of the lowest in the city.[10] These statics show that the Westlake district continues to be one of the most disenfranchised communities in Los Angeles. They reaffirm American studies scholar Laura Barraclough's claim that "racialized economic divisions are literally mapped onto social space in Los Angeles, which was more segregated between whites and non-whites in 2000 than 1940" (2008, 172).

The dilapidated buildings in the Westlake district continue to visually mark the substandard living conditions of young Maya immigrants, families, and children. Their living spaces tend to be crammed since it is not unusual for four to seven people to share a one-bedroom apartment as a way of reducing living expenses. In these crammed apartments there is often no space for privacy. The Maya immigrants' living conditions demonstrate that their citizenship status and precarious economic situation restricts their movement and contact with other parts of the city. As Doreen Massey stresses, understanding these power relations in the movements of people as well as the place given to different social groups in migratory flows allows for us to also recognize that mobility is impacted by ethnicity, gender, and socioeconomic conditions (1993a, 1993b). The limited mobility experienced by undocumented Maya immigrants in Los Angeles highlights the ways in which anti-immigration laws, labor exploitation, and historical racial segregation have carved substandard living spaces in the city for poor undocumented immigrants and ethnic communities. It also illustrates how sociopolitical ideas that maintain ethnic, gender, and class hierarchies have historically been encoded in the city's topography.

Confronted with a precarious social position in a racially segregated city and country, Maya immigrants employ varied forms of cultural and economic survival strategies. Through my engagement in collaborative work with Maya immigrants in the area, as well as accounts by residents in the community, I have observed that there are several apartment buildings housing members of specific Maya Guatemalan hometowns and linguistic regions. For example, one of the buildings mainly houses Mayas from Huehuetenango, while in another building the majority of the tenants are from northern El Quiché, Guatemala. The makeup of these apartment buildings illustrates the multifaceted aspects of transnational community networks that include employment opportunities as well as housing and social relations (Menjívar 2002). They also demonstrate another coping mechanism employed by Mayas as a way to survive the increased hostility and criminalization they experience daily as undocumented indigenous immigrants. By populating the apartment buildings with members of their hometowns or linguistic regions, the Maya tenants transpose elements of their community's social connections and relations. For instance, the proximity to members of the same hometown and linguistic region can allow for the creation of supportive spaces during difficult personal, familial, and community challenges. This is particularly evident during the death of a family member in the United States or Guatemala, loss of employment, and illness. On several occasions, I have observed Maya residents in the mentioned apartment build-ings gather to raise funds for funerals. Another moment of communal social relations takes place through the sharing of food when there is a birth. And while these types of collaborative dynamics take place in some apartment build-ings and not others, the sounds of marimba music and Maya languages are audible in several of the buildings housing Mayas and nonindigenous Latina/o immigrants in the area. Similarly, the creation of the public weekend mercado in the neighborhood asserts other forms of cultural and economic survival strat-egies used by Maya immigrants in a city that continuously segregates, criminal-izes, and erases their existence.

THE MAYANIZATION OF WESTLAKE/MACARTHUR PARK

Through my work with Maya organizations in Westlake/MacArthur Park, I have observed that most Maya immigrants living in the area are young men, some leaving wives and children, many leaving parents, siblings, and grandpar-ents behind. In informal and formal conversations, these young Maya immi-grants have noted that the survival of their families in Guatemala depends on the remittances they send periodically. Similarly, I have noticed an increased number of Maya women immigrants. This is particularly evident at the weekend mercado on Sixth Street, where Maya women wearing *traje* sell and consume regional food like tamales and *atoles*.[11] Consequently, in the past two decades there have been more families with children born in the United States visible in the area. This presence is evident as the families publicly interact in the mercado created by the vast number of Maya vendors on Sixth Street.

While street vending exists throughout several immigrant and working-class ethnic communities in Los Angeles, what makes the public vending on Sixth Street a form of Maya mercado is the spatial (re)organization as well as the participation of numerous Maya vendors in that particular place and on those specific days and time. The layout and presence of Maya vendors on Sixth Street differ from other neighborhoods in the city where street vending is vis-ible. Outside of Sixth Street there are mainly food vendors, and their presence does not reproduce a central location for Mayas. In this way, anthropologist Walter Little's analysis of Guatemalan street vendors in Antigua is useful since he highlights that "interaction of people and place allows not only for the social construction of place, but also for the social construction of identity" (2004, 6).

Likewise, the Sixth Street Maya mercado aids in constructing a sense of community in Los Angeles through the recreation of an essential site for social interaction, which fortifies informal social networks. Moreover, the public space where the mercado is located allows for visual forms of cultural affirmation to take place. This is particularly illustrated through culturally marked textiles that are worn and sold, the languages spoken, and the food cooked and consumed on the neighborhood's public sidewalks. Thus, the Maya cultural practices performed in the mercado simultaneously engage and are in tune with a variety of sensory elements like sound, smell, and vision, which enable a reinscription of that public space's symbolic meaning.

The social mercado practices on Sixth Street assert a public Maya identity since, as Little highlights, for some Maya vendors in Guatemala "being Maya is living, working, socializing, and worshipping in a particular place with others mutually identified as part of the same socio-cultural group. To not be intimately involved in that place with other people is not only 'sad' according to Maya vendors, it threatens to undermine one's identity and sense of self" (2004, 6). While Mayas in Los Angeles are not living, working, socializing, and worshiping in their ancestral lands, the space recreated through the mercado as well as the surrounding businesses owned and operated by Mayas (restaurants, couriers, indoor swap-meet stores) reconstruct a familiar and intimate space. In doing so, the Mayanization of the area opens possibilities for other forms of community empowerment like the creation of more formal networks and organizations. Though the majority of street vendors on these four city blocks are Mayas, there are also ladino and non-Guatemalan vendors who participate in that space. The heterogeneity of the mercado space "provides a context in which interethnic relationships can take place" (Little 2004, 101). Hence, the construction of this space opens possibilities for varied forms of solidarity that may be informal, like notifying each other when Los Angeles Police Department (LAPD) officers are ticketing, or more formal modes of solidarity visible in the participation of some vendors with the Asociación de Vendedores Ambulantes en Los Angeles (Los Angeles's Street Vendors Association) and their efforts to legalize street vending in the city.

In this context, the weekend mercado created on Sixth Street allows Maya residents of different generations and linguistic communities a space to connect as well as have access to a variety of goods that would otherwise be difficult to obtain because of their low income, limited Spanish- and English-language skills, and undocumented status. These products include work tools, home appliances, clothing, and shoes as well as home-cooked meals, bread from the Guatemalan highlands, Mesoamerican produce, and CDs and DVDs in Spanish and Maya languages. Familiar medicine like muscle rubs, creams for cuts and bruises, and cold remedies are sold in individual pill packages much like in Guatemalan stores and unlike the box of twelve or twenty-four pills sold in U.S. pharmacies. This economic exchange not only helps maintain cultural practices through the products sold and consumed but also addresses immediate survival needs like access to medicine that would otherwise be costly or inaccessible to undocumented Maya immigrants. Sociologist Cecilia Menjívar notes that "due to their inaccessibility to formal health care (because of an undocumented status or low-paying jobs offering no health benefits—as well as language barriers, cultural differences in the interpretation of illnesses, or lack of knowledge of the formal system)," when facing an illness, Guatemalan immigrants living in the sociopolitical contexts described will "assemble something akin to a 'package' of biomedical treatments and 'traditional' medicines" (2002, 441). Thus, the Maya mercado constructs a physical space from which to access these forms of healing practices that are necessary to survive in a country that has severely "constrained legal and financial opportunities" for undocumented immigrants (441).[12] In addition to the selling and purchase of familiar medicines, regional bread like wheat *cemitas* from El Quiché and large *xecas* made in Quetzaltenango are also brought from Guatemala and sold on the Sixth Street market days.[13] Spices like *achiote* (annatto paste used in sauces) and India Quiché sodas are also sold. Mayas with U.S. residency or citizenship that are able to travel back and forth bring the products directly from Guatemala. As I have observed, a similar strategy is employed in small highland communities, where primarily men travel to Guatemala City and bring back products to sell in the local markets.

Since most of the Maya residents in this neighborhood are undocumented, their mobility and participation in the U.S. formal economy is limited. Thus, the money vendors earn from sales in the mercado occasionally functions as supplemental income and too often as a primary source of economic survival. For day laborers that work in construction and are unable to find employment in the fall and winter as a result of weather conditions, the sales in the mercado serve as a short-term economic survival strategy. Other vendors, like women with children, depend on the sales as a primary income. The majority of vendors use the money from their sales to provide basic necessities such as food, housing, and education for families in the United States as well as Guatemala. In this way, the Sixth Street mercado is also economically important because the vendors participate and contribute to both local and transnational (in)formal economies. This is particularly illustrated through the goods brought back from Guatemala that are sold and consumed in Los Angeles. As Hamilton and Stoltz Chinchilla note, "street vending responds to a need among a relatively low income segment of the population in a declining economy by providing food, clothing, household items, and other items at a reduced price" (1996, 31). Additionally, the vendors provide these items in their own neighborhood as a response to their limited mobility throughout the city because of their undocumented status as well as their minimal English- and Spanish-language skills.

For many outsiders, particularly city officials, walking through Sixth Street on a late weekend afternoon the sidewalks may appear disorganized, cluttered, chaotic, and even dirty. This spatial conceptualization diverges from the ways space is packaged, ordered, and enclosed in U.S. supermarkets, farmers' markets, and department stores. The space recreated on Sixth Street reproduces visual and audible characteristics of mercados in Central America. In his scholarship on marketplaces in Costa Rica, Miles Richardson notes that open public Mesoamerican markets tend to be vibrant, bustling, and loud (1982, 425). He further explains that these markets are filled with a variety of colors and smells from the products sold and consumed (425). For Little, mercados in Guatemala "are common arenas for . . . social interactions" (2004, 99). He highlights that for Maya communities these public spaces aid in the creation of "meaningful social and economic relations" (99). Little also argues that they produce "a neutral locale where families can meet and exchange news. Here persons meet their future spouses" (100). Similarly, the frequent interactions in the mercado on Sixth Street between vendors, customers, and members of the community allows for the reproduction of these types of relations to take place in Los Angeles. A closer analysis of the layout on Sixth Street or *la sexta*, as Mayas in Los Angeles refer to the street, referencing a similar area in Guatemala City, illustrates its own organization and dynamics much like mercados in Guatemala.[14]

On *la sexta*, there are specific spaces on the sidewalk and side streets allocated for the products sold. Food is often on the side streets. In the spaces of food and produce the majority of those selling are women, who more frequently wear regional textiles. The type of food sold by Maya women blurs the lines between private and public spaces since the food is often cooked in the private home space of the vendor. This traditional Maya food vended as well as the ways in which it is prepared and presented maintains a sense of "home cooking" from the "homeland" that is sold and consumed in the neighborhood's public city streets. The participation of men is also visible in the food sites of female vendors. In these spaces, where food and produce are sold and consumed, men regularly perform supportive roles. This is similar to market relations in Guatemala, where Little observed, "few women were without male assistants. Some Kaqchikel couples, four to be specific, are almost equal partners, but even in these cases the women decided what was to be purchased from the middlepersons" (2004, 147). In Los Angeles, many of the men who perform these supportive roles are also responsible for carrying *bultos* (containers) of food, produce, and products sold on the mercado days. Moreover, men often assist in setting up and taking down the crates used at the vending site as well as collecting money from costumers. Maya women vendors in Los Angeles are usually in charge of deciding what meals will be cooked and sold. Unlike Guatemala, in some food-vending sites in Los Angeles both men and women serve the food. Similarly, women and men at the vending locations socialize with regulars that stand around the site to eat tamales or drink *atoles*. Fewer male vendors cook in the food section. These male vendors often sell traditional street food as opposed to the home-style meals vended by women. Some of these more traditional street foods are hot dogs and *garnachas* (small fried tortillas topped with meat, shredded cabbage, and tomato sauce) usually sold in Guatemalan community *ferias* (fairs) during patron saint festivities.

In addition to cooked meals, fresh produce native to the Mesoamerican region like *chipilín*, *yerba mora*, *loroco*, and *chilacayote* are also sold.[15] Most of these items are not readily available or perhaps are more expensive in U.S. Central American and Mexican markets. While selling and consuming native Mesoamerican produce has taken place in the area since the 1980s, how these products are sold and consumed has changed in the past three decades. In the '80s, Central American vendors sold exported items already packaged, like frozen green mangos, pickled chilies, and *loroco*, but today on Sixth Street the Maya vendors sell them fresh. When asked where they find the produce, women vendors said they grow them in rented lots around Los Angeles or in Maya homes around the city with backyards.[16] Sociologist Pierrette Hondagneu-Sotelo notes that these urban community gardens are "a pocket-sized oasis of trees, flowers, and Mesoamerican vegetables and herbs growing in an otherwise very cemented part of inner-city Los Angeles" (2014, 88). Moreover, the act of harvesting Mesoamerican greens, vegetables, and fruits reinscribes ancestral practices found in ancient Maya ways of knowing. These locally grown produce, just as is done in highland Guatemalan markets, are taken by the Maya growers to the Sixth Street mercado and sold mostly to members of the community.

On the main streets, the vendors sell electronics, used clothing, appliances, CDs, and DVDs. This physical reformulation of public space illustrates a reproduction of Maya social and cultural dynamics, where the mercados serve not only for economic exchanges but also social connections and relations. Yet, in Los Angeles these social dynamics and informal economic activities take place within a racialized, segregated city that criminalizes these informal labor and social practices. As several scholars have noted, Los Angeles has one of the most aggressive anti-vending ordinances in the United States (Hamilton and Stoltz Chinchilla 2001; Rosales 2013). Thus, the mercado highlights not only the visual presence of Maya vendors and residents in the city landscape but also the marginality of their existence. At the same time, the Maya immigrants' precarious position is often further reinforced by locals gangs that harass and demand payment for protection and/or permission to sell in the neighborhood's public sidewalks (Hamilton and Stoltz Chinchilla 2001).

It is from within this marginal space that Maya cultural practices and dynamics are transposed, performed, and transformed in the Los Angeles mercado. For instance, unlike Guatemalan marketplaces, around the Sixth Street mercado city light posts function as community boards with flyers addressing a variety of issues and needs, like someone searching for a person willing to "share the living room in an apartment." Flyers also advertise other services, such as a private automobile or taxi for undocumented immigrants who cannot obtain a driver's license or are unable to take a flight to any other state. These flyers are often handwritten and at times illustrate the author's limited grammatical skills. Many assure those calling that the car, which will taxi them to other parts of the city or country, is secure. Some of these "private taxis" provide transportation services anywhere in the United States and specifically to cities and states where Mayas have already created communities. The state of New York is often written in Spanish as Nueva York. North and South Carolina are simply "Carolinas." More than the type of services provided, the flyers illustrate that although anti-immigration laws, precarious economic conditions, and local policing of immigrants limit their contact with other parts of the city and country, these policies are not able to fully determine the movement of people since some of the boundaries are subverted. In another flyer placed on the same light post, there is a request for participants to wear black as they march against police brutality, while another offers babysitting services. These city light posts in the four blocks where the mercado takes place become a space for a variety of "co-operations," as Massey reminds us, that help establish formal and informal networks for Mayas living in that neighborhood (1993b).

In addition to the mercado, in the past decade approximately six new restaurants offering variations of Guatemalan regional food have opened in those four city blocks, replacing Mexican, Chinese, and Salvadoran restaurants, or at times adding regional Guatemalan food to those existing places.[17] The restaurant Punto Chapin (the name already suggests a space of contact for Guatemalans) replaced a former Chinese catery. Next to this restaurant is Mazat Express, which delivers packages to small communities in the highlands. The name of the business uses the K'iche' word *mazat* (deer). In doing so, the sign, like the residents of Westlake/MacArthur Park that use Maya languages in their public social interactions with others in the community, visually inscribes Maya linguistic practices and culture onto the Los Angeles city landscape.

Other businesses owned and operated by Mayas are located in three indoor swap meets in the area. Tienda Tipica is precisely what the name suggests, a "typical" small store like those found in different communities in Guatemala. In this typical store folks stop to buy Maya Guatemalan products and chat with the owners as well as exchange a variety of information that includes afterschool and educational programs in local schools, as a flyer posted below the tienda's name sign illustrates. The store sells a variety of items, from textiles and shoes used in the highlands to snacks, music DVDs in Maya languages, and soft drinks.

The selling and use of textiles, like Maya languages, is an essential visual marker of Maya culture and identity. At Tienda Tipica a young customer told me, "When ladinos walk by and see the *cortes*, they make negative comments. You know, like they don't understand why we continue to wear *corte* in Los Angeles." Her statement illustrates the ways wearing Maya regional textiles challenges not only U.S. but also ladino U.S. Central American and nonindigenous Latina/o assimilation processes and ethnocultural marginalizations. This is evident in the ways that public use of Maya regional clothing also functions as a "lesson [to the world] of [Maya] active cultural resistance. Thus, Maya *traje* also provides the world a [cultural] text to be read" (Otzoy 1996, 27). At the same time, Maya scholar Irma Otzoy argues that textiles speak "of the Maya as a people, of their roots, of their lives, and of their causes" (1996, 149). In this way, stores like Tienda Tipica as well as their customers continuously participate in an active act of cultural resistance both in Guatemala and the United States. And though Tienda Tipica was the first store in this indoor swap meet to sell Maya *cortes* and *huipiles*, in the past decade several other stores have opened in the vicinity. These new businesses not only illustrate that there is a market for

FIGURE 7.1. Sixth Street *mercado*. Photo by Manuel Felipe Pérez.

Maya women's textiles in the area but also visibly transpose Maya cultural texts, through selling and wearing textiles, onto the city's topography.

The three indoor swap meets on Sixth Street also provide other services: barbershops, internet cafes, cell phones, calling cards, money orders, and exchange rates. Additionally, one store functions as a photo and print shop where images of Maya women and children wearing regional clothing are often superimposed onto a background of the downtown Los Angeles skyline. These images literally carve a space in the city for the Maya community. They symbolically illustrate the efforts by members of the Maya diaspora to affirm their culture even as state-sponsored policies like police crackdowns of vendors and vast deportations attempt to erase their presence. The photos with the city skyline also express defiance to the state's erasure of the Maya immigrants' existence. Similarly, the photos assert the Maya immigrants' place and belonging in the cityscape.

It is important to note, however, that unlike Maya nonprofit organizations in the neighborhood or spaces like the Los Angeles radio program *Contacto Ancestral*, which clearly claim a politicized Maya identity, the dynamics that take place during the weekend mercado and in the surrounding businesses are not overtly affirming a Maya identity that is tied to larger pan-indigenous movements (Estrada 2013). Yet, the mercado dynamics do demonstrate varied forms of Maya cultural embodied knowledge, which serves as an important element in community survival and construction. These embodied cultural practices illustrate immediate modes of daily survival that become particularly pressing given that Mayas in the United States continue to be denied what Hannah Arendt calls their "rights to have rights" (1973, 296). That is, Mayas are not only subjected to state and transnational laws that criminalize and erase their existence, they are "denied both the political legitimacy and moral credibility necessary to question them" (Cacho 2012, 6). This is evident in the literal and metaphorical disposability of Mayas, who have been largely impacted by mass deportations during the George W. Bush and Barack Obama administrations.[18] In this way, the mercado on Sixth Street in the Westlake/MacArthur Park neighborhood demonstrates an informal response to these forms of structural violence and dehumanization.

MAPPING NEW ROUTES

The diverse forms of social, economic, and cultural exchanges that take place in the weekend mercado illustrate the multiple ways in which Mayas in this part of Los Angeles transmit, learn, and affirm their embodied cultural knowledge and memory. However, the efforts by Maya immigrants to (re)claim the public city sidewalks on Sixth Street need to be understood as taking place within a contested space where the vendors redefine the public streets and attempt to defy city cultural and legal regulations. These contestations occur within unequal power relations in which the Maya vendors, many undocumented, risk not only getting a ticket and having their merchandise and work tools confiscated but also experiencing jail time or deportation. Yet, the weekend mercado, coupled with the Maya residents in the surrounding apartment buildings, indoor swap-meet stores, and restaurants on Sixth Street, shows the ways Mayas attempt to survive in a city that severely marginalizes and limits their mobility. They illustrate the varied creative ways in which Mayas survive by asserting and maintaining their ethnic identity. The reconceptualization of those four city blocks provides a public space for multiple generations, Maya linguistic communities, religious denominations, and hometowns to meet and (re)connect within familiar cultural contexts and dynamics.

Thus, the remapping of this public space opens possibilities for informal and formal collaborations between members of the community and creates the potential for constructing cross-ethnic solidarities. It is in this type of public space, for example, where often men and women meet and exchange information that might help heal a physical, emotional, material, or community problem. This becomes an essential tool of daily survival since it is through some of these informal exchanges that many are able to live and work in a city and country that continuously criminalizes, dehumanizes, and erases their presence. For instance, the criminalization and disposability of Maya immigrants in Westlake/MacArthur Park was particularly evident in the shooting of the Maya-K'iche' day laborer Manuel Jaminez Xum by LAPD officer Frank Hernández. His murder in this predominately working-class Maya community was not the first. Yet, it was the first to receive local media attention as a result of rallies created by community members, organizations, and immigrant rights groups that protested for days demanding justice. Hence, the Maya residents' construction of alternative social spaces like the informal mercado on Sixth Street aid in community-building efforts that can potentially rally people together to demand their "rights to have rights." At the same time, these varied spatial practices by Maya immigrants collectively affirm their place in a city and nation that attempts to erase their existence.

NOTES

1. In Guatemala and in the diaspora, those who identify as Maya assert a politicized identity by taking part in a historically grounded and socially constructed collectivity that is tied to common indigenous ancestors, history, and culture (Bastos and Camus 2003; Fischer and McKenna Brown 1996).

2. Daily, open, and public mercados date back to the pre-Hispanic period in countries with large indigenous populations like Guatemala, Mexico, Bolivia, Peru, and Ecuador (Dahlin et al. 2007; Chase and Chase 2014). These mercados are built and dismantled on the same day in a similar way to what archaeologists suggest took place during the pre-Hispanic period. Today,

Latin American mercados provide for local residents a variety of products that include fresh food, produce, work tools, clothing, toys, and household items, among other goods.

3. See, for example, my articles "*Ka Tzij:* The Maya Diasporic Voices from *Contacto Ancestral*" (2013) in *Latino Studies Journal* as well as "*Latinidad* and the Maya Diaspora in the United States" (2015) in *Latinos and Latinas: Risks and Opportunities*. Also, see Alan LeBaron's "When Latinos Are Not Latinos: The Case of Guatemalan Maya in the United States, the Southeast and Georgia" (2012) in *Latino Studies Journal*.

4. There are numerous Maya hometown associations in the area, like those from San Pedro Soloma, Santa Eulalia, San Juan Barillas, among countless others. These hometown organizations have a variety of gatherings, including large *fiestas patronales* (patron saint festivities.) From 2009 to 2012, Pastoral Maya also held summer Maya-language classes in the area. I've attended other informal community events as well as community meetings and gatherings that address a variety of pressing issues like the shooting of Manuel Jaminez Xum by LAPD officer Frank Hernández and the death of community members as a result of illness, work injuries, suicide, and drug abuse.

5. Since the colonial period in Guatemala, the term *ladino* has referred to a variety of indigenous and mestizo subject positions. Today, ladino identitty is often understood as the negation of indigenous identity (Guzmán Böckler and Herbert 2002; Martínez Peláez 2009). Anthropologist Charles R. Hale also explains that "people who identify as ladino generally have absorbed an ideology of racial superiority in relation to Indians: viewing themselves as closer to an ideal of progress, decency, and all things modern, in contrast to Indians, who are regrettably and almost irredeemably backward." (2006, 4). Hale notes that ladinos reject racism but at the same time maintain and desire racial privileges (2006, 19).

6. *Pupusas* are handmade corn tortillas that are filled with any, or a blend, of the following: cheese, refried beans, pork meat, and other types of native produce from Mesoamerica. Often *loroco*, a Mesoamerican vine with edible buds and flowers, is used in pupusas.

7. James Loucky and Marilyn Moors (2000) remind us that by the late 1970s there were Maya residents living in the Westlake/MacArthur Park neighborhood.

8. See the following *Los Angeles Times* news briefs: "Fatal Fires," http://articles .latimes.com/1993-05-05/news/mn-31541_1_house-fires; and "Two Members of 18th Street Gang Charged with 10 Murders," http://articles.latimes.com/ 1998/nov/26/local/me-47932.

9. See the *Los Angeles Times*'s local news brief "Landlord Convicted of 23 Slum Charges," June 27, 1990, http://articles.latimes.com/1990-06-27/local/me-458_1_slum-conditions.

10. See http://maps.latimes.com/neighborhoods/neighborhood/westlake/.

11. In Guatemala, *traje* refers to the regional Maya weavings worn by women and men. Women wear blouses called *huipiles*, skirts called *cortes*, and a cloth belt referred to as a *faja*. *Atoles*, from the Nahuatl *atolli*, are hot drinks usually made from cornmeal.

12. Ester E. Hernández reminded me that these packages of "biomedical treatments and traditional medicines" are practices that are also criminalized since the police often conduct stings to capture people selling unauthorized medications.

13. *Cemitas* are Guatemalan sweet bread. *Xecas* are also sweet but made from anise and wheat flour.

14. Sixth Avenue, or *la sexta*, in Guatemala City is located at the heart of the Centro Histórico (Historical Center). The area is full of commercial activity that includes a variety of shops and restaurants. In addition, all around *la sexta* street vendors sell food and a variety of products that range from clothing items and toys to calling cards and herbal medicines.

15. The vegetables listed are native to the Central American region and Southern Mexico. *Chipilín* is a leafy vegetable. In Guatemala it is often used in tamales and soups. Like *chipilín*, *yerba mora* is a leafy vegetable but usually eaten in soups or sautéed. *Loroco* is a vine with edible flowers. In Guatemala and El Salvador it is often used as filling for *pupusas*. Guatemalans also use *loroco* in scrambled eggs. *Chilacayote* is a type of squash. Guatemalans use *chilacayote* as a sweet dessert and to make *refrescos/aguas frescas* (non-alcoholic sweet beverage).

16. On Central American and Maya urban community gardening in Los Angeles, please see Pierrette Hondagneu-Sotelos's "Paradise Transplanted: Paradise Lost?" (2014) in *Boom: A Journal of California* 4 (3): 86–94.

17. Hamilton and Stoltz Chinchilla note that in the 1980s there were a number of conflicts between formal businesses and restaurant owners with informal street vendors. These tensions continue to be visible among business owners and vendors in the area. More recently, business owners in the vicinity have participated in efforts to carve specific Latin American spaces in Los Angeles. The Guatemalan business owners have proposed what they call a "Guatemalan Mayan Village." This "Mayan Village" would be located between West Sixth

Street and Alvarado to South Lucas Avenue. According to *Los Angeles Times* journalist Esmeralda Bermudez the proposal suggests that local businesses would be "painted in vibrant colonial colors and a statue of Tecun Uman, the great Mayan ruler, will guard the entrances of the corridor." (See "Advocates Seek to Carve Out Official Latin American Areas in L.A.," http://articles .latimes.com/2014/apr/02/local/la-me-little-latin-america-20140403/2). The tensions between business owners and Maya vendors on Sixth Street are economic as well as conceptual.

18. Two of the largest immigration raids in U.S. history mainly impacted undocumented Maya workers. The New Bedford, Massachusetts, raid on March 6, 2007, at the Michael Bianco Inc. factory arrested about 300 workers. Approximately a year later, the Postville, Iowa, raid on May 12, 2008, at Agriprocessors Inc., which is considered the largest raid in U.S. history, detained 400 workers. Of those workers detained, 300 were convicted on fraud charges and 389 were placed on a fast-track deportation process, and of those in the deportation process 290 were Guatemalans. The majority of the Guatemalans were undocumented Mayas, including minors. While these ICE operations received wide media coverage, few noted that most of those detained and deported were mainly Guatemalan Mayas.

REFERENCES

Arendt, Hannah. 1973. *The Origins of Totalitarianism*. New York: Harcourt Brace Jovanovich.

Barraclough, Laura R. 2008. "South Central Farmers and Shadow Hills Homeowners: Land Use Policy and Relational Racialization in Los Angeles." *The Professional Geographer* 61 (2): 164–86.

Bastos, Santiago, and Manuela Camus. 2003. *Entre el mecapal y el cielo: Desarrollo del movimiento Maya en Guatemala*. Guatemala: FLACSO.

Batz, Giovanni. 2014. "Maya Cultural Resistance in Los Angeles: The Recovery of Identity and Culture Among Maya Youth." *Latin American Perspectives* 41 (3): 194–207.

Bermudez, Esmeralda. 2014. "Advocates Seek to Carve out Official Latin American Areas in L.A." *Los Angeles Times*, April 2. http://articles.latimes.com/2014/ apr/02/local/la-me-little-latin-america-20140403.

Bhimji, Fazila. 2010. "Struggles, Urban Citizenship, and Belonging: The Experience of Undocumented Street Vendors and Food Truck Owners in Los Angeles." *Urban Anthropology and Studies of Cultural Systems and World Economic Development* 39 (4): 455–92.

Brown, William, and May Odem. 2011. "Across Borders: Guatemala Maya Immigrants in the US South." *Southern Spaces: An Interdisciplinary Journal About Regions, Places, and Cultures of the US South and Their Global Connections.* February 16. http://southernspaces.org/2011/living-across-borders-guatemala-maya-immigrants-us-south#sthash.HrqXRsXb.dpuf.

Cacho, Lisa. 2012. *Social Death: Racialized Rightlessness and the Criminalization of the Unprotected.* New York: New York University Press.

Chase, Diane Z., and Arlen F. Chase. 2014. "Ancient Maya Markets and the Economic Integration of Caracol, Belize." *Ancient Mesoamerica* 25 (1): 239–50.

Dahlin, Bruce H., Christopher Jensen, Richard Terry, David R. Wright, and Timothy Beach. 2007. "In Search of an Ancient Maya Market." *Latin American Antiquity* 18 (4): 363–84.

Estrada, Alicia Ivonne. 2013. *"Ka tzij:* The Maya Diasporic Voices from *Contacto Ancestral." Latino Studies* 11 (2): 208–27.

———. 2015. *"Latinidad* and the Maya Diaspora in the United States." In *Latinos and Latinas at Risk: Issues in Education, Health, Community, and Justice,* edited by Gabriel Gutiérrez, 145–50. Santa Barbara, CA: Greenwood.

"Fatal Fires." 1993. *Los Angeles Times,* May 5. http://articles.latimes.com/1993-05-05/news/mn-31541_1_house-fires.

Fischer, Edward F., and R. McKenna Brown, eds. 1996. *Maya Cultural Activism in Guatemala.* Austin: University of Texas.

Guzmán Böckler, Carlos, and Jean-Loup Herbert. 2002. *Guatemala: Una Interpretación Histórico-Social.* Guatemala: Cholsamaj.

Hale, Charles R. 2006. *Más Que un Indio (More Than an Indian): Racial Ambivalence and Neoliberal Multiculturalism in Guatemala.* Santa Fe, NM: School of American Research Press.

Hall, Stuart. 1996. "New Cultures for Old." In *A Place in the World? Places, Cultures and Globalization,* edited by Jess Massey, Pat Jess, and Doreen Massey, 175–214. Oxford: Oxford University Press.

———. 1997. "Old and New Identities, Old and New Ethnicities." In *Culture, Globalization and the World System: Contemporary Conditions for the Representation of Identity,* edited by Anthony King, 41–68. Minneapolis: University of Minnesota Press.

Hamilton, Nora, and Norma Stoltz Chinchilla. 1996. "Negotiating Urban Space: Latina Workers in Domestic Work and Street Vending in Los Angeles." *Humboldt Journal of Social Relations* 22 (1): 25–35.

———. 2001. *Seeking Community in a Global City: Guatemalans and Salvadorans in Los Angeles.* Philadelphia: Temple University Press.

Hondagneu-Sotelo, Pierrette. 2014. "Paradise 'Transplanted: Paradise Lost?" *Boom: A Journal of California* 4 (3): 86–94.

Jiménez Mayo, Eduardo. 2010. "Maya USA: The Immigration Reform and Control Act of 1986 and its Impact on Guatemalan Maya in the United States." *International Journal of Critical Indigenous Studies* 3 (2): 29–44.

LeBaron, Alan. 2012. "When Latinos are Not Latinos: The Case of Guatemalan Maya in the United States, the Southeast and Georgia." *Latino Studies* 10 (1–2): 179–95.

Little, Walter. 2004. *Mayas in the Marketplace: Tourism, Globalization and Identity.* Austin: University of Texas Press.

Loucky, James, and Marilyn Moors, eds. 2000. *Maya Diaspora: Guatemalan Roots, New American Lives.* Philadelphia: Temple University Press.

Martínez Peláez, Severo. 2009. *La Patria Del Criollo: An Interpretation of Colonial Guatemala.* Durham, NC: Duke University Press.

Massey, Doreen. 1993a. "Politics and Space/Time." In *Place and the Politics of Identity*, edited by Steve Pile and Michael Keith, 139–59. London, New York: Routledge.

———. 1993b. "Power-Geometry and a Progressive Sense of Place." In *Mapping the Futures: Local, Cultures, Global Change*, edited by Jon Bird, Barry Curtis, Tim Putnam, Lisa Tickner, 60–70. London, New York: Routledge.

Menjívar, Cecilia. 2002. "The Ties that Heal: Guatemalan Immigrant Women's Networks and Medical Treatment." *International Migration Review* 36 (2): 437–66.

Otzoy, Irma. 1996. "Maya Clothing and Identity" In *Maya Cultural Activism in Guatemala*, edited by Edward F. Fischer and R. McKenna Brown, 141–55. Austin: University of Texas Press, Institute of Latin American Studies.

Popkin, Eric. 1999. "Guatemalan Mayan Migration to Los Angeles: Constructing Transnational Linkages in the Context of the Settlement Process." *Ethnic and Racial Studies* 22 (2): 267–89.

———. 2005. "The Emergence of Pan-Mayan Ethnicity in the Guatemalan Transnational Community Linking Santa Eulalia and Los Angeles." *Current Sociology* 53 (4): 675–706.

Richardson, Miles. 1982. "Being-in-the-Market versus Being-in-the Plaza: Material Culture and the Construction of Social Reality in Spanish America." *American Ethnologist* 9 (2): 421–36.

Rosales, Rocio. 2013. "Survival, Economic Mobility and Community Among Los Angeles Fruit Vendors." *Journal of Ethnic and Migration Studies* 39 (5): 697–717.

Taylor, Diana. 2003. *The Archive and the Repertoire: Performing Cultural Memory in the Americas.* Durham, NC: Duke University Press.

United States Census. 2010. "The Hispanic Population." http://www.census.gov/prod/cen2010/briefs/c2010br-04.pdf.

8

WEAVINGS THAT RUPTURE

The Possibility of Contesting Settler Colonialism
Through Cultural Retention Among the Maya Diaspora

FLORIDALMA BOJ LOPEZ

THE USE OF regional clothing by young second-generation Maya women in Los Angeles disrupts social and political hierarchies that exist around indigenous practices, beliefs, and people in Guatemala and the United States. In the diaspora, the use of this clothing—colloquially known as *traje*[1]—requires an intergenerational transmission of knowledge and the maintenance of a transnational practice rooted in Maya identity. The process of learning to wear Maya clothing and understanding its meaning and function in both home communities and within the diaspora allows for youth in particular to continue claiming and transforming traditions. While these transformations may be challenged, it is important to remember that changes are often a form of negotiating both their relationships to elders and their home country *and* the context of their lived experiences in Los Angeles. Referencing their own communities of origin, the use of Maya regional clothing creates the opportunity to recognize that the United States is also a place where multiple indigenous communities continue to struggle for survival and sovereignty. An investigation of how regional indigenous clothing functions socially helps us see that nation-bound understandings of Maya identity cannot encompass the cumulative experience produced by displacement since migration becomes an ongoing process as the structures, institutions, values, and meanings of the multiple local places we consider home become mobile. As Mayas form enclaves in places that are not their ancestral homes, Maya clothing becomes a critical and dynamic mechanism through which they can tap into longer historical trajectories of what it has meant to be Maya and to claim forms of being that also include the experience of migration in the twentieth and twenty-first century. It is necessary to acknowledge that Maya clothing as a practice of indigenous identity and spirituality does not exist in a vacuum and must be put in conversation with politics that already exist in the spaces to which Mayas migrate.

This chapter centralizes Maya women as the primary wearers of regional clothing to posit how it may be a teaching tool for young Maya women and men in the diaspora. I rely on formal interviews conducted with Maya youth in Los Angeles, participant observation at three annual conferences that bring various members of the Maya diaspora across the United States together, and attended community-specific celebrations organized by hometown associations in honor of the saint of each town.[2] The study is not meant to be comprehensive or representative of a homogeneous and singular Maya community. I could hardly assume the role of disinterested party, given that my personal experience as a Maya K'iche' informed both my methods and my analytical frameworks. This research is instead intended to represent one form of cultural analysis that could help us understand the reflexive, political importance of Maya clothing for youth. It is my explicit hope that it can help the conversation around Maya youth and cultural maintenance as people build on, agree with, or challenge the premises of this chapter.

GENDERED CLOTHING AND MAYA IDENTITY

Because Maya clothing is a visible marker of Maya identity, within the context of displacement and migration, it remains a terrain on which new identities and alliances are negotiated. In addition to how Maya clothing acts as a space of intergenerational meaning making, my interest in Maya clothing and the diaspora is rooted in the potential for alliances among Mayas and Native Americans. Maya migrants are often placed into larger Guatemalan and therefore Latina/o ethnic categories in the United States, preempting an otherwise apt analogy to Native American positionality. This casual lumping together within the Latina/o umbrella obscures the important differences that indigeneity makes for indigenous migrants from Latin America and a long-standing genealogy of hemispheric analysis through indigenous worldviews and histories that disrupts how national boundaries define indigenous experiences (Forbes 1994, 2001). In particular, this casual lumping conceals the racism that Maya migrants and other indigenous migrants face from Latinas/os who do not identify as indigenous. This form of racist discrimination that is informed by structures of inequality in the countries of origin are reinscribed and find new modes of expression in the diaspora. For example, Maya studies scholar Alicia Ivonne Estrada explains that some Mayas "noted that often non-indigenous immigrants used paternalistic and derogatory terms when interacting with Mayas, or other indigenous immigrants" (2013, 214). Giovanni Batz emphasizes the various strategies employed by Maya youth to maintain a sense of Maya identity in Los Angeles and acknowledges how discrimination from other Latinas/os plays a role in subverting Maya cultural practices (2014, 195). In particular, Alan LeBaron's (2012) and Hiller, Linstroth, and Vela's (2009) articles emphasize how conflicted Maya community members feel in regards to officially identifying as Latina/o or Native American and the implications for retaining a Maya identity. These articles critique the assumption that Maya are, or should be, labeled Latina/o. The articles mentioned also elide what it may mean for Mayas to disrupt categories and politics of indigeneity that are already in place in the United States.

Articulating how Mayas weave in, out, and through racial structures and political economies of multiple nations to produce notions of Maya identity that simultaneously inhabit multiple frames and spaces is crucial to the Maya diaspora. Closely reexamining the academic frameworks that are often taken for granted to think about the migrant Maya diasporic experience is crucial to generating an understanding that grapples more directly with indigenous cultural practices. For example, Lynn Stephen argues that Mixtec and Zapotec migrants should be understood through a transborder rather than transnational lens (2007, 6). According to her, a transnational lens often centers on the physical movement of people and goods between two nation-states (6). She proposes that we instead displace the national scale as a central unit of analysis and examine how migrants cross not only physical national borders but also boundaries of race, class, and gender in the process of migration (6). A transborder framework becomes less about a rigid frame and more an open-ended investigation of how Maya youth engage and position themselves within multiple, at times overlapping or contradictory, ethnoracial hierarchies.

In order to understand how young Mayas in Los Angeles, California, engage with the use and meaning of Maya clothing, it is important to begin with an overview of why the clothing is a critical expression of identity, history, and spirituality within Guatemala. Maya clothing in particular has served multiple functions in Guatemalan history and has often marked Maya women as outside, yet central to, the formation of the nation-state. According to Irma Otzoy (1996) and Greg Grandin (2000), Maya men were forced to discontinue the use of regional clothing in order to enter mainstream institutions of politics, government, education, and the economy. Grandin, who writes about Quetzaltenango specifically, argues that the historical production of Maya clothing as a feminine cultural practice was essential to allowing K'iche' patriarchs to participate in public positions while maintaining their ethnic identity (2000, 6). This means that while Maya women were left out of popular and mainstream understandings of what it meant to be Guatemalan, their exclusion was also the foundation for ladino[3] and K'iche' elite men to also lay claim to the masculine national subject. The gendering of this cultural practice is especially significant because, unlike other cultural markers, it literally imprints ethnic identity on the body, making it highly visible as gendered Other.

In the contemporary moment, discrimination against Maya women has persisted in Guatemala. However, the use of Maya *clothing* remains a political praxis founded on Maya worldviews. Maya scholar and activist Irma Alicia Velásquez Nimatuj, for example, has publicly denounced the discrimination she encountered because of her use of traditional clothing. In one instance, she sued the exclusive restaurant El Tarro Dorado in Guatemala for denying her entrance into the establishment because she was wearing Maya clothing. After detailing this particular situation in an article called "Transnationalism and Maya Dress," Velásquez Nimatuj explains the politics at issue: "Whenever we are seen in regional *traje*, the ruling classes are reminded of the failure of their efforts to make us disappear, which have ranged from genocide to ideological coercion. Five centuries of humiliation have not succeeded in bringing the Maya people to their knees" (2011, 524). Maya clothing continues to mark Maya women as easy targets of racism and discrimination, but in Velásquez Nimatuj's view, it also serves as a visual marker of Maya resilience against the multiple projects of genocide and ethnocide. She argues that neoliberal changes in the global market have resulted in an increased national economic dependency on tourism that has exacerbated the folklorization of Maya textiles often completely divorced from the lived realities of Maya people (527–28). One of the most recent examples of neoliberalist appropriation is Caroline Fuss's designer line Harare, which used textiles woven by Maya women from Atitlan, Sololá as part of their New York Fashion Week show in 2014 (Bobb 2014). While products manufactured by designers like Fuss thrive and retail hundreds of U.S. dollars under the free market's consumption patterns, the free market does little to change or even acknowledge the structural marginalization that creates and constantly reproduces the inequality most Maya women encounter. Harare and projects like it often generate and uphold the interchangeable use of Guatemalan and Maya, thereby ignoring how dominant Guatemalan society has historically structured Maya communities as folkloric, backward, and exotic (Guzmán Böckler and Herbert 2002, 117).

While much of the emphasis in research about Maya clothing focuses on Maya women and that weaving and wearing regional clothing is often a gendered activity (Hendrickson 1995; Macleod 2004), little research focuses on how Maya men take up traditional clothing. For example Betsy Konefal observes that "some men in communities such as Sololá, Santiago Atitlán, and Todos Santos, and within a new class of urban professionals, wear traditional and 'neotraditional' clothing" (2009, 48). This increased use of Maya clothing among Maya men along with an analysis of communities in which men have also maintained a visible and consistent practice of wearing regional clothing has yet to be fully addressed in academic research. Transborder frames will also be crucial to future analysis on the clothing practices of Maya men because it is also present in places like Los Angeles where Maya community leaders and young men increasingly connect spiritual practice and cultural performance to the use of the *capixay* (men's shirt often used by Maya-Q'anjob'al men in Huehuetenango and Los Angeles) or other regional textiles and shirts.

MAYAS AND SETTLER COLONIALISM

As a rubric for analysis, settler colonialism has gained prominence within Native American studies because it is particularly useful in understanding how the United States frames indigeneity in relation to territorial dispossession. Patrick Wolfe's work in particular claims that because the ultimate goal of settler colonialism is the occupation and ownership of land, it continuously reinscribes the notion that Native people, communities, and worldviews have disappeared and that the lands they once occupied are free for settlement. He argues that contrary to the policies geared toward enslaved Africans that served to grow the population in order to augment owners' wealth, "the restrictive racial classification of Indians straightforwardly furthered the logic of elimination" (2006, 388). An important distinction to his theory is that in the formation of the Guatemalan nation-state, indigenous populations represented a substantial and free labor force for colonial elites and those who eventually became national leaders (Arzú 1998, 30). However, these multiple logics collide and at times complement each other in the experience of indigenous migrants. Faced with both anti-indigenous racism from other Latinas/os, and what Mark Rifkin (2014) terms a "settler common sense" that is so entrenched it actively obscures itself, young Mayas understand that the difference their clothing represents will need to be explained within a context where Native people are constantly erased as contemporary and dynamic nations and communities.

Putting the experience of Maya migrants in conversation with settler colonialism literature recognizes that the transborder experience for indigenous people must also contend with how indigeneity is understood within the dominant society Mayas are displaced to or migrate. As a result, research about the Maya diaspora must always be transnational since it has to account for a minimum of three experiences: the community of origin, the nation-state of origin, and the nation-state to which people arrive. This layered experience, especially in relation to Maya clothing, helps us identify how power moves through the clothing, in part because the clothing is a visible marker of difference even if outsiders do not always recognize its specificity as Maya difference.

Maya migration across the U.S.-Mexico border also complicates how settler colonialism is developed. While some researchers have centered the settler-indigenous binary and considered how multiple colonial and imperial projects operate through this structure (Morgenson 2011; Byrd 2011), other research highlights how settlers of color may not create the settler colonial structure but do uphold it and at times use it to their benefit. For instance, Dean Itsuji Saranillio writes, "What has been less visible to many, if not rendered natural and normal, is how Asian projects for equality with white settlers and inclusion into the United States have actually helped form political projects and identities in opposition to or at the expense of those Native Hawaiians seeking self-government" (2010, 300). Analyzing the Maya diasporic and transborder experience within a framework of settler colonial critique gives us tools to push back on the notion that Mayas have or automatically will submit to a Latina/o category. Instead, what I am arguing is that settler colonial theory allows Mayas to center a conversation about Mayas that does not automatically reinscribe Native dispossession by reproducing a settler common sense that would have Mayas believe that we do not have to think about Native genocide, survivance, and sovereignty.

MY STUDY

By highlighting salient moments exposed in the research, I consider how subjectivity is formed through the use of Maya clothing in the diaspora. Araceli was one of the young people I interviewed; the daughter of a Maya-Q'anjob'al father and ladina mother, Araceli was seventeen at the time of the interviews. When I asked her if she had worn Maya clothing, she responded, "Yes! Right when I came back from Guatemala, it was like two years ago. We came back early in the morning and we went to visit my *tíos* and my *tías* because it was the first time both my great grandma and my grandma came here. So it was a really, really big deal" (February 3, 2010). Araceli's grandmothers' visit motivated her to wear the regional clothing during her trip back to the United States. This is crucial because in addition to providing inspiration for wearing Maya clothing, women elders play an important role in teaching younger women how to wear the regional clothing (Boj Lopez 2015). For second-generation young women who are not raised wearing region-specific clothing as an everyday practice, the support and skills provided by elders are essential to their participation. It is not uncommon during the conference and *fiestas* (community celebrations) to hear young women ask older women if their *corte* (skirt) is on correctly or to help them tighten the *ranta* or *faja* (waist belt). This is crucial because contrary to research that emphasizes intergenerational conflict (Harman 1996), the continued use of Maya clothing by young women in Los Angeles is reliant on dialogue and transmission between generations. Often these young women are gifted their clothing by family members. The average handwoven *huipil* (blouse) and *corte* (skirt) can cost anywhere between $300 and $500 for one whole outfit, which means that young women cannot usually afford to buy their own, and rely instead on gifts from their parent or extended relatives to either make or buy them their clothing.

In addition to the oral transmission of information about how one wears the clothing appropriately and the gifting of the actual outfit, this cultural practice creates the opportunity for stories that can also help second-generation youth learn about the economic and sociopolitical hierarchies that exist in Guatemala, even among Mayas. One of the conferences I attended with Maya Pastoral in 2012 gathered community leaders across the country in Alamosa, Colorado, to discuss and share experiences of violence and resistance during the genocide as well as to partake in Maya cultural and spiritual practice. During the conference, I was sitting with a group of four other Maya women—one older, one younger, and two high school students. As the conversations turned to the Maya clothing we were each wearing, the older woman remarked that one can tell whether an outfit is cheap or expensive based on the weight and thickness of the material and the type of embroidery. One of the young women responded that the clothing was relatively expensive and that her relatives in Guatemala gifted her most of her outfits. The two younger students, whose skirts were significantly thinner than the *cortes* the rest of us were wearing, made no comment. While it is impossible to say with certainty what the intention of the comment was, nor how everyone in the group perceived it, it nonetheless taught and reminded those present that hierarchies and differences abound even within the Maya diaspora. The incident is especially informative because it highlights that access to Maya clothing and Maya textiles more generally will vary across socioeconomic class in Guatemala *and* Los Angeles. That is to say that the socioeconomic class of youth in Los Angeles as well as their relationship to family in Guatemala and their socioeconomic status there will play a role in what type of clothing youth can obtain.

The stories of Maya youth that accompany the use of the *corte* and *huipil* can also provide them with key insights into other forms of Maya cultural practice. One of the young men I interviewed who mentioned the regional clothing was Luis, a twenty-four-year-old college student raised in Mid-City, Los Angeles, whose paternal grandmother is K'iche'. He mentioned that on a trip to Guatemala his grandmother showed him some of her *cortes*. He stated:

> She took out some *trajes* in the luggage that she had. She's like—see this, this is 60 or 80 years old. She puts on the, I don't know what you call it, I probably should know, but it's kind of like a blanket you put over your head. And when you go into church and if the ceremony is a funeral, you put it on like this. If it's a wedding, you put it on like that. She showed me some of the dances she used to do and how she would mourn people. So many little details that were really interesting to me. (August 18, 2010)

Luis's reference to the clothing of his grandmother and how it was a space for cultural transmission *across* gender was surprising. While Luis may not literally wear the Maya clothing, the clothing nonetheless acted as an important vehicle through which information about important ceremonies was acquired. This also represents an area for future research that emphasizes not just the significance of wearing Maya clothing but the role it plays in producing a Maya identity even for non-wearers.

Moreover, second-generation women employ dynamic clothing practices that transform their traditional use. In a follow-up conversation with Araceli, for example, she shared that sometimes she uses her *corte* as a blanket. Araceli further stated, "Actually I just wore my *rebozo* on Friday for school . . . I do wear them, not the *corte* like the dress, the skirt [but] I do wear the shirts and my *morrales*, my bags" (May 23, 2010). This was also true for another participant: Jessica, an eighteen-year-old being raised by her Mexican and Guatemalan Maya maternal grandparents. During the interview, I asked her about the regional clothing. She commented, "I like wearing the *camisa* [shirt] with jeans, and I think that looks nice. You can still show who you are with a different look to it" (June 26, 2010). This can be a point of contention, given that the clothing is meant to be an entire outfit and each piece has its own function and significance within the whole. As Morna Macleod writes, "Mayan dress has a deep significance for those versed in the Mayan worldview who can read and interpret the symbols represented in the weavings. Such depth of knowledge is not shared by all community members; different people have different levels of ethnic consciousness" (2004, 682–83). Despite the fact that Maya dress varies across regional geographies, each garment represents an aspect of Maya cosmovision and is most often a reflection of more localized histories and landscapes. Whether it is the sacred numerical values that are present in the technique of weaving, which correspond to numbers of key significance in the sacred calendars of the Mayas, or the actual figures and designs that speak to important landmarks in the area (lakes, mountain ranges, or volcanoes), the regional clothing is, as Macleod and Hendrickson have noted, a crucial form through which not only identity but spirituality is engaged.

When second-generation Mayas then decide to adapt the use of regional clothing in ways that make sense to them, it can lead to a slippery slope toward questions of tradition and authenticity. However, rather than consider this difference a rupture, we can see this practice as an extension of regional dress since second-generation youth want to connect their cultural practices to their everyday realities, which require that those practices be flexible. Perhaps the most unique use of the *corte* textile that I have witnessed was a handmade tube-top dress worn by the daughter of one of the leaders of the national Maya organization I participated with. When I asked her where she had gotten her dress she replied that she had actually made it herself. There is also a cross-gender aspect to the shifting use of textiles, and at the same conference I saw a young man wear a similar textile in the form of a men's dress shirt. In the context of displacement we cannot assume that these changes are representative of a cultural loss rather than an attempt to continue identifying as Maya even in the face of migration. It should also be noted that, with few exceptions, it is uncommon to see women in Maya clothing in Los Angeles. Those spaces of family or community celebrations like the ones I attended where many women wear their Maya clothing are a far cry from the everyday contexts of places like public schools or the workplace. As a result, young Mayas often negotiate the desire of wanting to embrace their distinctive culture with also knowing that it will mark them as different from their peers. This fear of difference needs to be understood in the framework of settler colonial perception of Native people as completely extinct or disappearing.

However, Maya clothing is a visible marker not just of difference but of being rooted in a Maya worldview. As Macleod (2004) mentions, being able to read the spirituality and history embedded within regional clothing is linked to the knowledge one has access to. For example, when I directly asked both Araceli and Jessica if they knew the significance of their clothing, they responded that they did not. They engaged the practice because it represented a connection to older generations and to a Maya identity, without necessarily being able to articulate what each textile meant. However, it is ultimately unhelpful to write off second-generation (mis)understandings of Maya clothing; instead, we should understand that the whole signifying world of Maya clothing is augmented by their own creativity. Irma Otzoy writes, "the incorporation of new symbols into the Maya meaning system permits textiles to serve as a dynamic expression of the Maya experience" (1996, 144). Referring specifically to the charge that changes in the colors and designs used within *huipiles* and their production through foot looms as opposed to back-strap looms made some of them less authentic than others, she instead argues that the fact that members of the Maya community accept and integrate these new techniques and designs are part of what makes them Maya. I pose that, in a similar fashion, the incorporation of the experiences and perspectives presented demonstrates that the clothing continues to be a dynamic space in which young Maya women (and men) in Los Angeles negotiate their identity in the diaspora. Rather than view

Maya epistemologies or worldviews as static and rigid, it recognizes the ways in which these aspects shift and change depending on the needs and views of Maya people themselves. While not stated outright, the experience of existing at the intersection of multiple worldviews that are also dynamic highlights what autonomy looks like in practice. To acknowledge the critical role of tradition, or elder knowledge, and at the same time leave space for migrants and others to play with and create new modes is part of what will allow us to understand the ways in which sovereignty for Native nations is rooted in long, dynamic histories.

Even older generations of Mayas in Los Angeles are resignifying regional clothing in their use—or nonuse—of it, although their motivations can be decidedly more practical and consequential. Luis, in reference to his K'iche' grandmother, commented, "there's [a picture] where she was only in L.A. for two or three months, and she was no longer wearing her *traje*, she was just wearing a skirt, and whatever she wears now—she looks all sad" (August 18, 2010). In Luis's view, his grandmother's inability to continue wearing Maya clothing was directly linked to the fact that she was undocumented and that her clothing would mark her as such. In "Mexicanization: A Survival Strategy for Guatemalan Mayans in the San Francisco Bay Area," Davenport, Castañeda, and Manz (2002) find that Maya identifying as Mexican minimizes the negative consequences of being identified as an undocumented migrant, an indigenous person, and a Guatemalan in a state where the majority of Latinas/os are of Mexican origin or descent. In addition, Batz also finds that "for undocumented Maya, wearing traditional dress may represent an increased risk of being deported or being discriminated against while crossing Mexico and settling in the United States" (2014, 199). Within the context of displacement and migration, Maya clothing marks a difference that some fear will be read as "illegal" citizenship status. Within the diaspora, the first generation not only relates their use of the clothing to their experiences in Guatemala but may at times also connect it to the realities of being undocumented migrants to then communicate those experiences to the second generation. I argue that this is an aspect that makes Maya migrants occupy a different type of position as arrivants. While gaining legal citizenship may place them more firmly into a settler colonial structure, the fact that many remain undocumented also means that they may not be benefiting from the settler colonial structure of the United States in the ways that other Latinas/os may.

IN CLOSING

Earlier I discussed that Maya clothing acts as a visible cultural marker that denotes not just a generalizable Maya identity but is also a form of indigenous geography that links migrants to particular histories and landscapes of the regions they are from. It is through this specificity that Mayas connect to their ancestral places of origin and that the use of Maya clothing in the diaspora can also create the opportunity for an aesthetic expression of indigenous alliance. In one such instance, when I attended a national conference for Maya migrants in June of 2012, held in the small town of Alamosa, Colorado, I was struck that during the opening ceremony, elders from the Taos Pueblo were invited to pray and bless the conference. As the night grew colder, one of the conference organizers went and draped her *peraje* (shawl) on the shoulders of one of the Taos Pueblo women who seemed to be cold. I was astonished by the waterfall of meaning in this one gesture. The textile given by the Maya woman said as much about her presence in Alamosa as it did about her absence from the hometown that she nonetheless continued to claim through her regional clothing. The shawl that to some extent symbolized "home" for a migrant now provided momentary warmth and comfort for an elder of a Native nation thousands of miles away from that place. Here we have a dynamic that defies the principal terms employed by settler colonial theory, one of the dominant interpretive and political lenses used in Native studies, which employs categories that do not adequately address moments of intercultural embrace like the Taos Pueblo–Maya interaction.

If there exists, as expressed in the example and articles mentioned above, an affinity for understanding the Maya experience as somewhere in between a Latina/o or Native American experience, it is also critical to think about how we enter a settler colonial political project that is premised on elimination. Alliances with Native communities would force us to always consider that we are visitors, that in order to not become settlers and reproduce Native dispossession we must always refute the notion that we are occupying emptied land and instead work to actively and concretely build solidarity networks with Native nations. However, in the absence of continual and structured relationships between organizations or clearly defined communities, the persistence of Maya clothing among the diaspora will remain a critical avenue through which

Mayas can contest these problematic logics. Ironically, by marking Mayas as outsiders to the U.S. nation-state and indigenous to specific towns or regions in Guatemala, Maya clothing, for that same reason, has the potential to be a practice through which geographies of belonging, identity, history, and spirituality can be retained through intergenerational dialogue and simultaneously be the foundation for an indigenous anti–settler colonial politic. Saranillio poignantly ends his article stating, "Perhaps until we become multilingual in each other's histories, we will continue to renew a system of imperial violence and capitalist exploitation" (2010, 304). It becomes important then to consider how Maya cultural practices like regional clothing blur the boundaries between settler, Native, and migrant in ways that may challenge what it means to be an indigenous migrant in a settler society. In her work on the ways in which Native women produce decolonial spatial logics through narrative, Mishuana Goeman challenges the idea that mobility and Native subjectivity are often considered oppositional. She writes, "I contend that instead of ingesting the norm of immobile native women, we open up the possibility of (re)mapping the Americas as Indigenous land, not only by rethinking dominant disciplining narratives but also critically examining how we become a self-disciplining colonial subject" (2013, 12). While this is a challenge to how we conceptualize the hemisphere, including the lands bound up within the territory of Central America as a region, it is also a call to conceptualize and build the field of U.S. Central American studies with a particular emphasis on the heterogeneity of experience and form frameworks that account for the commonalities and vast differences of being Central Americans in the United States.

This chapter focused on how Maya cultural continuities can also build responsible and generative relationships to Native transborder and local communities. This shift in meaning is rooted in the notion that part of what it means to be Maya in Los Angeles is, or perhaps should be, to disavow the dispossession of the indigenous peoples in whose lands we navigate the maintenance of our own cultural practices. Native communities are in themselves complex, diverse, and face a series of challenges. Understanding the multiple geographies of Maya identity that exist in regional clothing may help us move toward a common politic that challenges settler colonialism. Finally, demonstrating how Maya migrants and second-generation Mayas in Los Angeles work collectively to navigate and negotiate Maya clothing practice also highlights that these practices remain a dynamic terrain through which Mayas also respond to mobility by transforming cultural practice. These shifts across time, geography, and generation remind us that Maya communities live in transborder communities that coexist alongside many indigenous nations. This coexistence creates new opportunities for indigenous alliance across borders and expands our definitions of what it means to be Central American in the United States.

NOTES

1. The shift from the term *traje*, which is popularly used in Guatemala and the diaspora among Mayas and non-Mayas alike, to regional or Maya clothing marks an ongoing conversation among scholars and activists to question the folklorization of Maya culture. The concern that the English translation of the term *traje* as "traditional clothing" does not clearly articulate the diversity of textiles that exist, their relationship to specific geographic and regional areas, and its specificity to the Maya experience are important considerations.
2. The data collection for this chapter was conducted with approval from the Human Subjects Committee at California State University, Northridge.
3. It is important to distinguish between the terms *ladina/o* and *Latina/o*. *Ladino* is a term used for Guatemalans who do not identify as indigenous and instead highlight their European ancestry. For an excellent analysis of contemporary ladino identity, I recommend Charles Hale's (2006) *Más Que Un Indio (More Than an Indian): Racial Ambivalence and the Paradox of Neoliberal Multiculturalism in Guatemala*.

REFERENCES

Araceli. 2010. Interview by Floridalma Boj Lopez. February 3.
———. 2010. Interview by Floridalma Boj Lopez. May 23.
Arzú, Marta Casaús. 1998. *La Metamorfosis Del Racismo En Guatemala*. Guatemala City: Cholsamaj.
Batz, Giovanni. 2014. "Maya Cultural Resistance in Los Angeles: The Recovery of Identity and Culture Among Maya Youth." *Latin American Perspectives* 41 (3): 194–207.
Bobb, Brooke. 2014. "A Proenza Schouler Alum Launches a Line Made from Traditional Guatemalan Textiles." *New York Times Style Magazine*, August 27. http://tmagazine.blogs.nytimes.com/2014/08/27/caroline-fuss-harare-proenza

-schouler-alum-fashion-line-made-from-traditional-guatemalan-textiles/ ?smid=pl-share.

Boj Lopez, Floridalma. 2015. "Maya Youth and Cultural Sustainability in the United States." In *Latinos and Latinas at Risk: Issues in Education, Health, Community, and Justice*, edited by Gabriel Gutierrez, 151–70. Santa Barbara, CA: ABC-CLIO, LLC.

Byrd, Jodi A. 2011. *The Transit of Empire: Indigenous Critiques of Colonialism*. Minneapolis: University of Minnesota Press.

Davenport, Allison, Xóchitl Castañeda, and Beatriz Manz. 2002. "Mexicanization: A Survival Strategy for Guatemalan Mayans in the San Francisco Bay Area." *Migraciones Internacionales* 1 (3): 102–23.

Estrada, Alicia Ivonne. 2013. "*Ka Tzij*: The Maya Diasporic Voices from *Contacto Ancestral*." *Latino Studies* 11 (2): 208–27.

Forbes, Jack D. 1994. *Apache, Navajo, and Spaniard*. 2nd ed. Norman: University of Oklahoma Press.

Forbes, Jack D. 2001. "Indigenous Americans: Spirituality and Ecos." *Daedalus* 130 (4): 283–300.

Goeman, Mishuana. 2013. *Mark My Words: Native Women Mapping our Nations*. Minneapolis: University of Minnesota Press.

Grandin, Greg. 2000. *The Blood of Guatemala: A History of Race and Nation*. Durham, NC: Duke University Press.

Guzmán Böckler, Carlos, and Jean-Loup Herbert. 2002. *Guatemala: Una Interpretacion Historico-Social*. 2nd ed. Guatemala City: Cholsamaj.

Hale, Charles R. 2006. *Más Que Un Indio (More Than an Indian): Racial Ambivalence and Neoliberal Multiculturalism in Guatemala*. 1st ed. Santa Fe, NM: School of American Research Press.

Harman, R. 1996. "Intergenerational Relations among Maya in Los Angeles." In *Selected Papers on Refugee*, edited by A. Rynearson and J. Philips, 156–73. Washington, DC: American Anthropological Associations.

Hendrickson, Carol Elaine. 1995. *Weaving Identities: Construction of Dress and Self in a Highland Guatemala Town*. Austin: University of Texas Press.

Hiller, Patrick T., J. P. Linstroth, and Paloma Ayala Vela. 2009. "'I Am Maya, Not Guatemalan, nor Hispanic'—the Belongingness of Mayas in Southern Florida." *Forum: Qualitative Social Research* 10 (3).

Jessica. 2010. Interview by Floridalma Boj Lopez. June 26.

Konefal, Betsy. 2009. "Subverting Authenticity: Reinas Indígenas and the Guatemalan State, 1978." *Hispanic American Historical Review* 89 (1): 40–72.

LeBaron, Alan. 2012. "When Latinos are Not Latinos: The Case of Guatemalan Maya in the United States, the Southeast and Georgia." *Latino Studies* 10 (1–2): 179–95.

Luis. 2010. Interview by Floridalma Boj Lopez. August 18.

Macleod, Morna. 2004. "Mayan Dress as Text: Contested Meanings." *Development in Practice* 4 (5): 680–89.

Morgensen, Scott Lauria. 2011. *Spaces Between Us: Queer Settler Colonialism and Indigenous Decolonization*. Minneapolis: University of Minnesota Press.

Otzoy, Irma. 1996. "Maya Clothing and Identity." In *Maya Cultural Activism in Guatemala*, edited by Edward F. Fischer and R. McKenna Brown, 141–55. Austin: University of Texas Press.

Rifkin, Mark. 2014. *Settler Common Sense: Queerness and Everyday Colonialism in the American Renaissance*. Minneapolis: University of Minnesota Press.

Saranillio, Dean Itsuji. 2010. "Colliding Histories: Hawai'i Statehood at the Intersection of Asians 'Ineligible to Citizenship' and Hawaiians 'Unfit for Self-Government.'" *Journal of Asian American Studies* 13 (3): 283–309.

Stephen, Lynn. 2007. *Transborder Lives: Indigenous Oaxacans in Mexico, California, and Oregon*. Durham, NC: Duke University Press.

Velásquez Nimatuj, Irma Alicia. 2011. "Transnationalism and Maya Dress." In *The Guatemala Reader: History, Culture, Politics*, edited by Greg Grandin, Deborah T. Levenson, and Elizabeth Oglesby, 523–31. Durham, NC: Duke University Press.

Wolfe, Patrick. 2006. "Settler Colonialism and the Elimination of the Native." *Journal of Genocide Research* 8 (4): 387–409.

9

ILLEGAL CHICKENS

The Art of Branding Poultry in
Central American Los Angeles

YAJAIRA PADILLA

RESIDENTS AND VISITORS of Echo Park and Silver Lake are no doubt familiar with the vibrant murals of cartoon chickens painted on several walls throughout these two Los Angeles neighborhoods. These murals are the work of a local graffiti writer turned street muralist from Guatemala who goes by the name of Cache (pronounced *caché* in keeping with the Spanish translation of the French *cachet*).[1] A unique balance between the whimsical and the political, Cache's wall art and colorful characters are a strategic means of social commentary. Inspired by Carlos Castañeda's theory of *humaneros* (human coops), Cache's chickens are visual metaphors for humans who are trapped in the "coop" of a socially and economically stratified society that is largely driven by consumerism and that emphasizes uniformity (Lurie 2008, 21). His chicken murals speak to both the oppressive reality of this entrapment and the possibility of fighting against it whether the chickens depicted are white, rotund, and cute or more humanized and multihued or brown (the latter recalling chicken breeds used in the poultry industry). Thus it is not uncommon to see Cache's chickens partaking in antigubernatorial forms of resistance such as antiwar rallies and "Occupy L.A." marches alongside a black-cad cartoon Zapatista—a symbol of popular struggle in the Americas and the signature character of fellow street artist Eyeone.[2] Nor is it unusual to see these same birds standing defiantly—in some cases even thrusting a clenched fist in the air—while rising above the bubbly murkiness and the far-reaching mechanical tentacles (of society) that threaten to encase them.

Like other forms of what has broadly been termed "street art,"[3] Cache's murals evince the production of an "oppositional political-aesthetic stance" that "registers dissatisfaction" with oppressive economic, social, and political structures (Boykoff and Sand 2008, 17). This critical intervention is enacted on the visual playing field of the public spaces and walls of the city and achieved precisely through Cache's unique use of branding, one that draws on contemporary street art practices as well as the identity and communal politics of graffiti. In keeping with the anticorporatist bent of street art production since the 1990s, Cache's trademark—his chickens—is, as he notes, a tool for combating the "censored and diluted media assault on the human psyche" by corporations and the government, an "assault" that not only engenders uniformity but also speaks to the visual power wielded by the marketing world and government institutions ("Cache" 2010).

Branding, however, also speaks to Cache's identity and communal responsibility as a graffiti artist. As was the case with the tag artists of the New York graffiti movement of the 1970s and '80s for whom tagging or writing "graff" (not only in the form of stylized letters but also cartoon characters) was a form of self-promotion and representation, Cache's chickens are a type of personal signature.[4] Along with distinguishing him from the crowd and solidifying his street credentials, this signature provides Cache an avenue for communal engagement and empowerment. As Cache states, he is "one of the few people in the community with a voice," and he wants to use it to affect change in and for that community, one largely composed of working-class and/or impoverished people of color, including undocumented immigrants, who are often relegated to the city's margins and barred from being "true" Angelenos (Lurie 2008, 21).

The fact that the majority of Cache's murals have been painted illegally plays just as pivotal a role in the "oppositional politico-aesthetic stance" taken up through his art as does branding (Alegría 2009). In producing unsanctioned art on city walls and private property, Cache reframes the aesthetic and official politics within and against which he works. In other words, he forces a reconfiguration of what is conceived of as "art" and "the law." Regardless of the fact that street artists and their work often straddle the line between the mainstream and the periphery, street art remains an art "from below," to borrow from Rebecca E. Biron's (2009) discussion of the city and art in Latin America. It is an urban art form meant to be accessible to everyday people in the communal spaces they inhabit and, as such, pushes back against the ideal of "high art." It likewise challenges legal discourses from "above" that tend to construe street art, particularly graffiti, as vandalism and those who produce it as criminals. The eleven-year mural moratorium (2002–2013) in Los Angeles, a city that has a long and vibrant tradition of public murals, speaks precisely to this last point. In banning uncommissioned murals on private property as unsanctioned forms of advertising, even in cases where the owner of said property had provided consent, the city, in effect, used official channels to wage a war on public art, vilifying and rendering unlawful street murals and street artists alike.

Contextualizing Cache's murals within this broader framework of street art and graffiti, oppositional politics is essential for understanding his work. In this chapter, however, I also endeavor to highlight the impact that Cache's immigrant background and ethnic identity as a Guatemalan and, more broadly, as a U.S. Central American has on his street art. Thus, I also read Cache's art as an example of what Paul DiMaggio and Patricia Fernández Kelly (2010) denote as "immigrant art." Such art functions through a dialectical exchange in which art constitutes a window into the immigrant experience in all of its complexities and, similarly, immigration constitutes a lens for comprehending the diverse employment and transformation of artistic genres by immigrants. Situating Cache's work at this provocative intersection between "street" and "immigrant" art imbues his cultural production with another layer of meaning as a visual expression of the Central American immigrant experience in the United States. Although admittedly not all of Cache's art lends itself to this type of interpretation, as the following analysis of two of his works suggests, being Central American is a key dimension of his work. This discussion of Cache's art not only presupposes an understanding of his identification as a Guatemalan in Los Angeles and his subjectivity as a graffiti artist as mutually constitutive elements, but also allows for a critical possibility with regard to his art that has gone unexplored due to the premium placed on anonymity within street art.[5]

As Martin Irvine (2012) argues, street art is invested in toppling "regimes of visibility" that distribute and regulate power through the partitioning of visibility. These are the regimes of government (politics, law, property) and the aesthetic (a legitimizing art world that decrees what is and is not art). Working within their own set of rules and codes, such regimes determine "what can be made visible or perceptible, who has the legitimacy to be seen or heard where, and who can be rendered invisible" (Irvine 2012, 250). Indeed, as Cache's use of branding and the illegality of his murals reveals, his street art works against such regimes. His art contests not only the appropriation and distribution of visibility in what concerns public space by corporations and the government but also the marginalization and silencing of disenfranchised communities that are relegated to the background of the broader urban landscape even while paradoxically being one of its most visible elements. Similarly, by painting unsanctioned murals on city walls so as to engage community, Cache disrupts the regime of art and its means of policing what is "high" versus "low" art and who has access to either one.

Viewed through the lens of Cache's Central American-ness and its manifestation in his street art, however, one can argue, as I do here, that his work also evinces a challenge to these and other regimes of visibility concerning how, when, where, and under what circumstances Central Americans are seen or not seen in Los Angeles and, to a certain extent, the greater United States. Although Central Americans have resided in Los Angeles since the 1940s and '50s, it was the massive influx of immigrants, primarily from El Salvador and Guatemala, fleeing dire economic situations and civil wars in the late 1970s and '80s, that paved the way for what is today the largest Central American immigrant community in the United States (Segura 2010, 9). Relative newcomers, Central Americans have marked their presence in the city through the establishment of businesses, cultural associations, and yearly celebrations as well as political organizations and community outreach centers. Similar to other immigrant groups and ethnic communities, they have also claimed a sector of the city as their own, the Westlake and Pico-Union neighborhoods, popularly known as "Little Central America." Ongoing endeavors to have portions of this area officially sanctioned as commemorative sites of Central American culture and history reveal the stake Central Americans have in acquiring a legitimizing form of visibility and the struggles they face in doing so.

Such efforts are complicated by the issue of undocumented migration that, like the history of Central America's revolutions, is vital to understanding the Central American experience in the United States. In 2009, it was estimated that 45 percent of the almost three million Central American immigrants living in the United States were undocumented (Terrazas 2011). Although it is difficult to account for what portion of this undocumented population resides in Los Angeles, one can wager that a significant number does given the fact that approximately one in five Central Americans in the United States live in this metropolitan area (Terrazas 2011). Indeed, the undocumented are discernible in the U.S. popular and political imaginaries in the form of "illegal aliens," construed as a criminal threat to American livelihoods and one that has been increasingly Latinized following 9/11. However, as an exploitable labor force they remain hidden from view. For these unauthorized Central Americans, being seen is not just a matter of competing for visibility and struggling against the regimes of city government that grant it; rather, it is a question of also negotiating the regimes of the law and industry that keep them in the shadows.

Cache's street art exposes and works against the bearing that such regimes of visibility have on Central American sociocultural and legal struggles for voice and belonging. The first piece I examine—a recently renovated street mural in Echo Park that Cache completed in 2013—is an expression of Cache's self-identification as a Guatemalan Angeleno as well as a testament to the transformative presence of the Central American immigrant population in Los Angeles. Although Cache's mural constitutes a similar attempt as that of other community-sponsored projects to legitimate Central Americans and their contributions, Cache's street art is more effective in this regard precisely because it challenges official structures and it offers a more inclusive and broader understanding of Central American visibility. The second piece by Cache that I analyze differs significantly from the first in that it is a sculpture-based installation featured in the "By the Time I Get to Arizona" show held at Mid-City Arts Gallery in June 2010. In keeping with the show's focus, Cache's art manifests a critical response to Arizona's controversial Senate Bill 1070 (The Support Our Law Enforcement and Safe Neighborhoods Act). In addition to the overt political commentary it makes concerning the exclusionary and racist underpinnings of this law, I suggest that Cache's piece can be read alternately as a statement regarding the paradoxical construction of Central American undocumented laborers as simultaneously visible and invisible subjects in the United States.

CENTRAL AMERICANS IN THE CITY

To a certain extent, Cache's mural located on Sunset Boulevard, just east of Coronado Street, is an ode to Los Angeles. A collaborative effort with fellow street artists ZES (from Los Angeles) and Askew (from New Zealand), the mural features as its central focal point the city's name painted in neon lime and written in graffiti. The futuristic style of the lettering channels the work of L.A. graff writers of the 1980s, whose influences included East Los Angeles *cholo* tags of the 1970s and whose own unique style set them apart from New York artists

(Deitch 2011, 166). The city's name appears against a space-like backdrop with red and orange hues that evoke the lights and nonstop movement of the city at night. The chickens that populate the piece, also painted in red, orange, and purple tones, are angular and edgy, reflecting the mural's ultramodern feel. As is also characteristic of Cache's artwork, the chickens and graffiti are immersed in a light blue cloudlike matter. And emerging from the depths of this matter are tentacles painted candy-striped light blue and white that seemingly threaten to overtake the city and those who inhabit it.

The graffiti of the city's name is the only remnant of a previous mural painted by Cache on the same wall. The older work featured an idyllic day scene of the city inhabited by a host of anthropomorphic and animated characters, including cats, dogs, turtles, chickens, aliens, and walking boom boxes. The visual priority of "Los Angeles" and its constancy from one mural to the next speaks to the fact that, if anything else, street art is an engagement with the city, one that gives way to a "city re-imaged and re-imagined" (Irvine 2012, 237). Notably, in this instance, Cache's process of re-imaging and re-imagining the city is one mediated through his sense of being Guatemalan in Los Angeles. When asked via e-mail on September 12, 2013, whether or not he considers himself to be Guatemalan American or U.S. Central American or if he even cares for such labels, Cache responded with the following: "I am a guatemalteco with a US citizenship, but consider myself an earthling that bleeds Los Angeles" (Cache, pers. comm.). This answer registers a wide range of subject positions that hinge on national affinities, notions of legal and global citizenship, and locality. Yet the emphasis placed on being Guatemalan and Angeleno are undeniable. In stating that he is a "guatemalteco with a US citizenship," Cache draws a distinction between what is his national and cultural identification with Guatemala and what is his legal status as a citizen of the United States. The latter does not necessarily connote a similar sense of American national and cultural belonging. A similar distinction is made in Cache's articulation of self as an "earthling that bleeds Los Angeles." Although Cache considers himself to be a global citizen or "earthling," he remains at his very core an Angeleno. He carries the city in his blood.

This notion of being Guatemalan Angeleno is manifested via the tentacles featured in the mural since the light blue and white are reminiscent of the Guatemalan flag. They are also, however, colors that appear on the flags of El Salvador, Honduras, and Nicaragua and constitute national markers of identity for immigrants from these countries. The blue-and-white sign of the Cuscatleca Bakery, a Salvadoran-owned business located across the street from Cache's mural, exemplifies the symbolic currency of these colors. In using such colors, Cache thus not only showcases his national background but also his belonging to a broader Central American immigrant community in Los Angeles, and he attests to the transformative presence of this growing population in the city. Unlike his other murals in which tentacles are connected to alien ships and painted gray, these Central American signifiers are unattached and devoid of their meaning as the extending arms of a stratified society that entraps humans. They remain, nevertheless, alien and somewhat threatening as they register the existence of a community that, like other ethnic groups before it, is changing the spatial and cultural logics of the city.

Cache's visual representation of Central Americans in Los Angeles parallels ongoing efforts by Central American groups and organizations to have the historical contributions and cultural heritage of Central Americans officially recognized by the city. Since 2007, groups have petitioned the Los Angeles City Council to declare the Westlake and Pico-Union neighborhoods "The Central American Historic District," or a similar derivative, "The Central American Cultural District," following designations such as "Little Armenia," "Korea-town," and "Historic Filipino Town" (Bermudez 2012). Even though this measure has yet to be approved, the Central American community has succeeded in having the city declare a section of Vermont Avenue populated with Salvadoran businesses the "El Salvador Community Corridor." They have likewise procured two commemorative sites honoring Msgr. Oscar A. Romero, the archbishop of El Salvador who was an advocate of human rights and a martyr of the Salvadoran civil war (1980–1992).[6] Such initiatives reflect a conscious understanding that visibility and, relatedly, the ability to control how one is seen equals power. What is of essence to a community whose quest for voice as one of the seemingly newer arrivals is further compounded by the fact that they inhabit one of the most impoverished and densely populated areas of the city.

Like these efforts, Cache's painting of the mural in question is invested in making Central Americans visible through the acquisition of public space and its redefinition as a marker of Central American-ness. Yet, whereas these same community-led initiatives remain beholden to the city council's power to partition visibility and, therefore, publicly validate Central Americans as Angelenos, Cache's mural does not. As a work of street art that illegally co-opts city space, Cache's artwork circumvents such official routes, calling them and the regime of governance and visibility they sustain into question. Furthermore, it is a work that espouses a broader and more inclusive notion of Central American visibility. The majority of the aforementioned endeavors to legitimize the place of Central Americans in the city have been spearheaded primarily by Salvadorans, whose status as the largest group within the L.A.-based Central American community as well as history of social activism in the United States dating back to the solidarity movements of the 1970s and '80s tends to eclipse the presence of other Central American groups. They are also initiatives that have centered almost exclusively on claiming space within the noted Westlake and Pico-Union neighborhoods. Though a logical and relevant objective given this area's historical and present significance to Central American immigrants and newer generations, it is one that, nevertheless, runs the risk of limiting the Central American experience to that of living in an enclave.

Inasmuch as Cache's strategic use of light blue and white conveys his individual identity as a Guatemalan Angeleno, it also connotes a sense of Central American collectivity or regional identity. Employing these colors without any specific identifiers for any one Central American country allows them to function as signifiers of a unified presence and of belonging for a number of Central American groups in the city. Similarly, by painting his mural in Echo Park—just a few miles north of the Westlake and Pico-Union neighborhoods, but still outside of them—Cache decenters the notion of where and under what circumstances Central Americans are and can be seen. "Little Central America" may be a key settlement site, but it also functions as a port of entry. Many Central Americans reside in other parts of Los Angeles such as Hollywood, Van Nuys, North Hollywood, and South Central, not to mention further-removed cities and suburban areas throughout Los Angeles County. Allowing Central Americans to be seen outside of the epicenter of their cultural, financial, and political activity shows that their transformative potential is not confined to a specific location. As the tentacles in Cache's mural suggest, Central Americans are rising from the depths and are spreading, slowly but surely, Central Americanizing Los Angeles.

UNDOCUMENTED CHICKENS REVEALED

The artwork produced for the Mid-City Arts Gallery show is a significant departure from Cache's street murals in terms of form and context. The untitled three-dimensional installation fashioned out of papier-mâché sculptures and other household materials features one of Cache's trademark chickens staring intently at a hamburger that is surrounded by a white picket fence. The hamburger has an American flag planted in its center and rests atop of a mousetrap, depicting it as bait for the chicken that desires it from the other side of the fence. Like the hamburger, the chicken, which is suggestively brown, is also encased by a thin wall of poultry mesh, the type used in the construction of chicken coops. The floor underneath the entire installation is covered with a thin layer of sand spotted with mini potted cacti and small black pebbles. Coupled with the walls of fence and mesh, this flooring evokes the treacherous desert terrain of the U.S.-Mexico border that undocumented migrants risk their lives to cross in their quest for the "American dream," symbolized here by a cornerstone of American popular cuisine, the hamburger.

Exhibiting such a piece in a gallery setting constitutes for Cache a notably different spatial interface than that of painting unsanctioned street murals on the public streets of the city. In fact, a case could be made that because this piece appears in a legitimizing institution such as a gallery that it does not hold the same agency as those works by Cache that are produced and displayed in the streets. To do so, however, would be to ignore the fact that the gallery in question is instrumental in the construction of what Nancy Fraser (1990) terms "subaltern counterpublics" that enrich rather than detract from the critical interventions made by Cache's artwork in what concerns the issues of undocumented Central American migration and labor exploitation. Owned by the street artist Viejas del Mercado, who is also of Guatemalan descent, Mid-City Arts Gallery is a composite of three different spaces: an exhibition hall, an aerosol paint shop, and an open-air performance space. Aside from being a meeting ground for street artists from all over the globe, the gallery constitutes a shared space that puts these same artists and their work in dialogue with the diverse community in which it is located. Notably, almost half of Mid-City is composed of U.S.-born Latinas/os and Latin American immigrants from Mexico and El Salvador ("Mid-City Profile"). It is also in close proximity to "Little Central America," just five miles west on Pico Boulevard.

With its emphasis on street art, the demographic of its patrons, and its location, Mid-City Arts Gallery challenges elite notions of art and the power of visibility wielded by hegemonic art world institutions. In essence, it functions as a zone of opposition from which alternate discourses can be launched that challenge the status quo of the public sphere. Moreover, given that the "By the Time I Get to Arizona" exhibit was an act of creative resistance against Arizona's exclusionary immigration measure, Senate Bill 1070, the alternate discourses articulated within this subaltern counterpublic are also ones that contest discriminatory and dominant views of undocumented immigration. Thus, what becomes most paramount within this particular setting and context is not necessarily debates related to the dichotomy between high and low art and how the exhibition of street art in a gallery robs or imbues it with different aesthetic and market signification (though these issues remain present), but rather what the art on display contests and, ultimately, reveals or exposes.

Arizona's Senate Bill 1070 makes it a state crime to be in the country illegally and requires police officials to check the immigration status of any individual they suspect of being undocumented. Opponents of the bill consider it a violation of civil rights, as it leads to racial profiling, and believe it to be a targeted attack against Mexicans and other Latina/o populations. Like many of the other works on display at the Mid-City Arts show, Cache's critical reflection on this controversial measure underscores sociopolitical issues such as racism, the violation of human and civil rights, racial inequality, and the anxiety that fuels what Leo R. Chavez (2008) terms "The Latino Threat Narrative." This narrative posits Mexicans and, by extension, other Latin American immigrants as "an invading force from south of the border that is bent on reconquering land that was formerly theirs (the U.S. Southwest) and destroying the American way of life" (Chavez 2008, 2). These are issues often sublimated by the hypernationalism, criminalizing and racializing discourses surrounding undocumented immigration from parts of the so-called Third World, and emphasis on sovereignty that have historically been and continue to be a part of immigration debates and policy making in the United States. Senate Bill 1070 is no exception.

Key elements of Cache's installation, the white picket fence and the "hamburger trap" it encloses, speak to the exclusionary politics and racism at the center of Arizona's bill. Although codified as a law to help secure Arizona's border and the state's legal inhabitants against the threat of illegal aliens, the law allows for the policing of undesirable migrants and ethnic others construed in the popular imaginary not only as criminals but also as foreigners who refuse to assimilate. Such individuals must be barred from the nation lest they corrupt the "American way of life." Cache's provocative inclusion of a white picket fence—what conjures an image of the predominantly Anglo suburban neighborhoods of 1950s America—underscores this seeming need for protection and the attempt to preserve what is "ours." The wooden barrier protects what it fences in—the cornerstone of "America's way of life," the "American dream"—while also establishing a territorial, cultural, and racial boundary for would-be trespassers and unwanted guests. Moreover, in using the metaphor of a hamburger, a highly commercialized form of fast food and one that in this installation is a bait for a mouse trap, Cache also forces viewers to consider the nature of the "American way of life" and ideal of success that U.S. citizens protect so vehemently and undocumented migrants risk their lives to attain.

In effect, Cache's installation posits the "American dream" as a commodity for sale that has been successfully marketed to U.S. citizens and foreigners alike. It remains valuable as long as everyone wants to buy it and buy into it. It is also clear that the undocumented migratory subject, represented by the chicken gazing at the hamburger, is willing to do so, but at what cost? Keeping in mind Cache's metaphorical use of chickens in his street art, the price to be paid by undocumented migrants is that of becoming individuals trapped in a consumerist-driven society plagued by economic, racial, and gender inequality. This predicament is made all the more dire for migrants by their criminalization as "illegals" and their existence as "impossible subjects," individuals "whose inclusion within the nation [is] simultaneously a social reality and a legal impossibility," being "barred from citizenship without rights" (Ngai 2004, 4). The poultry mesh that encases the chicken foregrounds this reality, symbolizing the migratory subject's entrapment in the "coop" of society and, by the same token, his or her potential imprisonment in a deportation facility.

The exposure of these discriminatory politics and the discourses that work to both obscure and fuel them are the basis of the overall critical commentary that drives Cache's piece. However, it is not the only form of unveiling that Cache's art performs. In *Double Exposures: The Subject of Cultural Analysis* (1996), Mieke Bal argues that exposition or the gesture of exposure, such as that of the artist who puts on display his or her work in a museum, can be conceived of as a performative speech act that produces meaning (2). The artist (first person) communicates with the viewer (second person) about the object (third person), which despite its silence remains physically present. Within this exchange, it is the object (third person) that is of most consequence given its function as a sign and producer of meaning. Despite its actual visibility, the object on display comes to stand for something else, the statement being made about it to the viewer by the artist or exposer. Equally imperative to this discursive exchange is the narrative that links the object's "present" to the "past" of its "making, functioning, and meaning" and that of the master narrative of the exposition as a whole that the viewer experiences as he or she tours the museum (4). These narratives act as filler between the object and the statement being made about it, creating the possibility for ambiguity and discrepancies. Conceptualizing exposition in this manner allows Bal to destabilize what is the subject/object dichotomy created by this act, which presupposes that the object is present only to substantiate the statement being made about it to the knowledgeable viewer by the artist. In essence, Bal suggests that, among other things, the object can exist or *mean* in ways other than those intended by the artist.

Bal's discussion is useful as it foregrounds the possibility of Cache's installation piece as capable of also producing meaning or making a statement in what concerns Central American undocumented migration and labor exploitation. Cache's portrayal of the undocumented migratory subject as a brown chicken insinuates a link between this subject and the meatpacking and poultry industry. It likewise hints at the important gendered dimensions of such a relationship. As noted previously, this particular brown chicken calls to mind breeds such as ISA Browns that are genetically engineered hybrids for the purpose of egg laying and others that are grown specifically for their meat. A high premium is placed on females given their capabilities as reproducers of marketable goods (eggs). Ironically, in this case, the chicken represented by Cache does not necessarily evoke the product itself but rather the cheap and highly productive workforce needed to guarantee its production. This is a workforce that in recent decades has become not only increasingly Mexican and Central American but also more female.

This seeming reference to the growing female presence within the poultry industry adds further nuance to the broader critique I argue is made via this installation piece regarding the exploitation of undocumented Central American workers.[7] Women employed in poultry plants are generally responsible for some of the most physically taxing and hazardous forms of assembly-line work, including having to hang, slice open, and empty chicken carcasses of their entrails at high speeds and in substandard working conditions. The intense and debilitating nature of this work is made all the more acute by abuses of supervisory power aimed especially at women, such as sexual harassment and being paid lower wages. Like the ISA Brown breeds Cache's chicken in this installation piece recalls, women employed in these plants are expected to be high producers, valued only for how quickly and efficiently they can move products through the processing line. Within what is already a disenfranchised population of undocumented workers who lack citizenship-based rights, immigrant women find themselves all the more stigmatized and subordinated on account of their gender.

The successful functioning of the agricultural industry depends on the purposeful obscuring and docility of the broader undocumented immigrant workforce it employs. Were this necessary invisibility to be compromised, however, undocumented Central Americans would indeed be seen, but only as criminal illegal aliens. Highly publicized events such as the 2008 immigration raid at the kosher meatpacking plant Agriprocessors Inc., in Postville, Iowa, are a case in point. Following the raid, approximately 290 undocumented Maya Guatemalans were convicted of document fraud. The majority served five months in prison and eventually were deported, while the owners of the plant were not charged with any criminal charges for violating immigration and labor laws. Embedded in an alternate narrative of immigrant labor and exploitation, Cache's installation piece, like his street mural, becomes an expression of another key facet of the Central American immigrant experience in the United States. In effect, it reveals the contradictory positioning of Central Americans as, on one hand, visible illegal aliens and, on the other, invisible laborers maintained as such by the regimes of government, law, and the agricultural industry.

CENTRAL AMERICANIZING THE UNITED STATES

This chapter is, at its core, an inquiry into the critical possibilities that exist when street art, immigration politics, and being Central American in Los Angeles converge. Seeing the art of graffiti writer Cache from this intersectional vantage point reveals his work to be, among other things, a unique visual engagement with the Central American immigrant reality. As street art that also functions, in many respects, as a form of immigrant art, the examples of Cache's work analyzed here not only expose but also challenge the regimes of visibility (those of government, the law, and industry) that determine to what extent, where, and how Central Americans are made visually legible and, consequently, deemed welcomed additions to Los Angeles's diverse community. In Cache's Echo Park mural, candy-striped light-blue-and-white tentacles provide an apt metaphor for Cache's representation of his own Guatemalan Angeleno identity as well as the transformative and growing presence of Central Americans in the city. In his sculpture-based installation for the Mid-City Arts show, it is his well-known signature as a street muralist—his politicized chickens—that serve as the signifier of Central American-ness, calling attention to the plight of undocumented Central American workers who are kept by the regimes of government, the law, and industry in the impossible predicament of needing to remain invisible as laborers and, when visible, seen only as "illegals" who are unauthorized to be within the confines of the nation.

Although different in many respects, both of these works of art are part of the same conversation, allowing Central Americans to be seen in and outside of the city. Whereas in the mural Cache remarks on the Central Americanization of Los Angeles he sees around him and that he is a part of, his installation piece shows this process to also extend beyond the city. The narrative of Central American immigrants as an exploitable labor force within the agricultural industry is one that has taken shape in the last decades not necessarily in Los Angeles but rather in other parts of the country. It is the narrative of thousands of Central American immigrants that left the city in the early 1990s, or never settled there, and that now call other destinations in the Midwest and the U.S. South home. It is likewise a narrative with increasing relevance to how we think about the Central American experience in the United States, and its importance is certainly not lost on someone like myself, a transplanted Angelena who currently resides in Northwest Arkansas. Aside from being the corporate home of Tyson Foods, one of the leading companies in the global poultry industry and an active recruiter of immigrant labor, this geographic region is the site of a growing Central American community, as evidenced by the *mercados*, *pupuserías*, and *panaderías* with their telltale light-blue-and-white signs. Thus, and although Los Angeles remains an *epicentro* of sorts for U.S.-based Central American communities, its reverberations are extending outward and being felt across the United States.

NOTES

1. Images of Cache's chicken murals are easily accessible on various Los Angeles–based blog sites via a general Google search. Also available via YouTube is the short documentary *Cache: Don't Be a Chicken* (2010). Unlike other street artists with whom Cache works, he does not have a web or blog site of his own.

2. For more information on Eyeone's art, see his web/blog site *Eyeone/Seeking Heaven* at http://www.eyelost.com/eyeoneblog/index.php?catid=11 and the YouTube clip "Art and Activism with Eyeone" (2013).

3. *Street art* is a broad term that refers to both a global movement that has steadily gained ground since the 1980s and to the wide array of urban art expressions

that characterize it. These include, but are not limited to graffiti (simple "tags" of the artist's name made with a marker or aerosol paint, or more complex pieces with highly stylized or bubble-style letters and images), stenciling, murals, stickerbombing (placement of stickers, usually with a distinct image on various public surfaces), subvertising (alterations made to advertisements), wheatpasting (the adhesion of posters previously made by the artist on walls or other surfaces), and street sculpture (the placement of objects made by the artist in public spaces). The class backgrounds and skill level of those who practice this form of art are as varied as the works they produce, ranging from self-taught or intuitive artists who have honed their skills in graffiti crews to classically trained artists who attended world-class art institutes and universities. Not all individuals who have been associated with the term embrace it fully, as in the case of Cache, who prefers to be referenced as a graffiti writer rather than labeled a "street artist" despite the fact that he does produce street art.

4. Concerning the beginnings, evolution, and broader social and cultural significance of this movement, see the studies by Joe Austin (2001) and Gregory Snyder (2009).

5. Although the work of many street artists, in particular those that have acquired broad notoriety such as Bansky or Shepard Fairey, reflects a unique style or trademark that is easily recognizable, in general such works do not reveal individual or personal attributes of the artists themselves. As Allan Schwartzman (1985, 62) suggests, unlike graffiti artists who use their art to stand apart from the crowd, street artists seek "to merge with the crowd" and "vehemently cour[t]" anonymity.

6. The first of these sites is a busy intersection at the corner of South Vermont Avenue and West Pico Boulevard declared the "Msgr. Oscar A. Romero Square" in 2012. The second is a plaza in MacArthur Park, a hub of Central American social and political activity located in the Westlake neighborhood, which was inaugurated in 2013.

7. This same nuance regarding women and gendered dynamics as they relate to undocumented immigrants is equally apparent in a related installation piece by Cache for the "Dreams Deferred: Artists Respond to Immigration Reform" art exhibit organized by the Chinese American Museum in December 2010. Like the art show held at Mid-City Arts Gallery earlier the same year, this exhibit also consisted of artwork by prominent street artists that directly engaged with the topic of immigration, specifically the bipartisan immigration bill known as the "DREAM Act" (Development, Relief, and Education for

Alien Minors Act). Cache's piece made use of many of the same props featured in his previous work, with one key exception. Rather than a "hamburger trap," the brown chicken on the other side of the white picket fence has her gaze fixated on two white eggs, which rest on a patch of artificial grass. Via this piece Cache comments on the threat of family separation faced by many immigrant families in which one or both parents are undocumented, while also underscoring the limitations of legislative measures such as the DREAM Act that focus on providing a means of legalization for undocumented youth but not their parents. At the same time, Cache also implicitly references discriminatory discourses regarding undocumented immigrant women from Latin America, which not only posit these women as highly fertile but also target their civil (reproductive) rights and those of their U.S.-born children. Both of these related commentaries speak to the seeming femaleness of the brown chicken barred from her unhatched eggs in this installation and, by the same token, the plight of undocumented immigrant women in particular.

REFERENCES

Alegría, Andrea. 2010. "Political Chickens in Whimsical Worlds." *Eastside Living LA*, February 21. http://www.eastsidelivingla.com/?p=808.

Austin, Joe. 2001. *Taking the Train: How Graffiti Became an Urban Crisis in New York City*. New York: Columbia University Press.

Bal, Mieke. 1996. *Double Exposures: The Subject of Cultural Analysis*. London and New York: Routledge.

Bermudez, Esmeralda. 2012. "Pico-Union Intersection to Be Named for Salvadoran Archbishop." *Los Angeles Times*, January 20. http://articles.latimes.com/print/2012/jan/21/local/la-me-romero-square-20120121.

Biron, Rebecca E. 2009. "City/Art: Setting the Scene." In *City/Art: The Urban Scene in Latin America*, edited by Rebecca E. Biron, 1–35. Durham, NC: Duke University Press.

Boykoff, Jules, and Kaia Sand. 2008. *Landscapes of Dissent: Guerrilla Poetry and Public Space*. Berkeley, CA: Palm Press.

"Cache." 2010. *Beautiful/Decay*. April 12. http://beautifuldecay.com/2010/04/12/cache/.

Chavez, Leo R. 2008. *The Latino Threat: Constructing Immigrants, Citizens, and the Nation*. Stanford: Stanford University Press.

Dietch, Jeffrey. 2011. *Art in the Streets*. New York: Skira Rizzoli Publications, Inc.

DiMaggio, Paul, and Patricia Fernández-Kelly, eds. 2010. *Art in the Lives of Immigrant Communities in the United States*. New Brunswick, NJ: Rutgers University Press.

Eyeone. 2014. *Eyeone/Seeking Heaven*. Accessed August 30. http://www.eyelost .com/eyeoneblog/index.php?catid=11.

Fraser, Nancy. 1990. "Rethinking the Public Sphere: A Contribution to the Critique of Actually Existing Democracy." *Social Text* 25 (26): 56–80. http://www.jstor .org/stable/466240.

Irvine, Martin. 2012. "Work on the Street: Street Art and Visual Culture." In *The Handbook of Visual Culture*, edited by Barry Sandywell and Ian Heywood, 234–78. London: Berg/Palgrave Macmillan.

LA Street Art Gallery. 2013. "Art and Activism with Eyeone." YouTube, January 14. https://www.youtube.com/watch?v=z65RAV5kwbA.

Lurie, Joshua. 2008. "Tastes like Revolution: Local Muralist Cache Spearheads a Chicken-Led Revolution." *New Angeles Monthly*, 12: 21. https://issuu.com/ newangelesmonthly/docs/may2008.

"Mid-City Profile." 2013. *Los Angeles Times*. http://maps.latimes.com/neighbor hoods/neighborhood/mid-city/.

Ngai, Mae N. 2004. *Impossible Subjects: Illegal Aliens and the Making of Modern America*. Princeton: Princeton University Press.

Schwartzman, Allan. 1985. *Street Art*. New York: Bantam Doubleday Dell Publishing Group.

Segura, Rosamaría. 2010. *Central Americans in Los Angeles*. Mount Pleasant, SC: Arcadia Publishing.

Snyder, Gregory J. 2009. *Graffiti Lives: Beyond the Tag in New York's Urban Underground*. New York and London: New York University Press.

Terrazas, Aaron. 2011. "Central American Immigrants in the United States." *Migration Information Source*, Jan 10. http://www.migrationpolicy.org/article/ central-american-immigrants-united-states-0.

10

CRITICAL REFLECTIONS ON U.S. CENTRAL AMERICAN STUDIES FOR THE FUTURE

KARINA O. ALVARADO, ALICIA IVONNE ESTRADA, AND ESTER E. HERNÁNDEZ

B ERTA CÁCERES'S ASSASSINATION in March 2016 stunned the international community. She was cofounder of Consejo Cívico de Organizaciones Populares e Indígenas de Honduras and 2015 Goldman Environmental Prize winner. Her death highlights the continued political violence against indigenous activists, community leaders, and women. Subsequently, the life-or-death struggle continues. As our histories have shown, violence of the past links to the present through global processes. To date, the United States and Canada continue to have a strong grip on land ownership and use as they promote development agendas focused on extraction and mining—an agenda that Cáceres and many activists like her call out as imperialistic. Central America's strategic location between South and North America places it at the crossroads of aggressive neoliberal projects, drug trade, and the U.S. War on Drugs. Significantly, the diasporas that resettled in the United States have remained integral to their communities through familial ties and the high level of remittances that are now central to the economies of many countries in the isthmus. In this volume we shift focus to lived experiences and representations of U.S. Central American identities in the context of cultural, political, and legal frames.

Connected and in opposition to the creation of Latina/o submarkets, these projects of historical memory and recovery underscore the significance of ethnic identities rather than national ones to invoke a conversation about pan-regional unity. The volume calls attention to questions of customs, language, and performance and insists on the importance of spaces such as parades, *mercados*, and public art. The murals and oral performances engage postmemory projects that bring to life and voice those stories and narratives that would link cohorts and generations together. As our contributors show, U.S. Central Americans produce art and counternarratives that disrupt sanitized versions of pan-ethnicity and pan-Latina/o identities. They highlight globalization and insist on historical specificity. All the contributors explore gendered social mobility and politicized identities in classed and racialized terms. Because this anthology represents but a smidgen of the necessary work needed in assisting our communities and in institutionalizing U.S. Central American studies, we close by offering areas of study important to consider in future scholarship. The following suggestions are neither comprehensive nor closed. We hope that the anthology and our recommendations represent entry points in our developing field to be expanded for further inquiry and fruitful dialogue. Suggestions are in alphabetical order.

CRITICAL INDIGENEITY AND AFRO-INDIGENEITY

Critical dialogues and approaches become particularly important given the rise of indigenous migrations to the United States. In this volume the scholarship on Maya enclaves expands and demands that we look at critical indigenous practices from more politicized perspectives as part of hemispheric identities. This lens thus challenges Eurocentric frameworks of analysis to propose analytical lenses grounded on indigenous *saberes* (knowledges and practices). In doing so, there is an opportunity for forming cross-alliances that both emphasize and demand expansive definitions of land-based identities and connect them to postmemory work for social justice. Indigenous diasporic memory functions as an important cultural text that stresses resistance against assimilation processes and as a site of solidarity with other indigenous nations. Moreover, recognizing Central America's ethnic heterogeneity entails that scholars break the mestizo ideology that continues to erase blacks and blackness in Central America and, consequently, that they challenge ideas and economic projects that become a justification for continued racism, political exclusion, and land theft of indigenous, Afro-indigenous, and black peoples. We hope that these contributions provide critical dialogues on the multiple struggles encountered and the survival strategies employed by indigenous diasporas in the United States. This volume engages structural and symbolic inscriptions of indigeneity from cultural and economic survival strategies to performative and oppositional social texts.

GENDER

Honduras, Guatemala, and El Salvador are countries with high femicide rates in the hemisphere. The United Nations reports that El Salvador has an average of twelve murders for every 100,000 women. In addition to the high numbers of tortured, mutilated, and/or murdered women, these countries also have a large percentage of impunity. For instance, in Guatemala only 2 percent of the more than 6,000 cases of murdered women led to prosecutions. Anthropologist Victoria Sanford (2008) notes that the impunity held by military officers in Guatemala, both as intellectual authors of genocide and attackers, continues and contributes to feminicide.[1] In Honduras, the UN reports that seven women are murdered for every 100,000 and that less than 2 percent of the cases lead to a prosecution. Thus, the recent murder of Berta Isabel Cáceres Flores, a Lenca environmental justice activist, directly links state violence against women and indigenous people as they struggle against the devastation brought to their communities by foreign capital through mining, hydroelectric dams, and megadevelopment projects. Similarly, the landmark Sepur Zarco trial in Guatemala and its historic verdict on February 26, 2016, makes visible the systematic forms of sexual violence against women and indigenous peoples directly and indirectly supported by U.S. aid to those nations' repressive and genocidal governments.[2]

These forms of varied state-sponsored violence have gendered outcomes that need to be centralized in analyzing the current migration "crisis." Once in the United States, Central American immigrants encounter a highly gendered labor-force landscape. The disproportionate presence of U.S. Central American women and men in domestic service and in various service economies continues as long as they are not recognized as legitimate refugees and accorded legal status. Furthermore, Central Americans are increasingly finding work in rural agricultural industries that rely on undocumented labor.

Within the cultures of Central American diasporas, we need to examine the stories and knowledges that women communicate as pedagogical lessons to their children, seriously considering the ways children talk back to affirm or contest identities.[3] Gendered stereotypes abound that reinforce patriarchal hegemonies as well as gendered violence at symbolic levels. For example, Central American women stereotypes include being domineering and promiscuous. These stereotypes are often deployed as microaggressions since they are usually voiced as "I heard Central American women are such and such," forcing Central American women to respond to the way they were demeaned through association. This raises issues about how Central American men live and represent their masculinities.

INSTITUTIONALIZATION OF CENTRAL AMERICAN STUDIES

As suggested in the anthology, there needs to be a conversation about institutionalizing Central American studies to create curricula and professional organizations and ensure that universities open faculty lines and departmental/program structures that fully engage our expertise and voices. The scope in this anthology also suggests that we move beyond a frame that situates U.S. Central Americans in the context of the civil wars (1960–1996) and consider our communities' varied histories, experiences, and contributions in the United States and the isthmus. Similarly, our focus on studies produced by 1.5- and second-generation U.S. Central American scholars emphasizes the need to expand the critical voices and methodologies used in the study of Central America and its diasporas in the United States. Moreover, instituting these changes, and promoting a more inclusive way of integrating Central American communities and topics in the classroom, should alleviate the level of marginalization and alienation U.S. Central American students experience in higher education.

LATINIDAD

While we focus in California, and center on Los Angeles, our contribution resituates the diaspora within the double movement of de- and re-territorialized embodiments. The project of Latinidad embraces Central Americans yet also creates the conditions for invisibility. This volume expands discussions of cultural and legal citizenship and insists that scholars engage U.S. Central

Americans in their analysis not as an afterthought but as fundamental to understanding the particularities of racialization, empire, and globalization.

MEDIA AND REPRESENTATION

We recommend that Central American individuals, artists, and organizations continue to use media and social outlets to bring visibility to Central American arts and issues. Promoting U.S. Central American film will greatly benefit diasporic communities to mark their presence and show their distinct cultures and interrelations with other U.S. ethnicities. As U.S. Central Americans we must be producers of our own realities and heterogeneities on and off screen. Central American diasporas must interrupt the top-down gaze that represents us as fragmented and unintelligible bodies from the *maras* to the silent domestic worker. Similarly, we recognize the importance of community radio programs, television shows, newspapers, and blogs that aid in the construction of transnational historical memories. These grassroots and community-based media outlets are essential in contesting one-dimensional dominant representations of Central American, Maya, and Garifuna diasporic communities. We propose more scholarship that makes visible these community-based efforts and resistance to stereotypical mainstream media representations.

MIGRATION/REFUGEE POLICY

The continued U.S.-supported social, political, and economic instability in the region drives Central American refugees to migrate. Women and children embark on harrowing journeys through Central America and Mexico to make their way to the U.S. border where they are intercepted by or surrender to immigration authorities. During the last three decades, Central Americans have been placed at the center of national immigration and border security debates. The U.S. government places undocumented Central American migrants in detention to "send a message" that the United States will not be a safe haven for them. At the detention centers, Central American migrants are placed on fast-track deportations, denying them legal counsel and interpreters. These state tactics of "sending a message" and placing migrants in fast-track deportations are also used at raids conducted by the Immigration and Customs Enforcement

Agency (ICE), where undocumented migrants are often violently denied their legal rights. Most of these immigrants caught in detention centers, either as they attempted to cross the border, or at raids conducted by ICE, are quickly deported and returned, for some, to a literal death sentence.

Future scholarship should document the role that Central Americans have played in the immigration movement, legislation, and policy. It is important to document individuals and organizations in the struggle for immigration reform currently taking place and also their long-standing contributions. Furthermore, prior research has not included the full impact of policies to integrate hemispheric refugee migrations and how those policies have been demanded and earned from the bottom up. We need to continue to explore how Central Americans identify and imagine themselves as international labor and how a path to a just, legal labor migration might be established. Research on immigration policies should include how these policies reproduce gender and racial asymmetries. Similarly, this research should be in tune with the specific sociopolitical conditions that displace indigenous communities as well as the varied struggles that indigenous migrants encounter in their perilous journey to the United States, specifically giving attention to the multiple forms of discrimination and racism that Maya and Garifuna migrants confront from state officials and nonindigenous migrants.

NEOLIBERAL POLICIES IN THE ISTHMUS

U.S. trade agreement and security policies in the hemisphere have defined globalization through the current extraction and mining model driven by U.S. and Canadian capital. International investors include China's stalled development plan for a canal in Nicaragua that threatens indigenous communities. In the area of communication, privatization of telecommunications (which brought Mexican and Spanish capital as well) and health care have further put pressure on agricultural and urban sectors where the poor continue to be made surplus, driving them out of their communities as is the case in the Northern Triangle. According to the Washington Office on Latin America, the Central American Free Trade Agreement (CAFTA), now ten years old, makes national development secondary to the needs of foreign investors. It does not benefit working people but instead exposes them to U.S. competition and reduces their access to low-cost generic medicine due to patents and copyright protections that favor investors. The free-trade agreements, and their patents on intellectual property and copyrights, work to the benefit of large corporations such as seed, pesticide, and fertilizer companies, ensuring that indigenous populations continue to lose their landholdings. At the same time, these patents force indigenous farmers to depend on commercial seeds, thus threatening indigenous food sovereignty. Likewise, commercial seeds, pesticides, and fertilizers have devastating impacts on the environment, health, and economy of indigenous Central American communities. Therefore, environmentalism must be conceptualized beyond preservation of ecodiversity to include race, class, and gender. Critical questions of sustenance and sustainability need to consider how global capital blocks people's access to land, agriculture, and food security.

SECURITY

The criminalization of Central Americans as undocumented aliens has disproportionately placed youth in the U.S. deportation path since 1996; youth gangs in Central America have become the eye of the storm in its security crisis. The United States has initiated and funded major drug interdiction operations through the 2008 Central America Regional Security Initiative (CARSI), whose objective is to control trafficking and reduce gang activity and corruption through policing and legal initiatives. U.S. deportation policies that placed gang members in precarious urban conditions fostered their growth, primarily in Honduras, Guatemala, and El Salvador. A larger issue arises of how CARSI promotes the remilitarization of Central America with the pretext of shoring up security. These security initiatives do not bode well for social protest campaigns and put control of policing Honduran citizens on the U.S. Drug Enforcement Administration (DEA), Southern Command,[4] and the Pentagon. Specifically, Intelligence Troop and Special Security Response Groups (Spanish acronym TIGRES, meaning "tiger")[5] have been created in Honduras and brought even more insecurity. This is preceded by the Honduran Congress's approval of "river concessions, tax enclaves or model cities, the Antiterrorist Law, the Private Communications Interception Law, and the Law for the Extradition of Hondurans to the U.S."[6] In other words, civil organizations such as Comité de Familiares Detenidos Desaparecidos en Honduras see these developments as creating an infrastructure of surveillance against social movements within urban areas as well. Even El Salvador, with a leftist elected government in power, is turning to the United States for assistance and clamoring for funds from the Alliance for Prosperity. It is important for us to remember that this translates to a deepening militarization of the region. With the history of military impunity, such regional integration initiatives challenge nascent democracies in the region.

Northern Triangle citizens have organized massive anticorruption demonstrations demanding greater transparency. Presidents and former presidents have faced corruption charges. Guatemala's Otto Pérez Molina and his vice president Roxana Baldetti were arrested for a customs-evasion scheme after massive demonstrations.[7] Similarly, late Salvadoran president Francisco Flores, of Alianza Republicana Nacionalista (ARENA), was jailed for laundering money and illicit enrichment in connection to relief funds from Taiwan. He was the president that dollarized the Salvadoran economy with little input from Salvadoran political sectors in 2001. More recently Mauricio Funes, the first president representing the Farabundo Martí National Liberation Front, who came to power in 2009, is facing charges of "illicit enrichment." He claims the charges are revenge for his role in pressuring prosecution against Francisco Flores. President Antonio Saca (of ARENA, 2004–2009) will also face trial.[8] Though many of these corruption cases led to arrests, the lack of a noncorrupt judicial system limits the possibilities for structural transformations in many of these Central American nations.

Additionally, while the security threat of the *maras* is whipped up to excite worries about generalized crime and violence, the Alliance for Prosperity, CARSI, and a host of other programs continue to orchestrate a dependent Central America, one that threatens economic resources and ecodiversity and that ultimately pushes women and children into the path of migration and the grip of a neoliberal model. This model calls for tourism, the deepening of energy projects that benefit huge corporations, and displacement of indigenous and peasant populations.

We recommend policies that reintegrate deported populations and that treat *maras* and deportees humanely, beginning with decriminalizing them. We call for economic models built not on militarization but on education, job training, and local economic investment. In order to intercept the cycles of gendered violence in gang formations, we need to study gangs beyond sensationalism to hear their own voices. Their narratives as explained by them might help us move beyond their foreclosed vilification to deconstruct their abjection from society and reintegrate them as life-affirming community members.

CLOSING

This volume unsettles the ways in which scholars, media, and other Latinas/os perceive the U.S. Central American condition. Small talk about U.S. Central Americans often centers on the overrepresentation in domestic service or the latest news montage or gang movie. Here we present U.S. Central Americans' ways of speaking back and demanding consideration of the spectrum of our cultural, artistic, and social dimensions. *U.S. Central Americans: Reconstructing Memories, Struggles, and Communities of Resistance* disrupts common ways of integrating Central American diasporas within discourses of Latinidad, immigration, and ethnic subjectivities to assert that we are transisthmian *aqui y alla* (here and there), in solidarity with our people's fight for land and dignity.

NOTES

1. See Victoria Sanford (2008), "From Genocide to Feminicide: Impunity and Human Rights in Twenty-First Century Guatemala" in *Journal of Human Rights* 7 (2): 104–22.
2. Approximately twenty years after the 1996 Peace Accords were signed in Guatemala, two high-ranking military officials, Lieutenant Colonel Esteelmer Reyes and former military commissioner Heriberto Valdez Asij, were charged in a Guatemalan court with crimes against humanity. These crimes specifically charged the military officers with sexual violence against fifteen Maya-Q'eqchi' women from Sepur Zarco.
3. See Ines Gomez, "A Space for Remembering: Home-Pedagogy and Exilic Latina Women's Identities," in *Engendering Forced Migrations*, ed. Doreen Indra, 200–217 (New York: Berghahn Books, 1999).
4. See "NEWS RELEASE: Marines set to deploy to Central America" regarding the deployment of 200 Marines in May 2005 to promote security. http:// southcom.mil/newsroom/Pages/NEWS-RELEASE-Marines-set-to-deploy -to-Central-America.aspx.
5. Training of Honduran TIGRES. Article is in Spanish in *El Heraldo*, July 4, 2014, http://www.elheraldo.hn/pais/571484-214/entrenan-200-efectivos -para-crear-fuerza-policial.

6. See "COFADEH: 'Tigres' Are Honduras' New Battalion 3–16," July 30, 2012. Communiqué from Comité de Detenidos Desaparecidos en Honduras (COFADEH) tying current security efforts to death squad battalion 3–16 or 316. http://quotha.net/node/2356.

7. See "From President to Prison: Otto Pérez Molina and a Day for Hope in Guatemala," by Francisco Goldman, September 4, 2015. http://www.newyorker.com/news/news-desk/from-president-to-prison-otto-perez-molina-and-a-day-for-hope-in-guatemala.

8. See "Salvadoran Ex-President Faces Corruption Trial," February 24, 2016. http://www.efe.com/efe/english/world/salvadoran-ex-president-faces-corruption-trial/50000262-2849492.

CONTRIBUTORS

Leisy Abrego is a 1.5-generation Salvadoran immigrant and an assistant professor in the César E. Chávez Department of Chicana and Chicano Studies at UCLA. Trained as a sociologist, she is interested in the study of families, Central American migration, and Latino immigrants' lived experiences of U.S. immigration laws. Her research investigates the opportunities for mobility and well-being of immigrants and their families in the home country, particularly as these are shaped by immigration policies and gendered expectations. In her first book, *Sacrificing Families: Navigating Laws, Labor, and Love Across Borders* (Stanford University Press, 2014), she highlights the role of gender and legal status in creating inequalities among Salvadoran transnational families. Her work on undocumented youth and transnational families appears in *Latino Studies*, *Law & Social Inquiry*, the *Journal of Marriage and Family*, *Law & Society Review*, and the *American Journal of Sociology*.

Karina O. Alvarado (co-editor) holds a PhD in ethnic studies from the University of California at Berkeley. Salvadoran born, she was raised in the Westlake and Pico-Union areas in Los Angeles. A President's Postdoctoral Fellow in the English Department at the University of California, Los Angeles (2007–2009), she has taught on U.S. Central American, Chicana/o, and Latina/o literature at Scripps college (2010) and UCLA. She is a visiting lecturer in the Chicana/o Studies Department at UCLA (2012 to current) where she designed undergraduate and graduate courses on U.S. Central American cultures, literatures, racial constructions, and cultural memory production, practices, and performativities.

She is interested in intercultural and gendered Latina/o narratives, cross-textual representations of Latinidad, and U.S. Central American transnational cultural recuperations. Alvarado's articles are found in *Studies in 20th and 21st Century Literature, Latino Studies Journal,* and in *ISTMO-Denison.*

Maritza E. Cárdenas is an assistant professor of English at the University of Arizona. A recipient of the Woodrow Wilson Fellowship, and the Center for Mexican American Studies Benson Fellowship at the University of Texas at Austin, her research and teaching interests focus on U.S. Central Americans, U.S. American ethnicities, Latina/o cultural productions, Latina/o identity and subjectivities, and transnational community formations. Her work has been published in the journal *Studies in 20th and 21st Century Literature.* Presently, she has essays under review on the topic of U.S. Central Americans and the media, Central American–American identity politics, and Central American cultural productions in the diaspora. She is also currently working on her book manuscript, which highlights the historical, sociopolitical, and economic processes that have facilitated the construction of a pan-ethnic transnational cultural identity (U.S. Central American) to emerge in the U.S. diaspora.

Alicia Ivonne Estrada (co-editor) is an associate professor in the Chicana/o Studies Department at California State University at Northridge. She holds a PhD in literature from the University of California at Santa Cruz. Her research focuses on Maya cultural productions in Guatemala and the United States. She has published articles on contemporary Maya literature, film, and radio. Her work has appeared in *Romance Notes, Latino Studies,* and *Revista Canadiense de Estudios Hispánicos,* among other journals and anthologies. Her current project is a book manuscript on Maya Guatemalan diasporic communities in Los Angeles. Since 2006, she has actively collaborated with the Maya radio program *Contacto Ancestral.* The show has been on the airwaves for over a decade and continues to air every Monday night in Southern California on the community radio station KPFK as well as on the World Wide Web.

Ester E. Hernández (co-editor) is a professor of Chicana/o and Latina/o studies at California State University, Los Angeles. She holds a PhD in Social Science from the University of California, Irvine. Born in El Salvador, she grew up in the Mid-Wilshire/Koreatown area of Los Angeles. Her work focuses on Central Americans' evolving identities, community formation, and social and economic adaptation. She has published in *Journal of American Ethnic History* and *Economy and Society*. She is the recipient of a Rockefeller Foundation Humanities Fellowship, and she has served on the executive board of the Coalition for Humane Immigrant Rights of Los Angeles (2010 to present) and Mujeres Activas en Letras y Cambio Social (2011 to 2013).

Floridalma Boj Lopez is Maya K'iche' and was raised in Los Angeles, California. She is currently a doctoral student in American studies and ethnicity at the University of Southern California. Her research interests include transnational Maya cultural and spiritual practice, with an emphasis on intergenerational relationships, memory, and Maya diasporic formations in the United States.

Steven Osuna is an assistant professor in the Department of Sociology at California State University, Long Beach. He received a PhD in sociology at the University of California, Santa Barbara with an emphasis in Black studies (2015) and a BA (2005) and MA (2008) in Chicana/o studies at California State University, Los Angeles. Steven was born and raised in the Echo Park district of Los Angeles. His mother migrated from Mexico in the late 1960s and his father from El Salvador in the late 1970s. Steven's research interests include comparative and relational ethnic studies; transnationalism, globalization, and migration; policing, militarization, and criminalization; and the history of race, class, and cultural struggles in Los Angeles.

Yajaira Padilla is an associate professor of English and Latin American and Latino studies at the University of Arkansas, Fayetteville. She received her PhD in literature (Spanish) from the University of California, San Diego. Her teaching and research interests include Central American cultural studies, U.S. Latina/o studies, and contemporary Latin Americanist literary, cultural, and social theory. She is the author of *Changing Women, Changing Nation: Female Agency, Nationhood, and Identity in Trans-Salvadoran Narratives* (SUNY, 2012) and has published articles in *Latin American Perspectives*, *Latino Studies*, and the *Arizona Journal of Hispanic Cultural Studies*, among others. Currently, she is working on a new project focused on the social, cultural, and political discourses and expressions of Central American belonging and nonbelonging in the United States.

Ana Patricia Rodríguez is associate professor in the Department of Spanish and Portuguese and the U.S. Latina/o Studies Program at the University of

Maryland, College Park, where she teaches classes on Latin American, Central American, and U.S. Latina/o literatures and cultures. She received an MA and PhD in literature from the University of California, Santa Cruz. Her research interests include Central American and Latina/o cultural production, transnational cultural studies, diaspora studies, and postwar/posttrauma studies. She has published widely on the cultural production of Latinas/os in the United States and Central Americans in the isthmus and the wider Central American diaspora. She is the author of *Dividing the Isthmus: Central American Transnational Histories, Literatures, and Cultures* (University of Texas Press, 2009) and co-editor (with Linda J. Craft and Astvaldur Astvaldsson) of *De la hamaca al trono y al más allá: Lecturas críticas de la obra de Manlio Argueta* (San Salvador: Universidad Tecnológica, 2013).

INDEX

CPSIA information can be obtained
at www.ICGtesting.com
Printed in the USA
FSHW021304270120
66532FS

9 780816 534067